S-TO

S0-DRW-299

INTERNATIONAL SERIES OF MONOGRAPHS IN
ELECTRICAL ENGINEERING
GENERAL EDITOR: D. J. SILVERLEAF

VOLUME 1

LIGHTING FITTINGS
PERFORMANCE AND DESIGN

LIGHTING FITTINGS PERFORMANCE AND DESIGN

by

A. R. BEAN,
C.Eng., M.I.E.E., F.I.E.S., F.R.S.A.

Senior Lecturer in Electrical and Illumination Engineering
Medway College of Technology

and

R. H. SIMONS,
B.Sc., A.R.C.S., M.I.Biol.

Manager, Lighting Development Group
British Lighting Industries Limited, Enfield

THE QUEEN'S AWARD
TO INDUSTRY 1966

PERGAMON PRESS

OXFORD · LONDON · EDINBURGH · NEW YORK
TORONTO · SYDNEY · PARIS · BRAUNSCHWEIG

Pergamon Press Ltd., Headington Hill Hall, Oxford
4 & 5 Fitzroy Square, London W.1
Pergamon Press (Scotland) Ltd., 2 & 3 Teviot Place, Edinburgh 1
Pergamon Press Inc., 44–01 21st Street, Long Island City, New York 11101
Pergamon of Canada Ltd., 207 Queen's Quay West, Toronto 1
Pergamon Press (Aust.) Pty. Ltd., 19a Boundary Street, Rushcutters Bay,
N. S. W. 2011, Australia, Sydney, N. S. W.
Pergamon Press S.A.R.L., 24 rue des Écoles, Paris 5e
Vieweg & Sohn G.m.b.H., Burgplatz 1, Braunschweig

First edition 1968

Library of Congress Catalog Card No. 68–18517

08   012594   8

1488972
CONTENTS

PREFACE

A GREAT deal of useful progress has been made in recent years in the design and prediction of the performance of lighting fittings. Until now most of this work has only been available in the various technical papers.

The aim of this book is to bring together much of this material and relate it to the more generally available information. It is hoped that it will provide an advanced text which will be useful to designers, lighting engineers, research workers, photometricians and students.

In keeping with our aim of dealing with advanced topics in a detailed but concise manner, we have assumed that the reader has a knowledge of the elementary photometric terms and has some familiarity with the basic laws of optics.

Chapter 8 has a different character to the rest of the book in that it is intended to be a practical guide to the routine calculations encountered by lighting engineers. To make for ease of reference, this chapter has been placed at the end of the book.

Since this is a book on "lighting fittings" we do not discuss light sources except where it is necessary to illustrate how the source to be used would dictate particular design features.

The authors gratefully acknowledge the assistance of Mr. V. T. Lilley for his suggestions for the section on capacitor design; Mr. W. R. Bloxsidge and Mr. D. F. Chapman for help with the section on choke design; Mr. J. G. Holmes for his comments on the section on the Holophane Lumeter; Mr. P. Markus for information on illumination meters; Mr. R. C. Kember and Mr. C. T. Hambleton for their comments on Chapter 6; Dr. J. Barnett for information on British Standards; and Mr. C. J. T. Greenslade for Appendixes A and B; and Mr. G. V. Lambert for Appendix C. Special thanks are due to Mr. H. Hewitt for bringing the authors together and for his interest in the book. Finally, we are indebted to the Illuminating Engineering Society, London, for permission to use a number of graphs and figures.

CHAPTER 1

LUMINOUS INTENSITY AND FLUX

LUMINOUS INTENSITY

The purpose of a lighting fitting and the associated light source is to produce an illumination and luminance pattern within the space surrounding the unit.

The performance of a lighting unit can be shown by diagrams of the distribution of illumination in each situation. However, a difficulty arises since the illumination pattern depends upon the size and shape of the enclosing space, and may be modified by interreflection. To overcome this difficulty a simple situation is chosen which provides information that can be used to predict the performance of the unit in all other situations. The unit is considered to be enclosed in a sphere of zero reflection factor and an orderly survey made of the illumination pattern at the inner surface of the sphere. The lighting unit defines the centre of the sphere and so the illumination values can be related to a system of angular coordinates (Fig. 1.1).

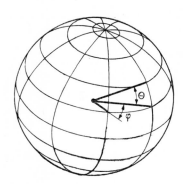

FIG. 1.1.

If the radius of the sphere is greater than five times the major dimension of the lighting unit, then the reduction of illumination on successive spheres of increasing radius is, to a close approximation (better than 1%), the same as that for a similar unit of infinitely small dimensions. The source therefore behaves as a point source, and the illumination at a similar point on each sphere is inversely proportional to the area of the sphere, i.e. inversely proportional to the radius squared. This is the inverse-square-law relationship, and may be written

$$E_{\theta,\varphi} = \frac{k_{\theta,\varphi}}{R^2} \qquad \text{or} \qquad k_{\theta,\varphi} = E_{\theta,\varphi} \, R^2,$$

where R is the radius of the sphere and $E_{\theta,\varphi}$ is the illumination at the point defined by θ,φ in lumens per unit area.

Thus for each radial light path specified by an angle of altitude θ, and azimuth φ, a factor $k_{\theta,\varphi}$ is obtained that is independent of the sphere size. For a given radius, the illumination is directly proportional to this factor, and so it is called the luminous intensity of the source in that direction. The symbol for luminous intensity is I, i.e.

$$I_{\theta,\varphi} = k_{\theta,\varphi}.$$

The unit of intensity is the candela.

The concept of luminous intensity can be used for sources that are too large to obey the inverse square law at working distances. Such a source may be treated as a series of point sources each providing part of the total intensity. The resultant illumination for

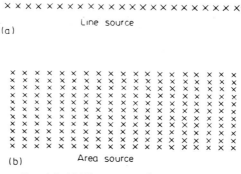

Fig. 1.2. (a) Line source. (b) Area source.

the whole source is obtained by summing the illumination values for each point source (Fig. 1.2(a)–(b) and Chapter 2).

The question arises how this intensity data once obtained can be conveniently displayed? The value of intensity in a particular direction could be marked on the surface of an actual sphere. Alternatively, a solid could be constructed in which the radial distance from a fixed point within the solid to the surface was proportional to the intensity in that direction.

The first method is the basis of the isocandela diagram. On this diagram points of equal intensity are joined to form lines similar to map contours.

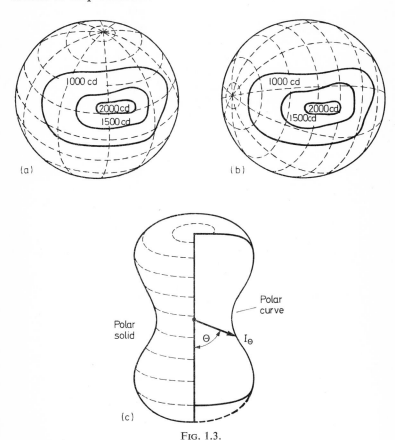

FIG. 1.3.

The direction of the angular coordinates has no effect upon the shape of the isocandela curves but it does alter the way in which a particular point on the sphere is specified. The coordinates shown in Fig. 1.3(a) are those used with the normal polar distribution photometers, Figs. 7.15–7.23, or the goniometer shown in Fig. 7.27(a). The coordinates shown in Fig. 1.3(b) are those used with the goniometer shown in Fig. 7.27(b), which is the type often used for projector photometry.

Although the solid angles (see below) represented by similar areas on either sphere are independent of the coordinate system, the flux in a given zone between two parallels would usually be different since the mean intensity within such a zone will depend upon the direction of the parallels relative to the isocandela curves.

The second method results in a figure called a polar solid of luminous intensity. In practice cross-sectional diagrams indicating the shape of the solid and called polar curves are used [Fig. 1.3(c)]. If the source distribution is the same through any vertical cross-section, then only one curve is required to describe the solid.

SOLID ANGLE

A concept which frequently occurs in lighting calculations is that of solid angle, and this is explained below.

Consider the relationship of an arbitrary area A to a point P

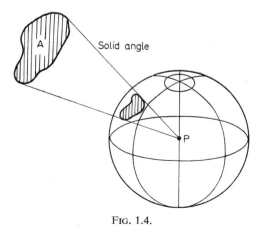

Fig. 1.4.

(Fig. 1.4). Two points on the boundary have been directly joined to point P. If all points on the boundary are joined to P in a similar manner, then a solid angle is formed. Let P represent the centre of a sphere as shown. There will be a boundary of intersection where the solid angle subtended by area A passes through the sphere. This area on the sphere surface and area A are regarded as subtending the same solid angle at P. Thus a convenient definition of solid angle is

$$\text{Solid angle } (\omega) \text{ subtended by any area} = \frac{\text{Area of intersection at sphere surface}}{(\text{Radius of sphere})^2}.$$

THE ISOCANDELA DIAGRAM

The method of representing the intensity distribution of a lighting unit by "contour" lines on a sphere allows a flat diagram to be made using a map-makers' projection. A commonly used projection is one in which the fraction of the total area enclosed by any element of the graticule is the same as it would be on the sphere. This equal area property simplifies the calculation of the flux emitted in any range of directions.

Consider an element of area δa on the surface of a sphere defined by the elemental angles $\delta\theta$ and $\delta\varphi$ (Fig. 1.5).

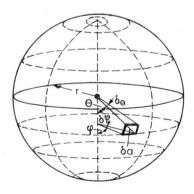

FIG. 1.5.

Let $\delta a \to 0$, then

$$da = r \, d\theta r \sin \theta \, d\varphi.$$

So area a defined by φ_1, φ_2 and θ_1, θ_2

$$= r^2 \int_{\varphi_1}^{\varphi_2} \int_{\theta_1}^{\theta_2} \sin \theta \, d\theta \, d\varphi.$$

Any scheme of graphical representation could be used which would satisfy the conditions of this equation. The one shown in Fig. 1.6(a) results in a diagram called Sanson's net or an "onion" diagram.

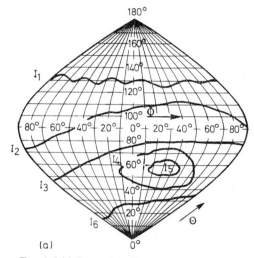

FIG. 1.6.(a) Isocandela lines on Sanson's net.

A vertical axis of length $2r$ is marked off in uniform increments of θ, and $\varphi \sin \theta$ is plotted against this axis. The scales are given by $\frac{1}{2}\pi = r$ for values of θ from $0°$ to π, and increments of φ from $-\frac{1}{2}\pi$ to $+\frac{1}{2}\pi$.

The diagram is a sinusoidal web on which "contours" of equal intensity are drawn with reference to the angular scales. The complete diagram represents one half of the sphere. It is useful for showing the performance of asymmetrical lighting units such as street lighting lanterns.

If the area of any part of the diagram is multiplied by the mean intensity over that range of directions, a quantity proportional to the flux emitted through that area is obtained.

Flux emitted through the area (F) = Mean illumination × area on surface of sphere (A):

$$F = E_{mean} \times A.$$

Now

$$E_{mean} = \frac{I_{mean}}{r^2}$$

therefore

$$F = \frac{I_{mean}}{r^2} \times A,$$

but

$$\frac{A}{r^2} = \omega \text{ (solid angle)},$$

and so

$$F = I_{mean} \times \omega. \tag{1.1}$$

The solid angle for half of the sphere is 2π.

Now the fraction of the total area on the surface of the sphere is equal to the fraction of the total solid angle, giving,

$$F = I_{mean} \times \begin{pmatrix} \text{fraction of total area} \\ \text{of the diagram} \end{pmatrix} \times 2\pi.$$

Also, from (1.1)

$$I_{mean} = \frac{F}{\omega}.$$

That is, the mean intensity over a particular range of directions or zone is the flux contained in the zone divided by the solid angle. If ω is infinitely small the intensity is no longer a mean value, but the value in a specific direction.

Thus the luminous intensity may also be defined by the equation:

$$I_{\theta,\varphi} = \mathbf{L}_{\delta\omega \to 0} \frac{\delta F}{\delta\omega} \quad \text{(see p. 2).}$$

From this result we may conclude that luminous intensity is a solid angular flux density where as illumination and luminous emittance are area flux densities.

ALTERNATIVE PROJECTION

An alternative projection to the "onion diagram" is shown in Fig. 1.6(b). Here a circular boundary is retained and a similar coordinate direction is used. As a consequence, in the resulting equal area diagram the "parallels" are curved as shown. This is of little importance, and the projection has several advantages over the onion diagram. One of these is that the isocandela curves are not distorted when they are rotated about the origin of the diagram, as occurs, for example, when the light source is tilted. (See Chapter 8. Street Lighting.)

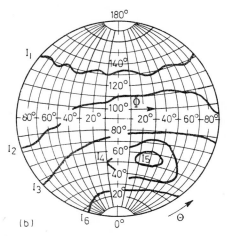

FIG. 1.6.(b) Isocandela lines on the normal zenithal projection.

THE POLAR CURVE

The idea of a solid of luminous intensity has already been introduced and the use of polar curves related to this solid has also been mentioned.

The polar diagram is most suited to the display of symmetrical distributions, such as those given by incandescent units for interior lighting purposes. They are also used for other fittings, such as those housing fluorescent tubes, which usually have a vertical distribution that changes gradually as the angle of azimuth is altered (Fig. 1.7)

The area of a polar curve is not related to the flux emitted by the source in the way that the area of an isocandela diagram is, and a different procedure must be adopted for flux calculations. Generally, the mean vertical polar curve for the lighting unit

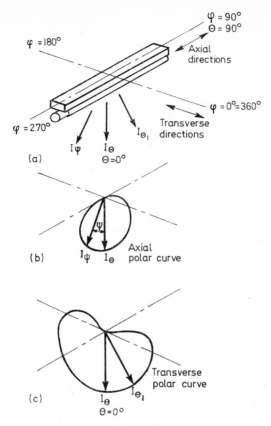

FIG. 1.7.

is obtained, and the method of achieving this is explained in Chapter 7. The polar solid related to this curve is considered to be enclosed in a sphere, and the flux emerging from the sphere through zones defined by the angular limits θ_1 and θ_2 (Fig. 1.8) is found as follows:

Since

$$I_{\theta, \varphi} = \mathbf{L}_{\delta\omega \to 0} \frac{\delta F}{\delta\omega}$$

$$dF = I_\theta \, d\omega$$

and

$$F_{\theta 1, \theta 2} = \int_{\theta_1}^{\theta_2} I_\theta \, d\omega.$$

The elemental solid angle $d\omega$ related to $d\theta$ is given by

$$d\omega = [\text{area of encircling strip between } \theta \text{ and } (\theta + d\theta)]/r^2$$
$$= r\, d\theta\, 2\pi r \sin \theta / r^2$$
$$= 2\pi \sin \theta\, d\theta.$$

Therefore
$$F_{\theta_1, \theta_2} = 2\pi \int_{\theta_1}^{\theta_2} I_\theta \sin \theta\, d\theta,$$

and the total flux emitted is given by:

$$F = 2\pi \int_0^\pi I_\theta \sin \theta\, d\theta.$$

If I_θ is a simple function of θ, such as $I_\theta = I_m \cos^n \theta$, then direct integration may be employed. However, in most practical cases, the equation to the curve is not known accurately, and graphical or numerical methods must be employed.

FIG. 1.8. Flux determination from a polar solid.

One method would be to plot a graph of $I_\theta \sin \theta$ against θ and determine the area under the curve, but this is tedious and seldom done.

The more common techniques employed are: 1, Zonal Constants. 2, The Rousseau Diagram. 3, Russell Angles.

1. ZONAL CONSTANTS

In this method the solid angles related to zones defined by angles of elevation from the downward vertical are calculated, and these are called the zonal constants. The flux contained in a zone is equal to the mean zonal intensity multiplied by the zonal constant.

In practice sufficient accuracy is obtained by using the mid-zone intensity and choosing zonal limits to give solid angles over which this value approximates to the mean value. Thus for a rapidly changing distribution 2° zones might be required, but with other distributions 5° or 10° zones might be used with similar accuracy. We have already established that elemental solid angle $d\omega = 2\pi \sin \theta \, d\theta$. Therefore in Fig. 1.8 the solid angle with the limits θ_1 and θ_2 is given by

$$\omega_{\theta 1, \theta 2} = 2\pi \int_{\theta_1}^{\theta_2} \sin \theta \, d\theta$$

$$= 2\pi \left(- \cos \theta \right)_{\theta_1}^{\theta_2}$$

giving

$$\omega_{\theta 1, \theta 2} = 2\pi(\cos \theta_1 - \cos \theta_2)$$

or

$$= 4\pi \sin \left(\frac{\theta_2 - \theta_1}{2} \right) \sin \left(\frac{\theta_2 + \theta_1}{2} \right),$$

which is a more convenient form for the purposes of calculation. Zonal constants for 2°, 5° and 10° intervals are given in Table 1.1.

TABLE 1.1. ZONAL CONSTANTS FOR 2, 5 AND 10 DEGREE ZONES

2 degree zones		5 degree zones			10 degree zones		
Zone limits degrees	Zonal constant	Zone limits degrees		Zonal constant	Zone limits degrees		Zonal constant
0–2	0·0038	0–5	175–180	0·0239	0–10	170–180	0·095
2–4	0·0115	5–10	170–175	0·0715	10–20	160–170	0·283
4–6	0·0191	10–15	165–170	0·1186	20–30	150–160	0·463
6–8	0·0267	15–20	160–165	0·1649	30–40	140–150	0·628
8–10	0·0343	20–25	155–160	0·2097	40–50	130–140	0·774
10–12	0·0418	25–30	150–155	0·2531	50–60	120–130	0·897
12–14	0·0493	30–35	145–150	0·2946	60–70	110–120	0·993
14–16	0·0568	35–40	140–145	0·3337	70–80	100–110	1·058
16–18	0·0641	40–45	135–140	0·3703	80–90	90–100	1·091
18–20	0·0714	45–50	130–135	0·4041			
		50–55	125–130	0·4349			
		55–60	120–125	0·4623			
		60–65	115–120	0·4862			
		65–70	110–115	0·5064			
		70–75	105–110	0·5228			
		75–80	100–105	0·5351			
		80–85	99–100	0·5434			
		85–90	90–95	0·5476			

The type of coordinate system shown in Fig. 1.3(b) is often used for the photometry of projectors having a narrow beam. With this type of distribution it is frequently necessary to determine the solid angle subtended by one of the "rectangular" areas (i.e. areas bounded by adjacent parallels and great circles). These are simply the appropriate fraction of the total solid angle between the two parallels (i.e. the lines running vertically). These have been used to find the flux values shown in Fig. 8.26.

2. THE ROUSSEAU DIAGRAM

This diagram has an area proportional to the flux emitted by the source, and from it both zonal flux and total flux may be determined. The construction is as follows.

Enclose the polar curve in a circle of radius r as shown (Fig. 1.9). At a suitable distance draw a line AB parallel to the vertical axis of the polar curve MN. Divide the circle into angular zones and

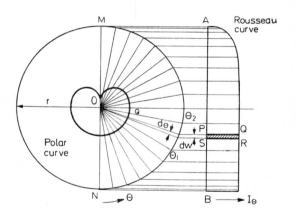

FIG. 1.9. Rousseau construction.

project the intercepts of the zonal limits and the circle horizontally to cut the line AB at right angles. Plot the intensity value related to each radial line along the corresponding horizontal line, the line AB being used as base line. For instance, in Fig. 1.9 PQ is made equal to OQ. Sufficient number of intensity values should be plotted to enable a smooth curve to be drawn through the points obtained.

The proof that the area of the diagram is directly proportional to the flux emitted is given below.

Area of elemental strip $PQRS$ on the Rousseau diagram

$$= dw \times I_\theta$$

and area between θ_1 and θ_2

$$= \int_{\theta_1}^{\theta_2} I_\theta \, dw.$$

Now $dw = r \, d\theta \sin \theta$.

Therefore area between θ_1 and θ_2 $= r \int_{\theta_1}^{\theta_2} I_\theta \sin_\theta \, d\theta$.

We have already established that the flux contained in any angular zone with limits θ_1 and θ_2 is given by

$$F_{\theta1,\theta2} = 2\pi \int_{\theta_1}^{\theta_2} I_\theta \sin \theta \, d\theta,$$

therefore the area of the diagram between θ_1 and θ_2 must be multiplied by $2\pi/r$ to obtain the flux in this zone. The total flux emitted is obtained by multiplying the total area of the diagram by $2\pi/r$. Since one axis of the diagram is scaled in intensity units, and the other in units of length, the area must be expressed in units of length × intensity if the actual value of flux is required.

An example of the use of this diagram is given under the section dealing with uniform diffuse sources in which it is used to obtain the relationship between the flux emitted by a uniformly diffusing element and the maximum intensity of the element.

3. RUSSELL ANGLES

An approach which is useful when total flux is required is to measure the intensities at the centre of equal solid angles. If this is done then the total flux can be calculated from

$$F = \frac{4\pi}{2n} \sum I_\theta,$$

where $2n$ is the number of equal solid angles into which the enclosing sphere is divided.

In the section on zonal constants we established that the solid angle is given by

$$\omega = 2\pi \int \sin \theta \, d\theta.$$

To determine the Russell angles we must calculate the value of θ for the mid-point of a series of adjacent solid angles.

Now the solid angle between $0°$ and $\theta_1°$, where $\theta_1°$ is the first Russell angle, is equal to half the chosen increment of solid angle, i.e. $\frac{1}{2} \times 4\pi/2n$.

Also

$$\omega_{0,\theta1} = 2\pi[1 - \cos\theta_1]$$

giving

$$\frac{1}{2} \times \frac{4\pi}{2n} = 2\pi[1 - \cos\theta_1]$$

or

$$\cos\theta_1 = \frac{2n - 1}{2n}.$$

The mid-point angle $\theta_2°$ of the second solid angle, measured from $0°$, occurs at

$$\frac{3}{2} \times \frac{4\pi}{2n} = 2\pi[1 - \cos\theta_2]$$

giving

$$\cos\theta_2 = \frac{2n - 3}{2n}.$$

Similarly for θ_3, where $\omega_{0,\theta3} = \frac{5}{2} \times \frac{4\pi}{2n}$

$$\cos\theta_3 = \frac{2n - 5}{2n},$$

and so on, until the last angle is obtained at

$$\cos\theta_n = \frac{2n - (2n - 1)}{2n} = \tfrac{1}{2}n.$$

In general, θ is given by $\cos^{-1}(M/2n)$, where M has the range of values, 1, 3, 5, 7, ..., $(2n - 1)$.

Table 1.2 gives Russell angles for 10 and 20 increments.

TABLE 1.2. RUSSELL ANGLES

20 angles (degrees)

18·2	31·8	41·4	49·5	56·6	63·3	69·5	75·5	81·4	87·1	92·9	98·6
104·5	110·5	116·7	123·4	130·5	138·6	148·2	161·8				

10 angles (degrees)

25·8	45·6	60·0	72·5	84·3	95·7	107·5	120·0	134·4	154·2

THE SECTOR SOLID AND THE *K* FACTOR METHOD

If the methods of obtaining flux which have so far been described are used for linear sources such as fluorescent fittings, then it is necessary to obtain a mean polar curve for the fitting.

An alternative approach[1]† is to consider a sector solid related to the source (Fig. 1.10), and to calculate the flux passing through the curved window *ABCD*.

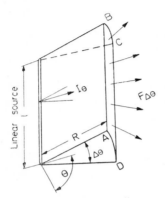

FIG. 1.10. Sector solid.

If the radial distance is diminished until $R \to 0$, then the flux passing through window *ABCD* will be the total flux emitted by the source in the sector. The flux passing through any range of sectors may be obtained by summation.

The flux passing through window *ABCD* when $R \to 0$ is given by

$$F_{\Delta\theta} = I_\theta K_L,$$

where I_θ is the mean transverse intensity of the source between the sector limits and is obtained from the transverse polar curve (Fig. 1.7(c)). The mid-sector intensity value can normally be used with negligible error provided the angle θ is kept small, say 10°. K_L depends only upon the axial intensity distribution (Fig. 1.7(b)) and $\Delta\theta$.

For the purpose of calculation, the equation of the axial polar curves of many fluorescent lighting units may be approximately represented by simple mathematical functions such as $I_\psi = I_\theta \cos \psi$,

† Superscript figures in parentheses are to the References at the end of the chapter.

$I_\psi = I_\theta \cos^2 \psi$, $I_\psi = I_\theta \cos^3 \psi$, etc., or more generally $I_\psi = I_\theta \cos^n \theta$, where ψ is the angle between the normal to the source in the plane of the polar curve and the direction of I_ψ and I_θ is the intensity in the direction of this normal. K_L factors for $10°$ sectors and a number of axial distributions are given in Table 1.3.

TABLE 1.3. LIMITING VALUES OF K FOR $10°$ SECTORS (K_L)

Distribution	K_L
Cosine (diffusing)	0·274
Cosine^2 (louvered)	0.233
Cosine^3 (deep louvers)	0·206
Cosine^4 (prismatic control)	0·186

The total light output of a linear source with a transverse polar curve that is symmetrical about a vertical axis could be determined by considering 18, $10°$ sectors, as follows:
Total flux emitted

$$\sum F_{\Delta\theta} = F = 2 \times (I_{\theta 1}K_{L1} + I_{\theta 2}K_{L2} + I_{\theta 3}K_{L3} + \cdots I_{\theta 18}K_{L18})$$

or, if the axial distribution is the same for each sector,

$$F = 2K_L(I_{\theta 1} + I_{\theta 2} + I_{\theta 3} + \ldots I_{\theta 18}).$$

As a simple example consider a fluorescent tube (Fig. 1.11); in this case both K_L and I_θ are constant. If we assume a cosine axial distribution and obtain K_L from Table 1.3,

$$F = 2 \times K_L \times 18I_\theta$$
$$= 2 \times 0·274 \times 18I_\theta = 9·86I_\theta$$

which agrees with the known value of $\pi^2 I_\theta$.

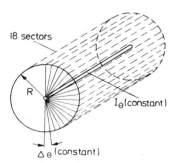

FIG. 1.11. Summation of sector solids.

K_L factors are directly proportional to the sector angle and hence factors for smaller or larger sectors may be obtained from $K'_L = K_L(x/10)$, where x is the new sector angle in degrees.

The derivation of K_L factors is given in Chapter 2.

FLUX DETERMINATION FROM AN ISOPHOT DIAGRAM

An isophot diagram is one on which "contours" of equal illumination are drawn.

The flux falling on a surface can be obtained from such a diagram, since:

Flux = Average illumination (lumens per unit area) (× area of the surface).

The area between two contours is multiplied by the average value of illumination between the contours to obtain the flux falling on this area. If this procedure is repeated for the whole diagram the total flux to the surface is obtained.

The method is useful for calculating the flux emitted by concentrating fittings where all the flux can be intercepted by a surface of relatively small area.

WOHLAUER'S METHOD OF REPRESENTING FLUX

Earlier it was pointed out that polar curves do not give a direct indication of the total flux emitted by a source, and the common methods for calculating the zonal fluxes were explained. There is,

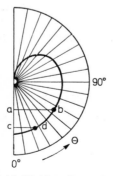

FIG. 1.12. Wohlauer's construction.

however, a simple construction which enables the flux contained in the different zones to be obtained directly from the polar curve. This construction is due to Wohlauer[2].

Figure 1.12 shows the polar curve for a point source having a distribution that is symmetrical about the vertical axis.

The flux in each zone is proportional to the length of lines such as *ab* and *cd*, which are horizontal and join the points representing the mid-zonal intensity to the downward vertical. This is only the case if the zones are of equal angular subtense.

The proof is as follows.

The flux $F_{\theta 1, \theta 2}$ in each zone is given by

$$F_{\theta 1, \theta 2} = 2\pi \int_{\theta_1}^{\theta_2} I_\theta \sin \theta \, d\theta$$

(where I_θ is the mid-zonal intensity)

$$= 4\pi \sin \left(\frac{\theta_2 - \theta_1}{2} \right) \times I_\theta \sin \left(\frac{\theta_1 + \theta_2}{2} \right) \quad \text{from p. 11.}$$

$\sin [(\theta_2 - \theta_1)/2]$ is a constant since the zones are of equal angular subtense. Also $I_\theta \sin [(\theta_1 + \theta_2)/2]$ is equal to the length of the horizontal line joining the point representing the mid-zonal intensity to the downward vertical. Hence the flux represented by any part of a polar curve can be found by adding up the appropriate horizontal lines (measured in units of intensity) and multiplying the answer by $4\pi \sin [(\theta_2 - \theta_1)/2]$.

If we use this construction we can see the contribution that each zone makes to the total flux immediately. For instance, in the example given, although the mid-zone intensity at point *d* is greater than at point *b*, the flux in the zone containing *b* is greater than that in the zone containing *d*. This method of representing flux will be used in the section on the optical design of specular reflectors (Chapter 4).

REFERENCES

1. BEAN, A.R., Monograph of I.E.S. (London), No. 7, 1963.
2. WOHLAUER, A. A., *Illum. Engng.* (*N. Y.*) **3**, 657 (1908).

ILLUMINATION FROM LINE
AND AREA SOURCES

LUMINANCE AND LUMINOUS EMITTANCE

When we describe the luminous appearance of a surface or source we sometimes refer to its "brightness". This term is a general one which can be interpreted in two different ways. It can be taken to mean either the brightness of the source as measured by some physical instrument such as a photoelectric cell, or the brightness of the source as evaluated by the human eye. Throughout this book it is the physical brightness which will be considered when deriving the various illumination formulae.

The physical brightness is termed its luminance, while the term luminosity is reserved for its apparent brightness as evaluated by the eye.

Luminance is generally defined as the intensity of a source or element of a source in a given direction divided by the orthogonally projected area of the source or element in that direction.

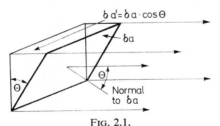

FIG. 2.1.

The orthogonal projection of any element of area of a surface δa is given by $\delta a = \delta a \cos \theta$, where θ is the angle between the normal to element δa and the direction of view (Fig. 2.1).

The element δa may have any size provided that this is small compared with the distance at which the intensity measurement is made.

British Standard 233, which deals with the terms used in illu-

19

mination and photometry, defines the luminance at a point of a surface and in a given direction as "the quotient of the luminous intensity in the given direction of an infinitesimal element of the surface containing the point under consideration by the orthogonally projected area of the element on a plane perpendicular to the given direction. Symbol L."

The authors have, as far as possible, limited the use of the symbol L to indicate luminance in intensity units per unit projected area, e.g. candelas/ft². However, there is another system of units; in this luminance is expressed in terms of the luminous emittance of a uniform diffuser. When related to a luminous emittance in lumens/ft² the unit is called the foot-lambert. This unit is defined as: the luminance of a uniform diffuser emitting one lumen/ft². Almost all the instruments for measuring luminance are calibrated in these units. The foot-lambert is a much smaller unit than the candela/ft². A uniformly diffusing surface having a luminance of one candela/ft² would emit π lumens/ft².

At the present time it is common practice to set up flux transfer equations in terms of luminance in foot-lamberts. This is done to avoid introducing the factor of π which would occur if candelas/ft² were used. The authors prefer to use luminous emittance, which is the flux emitted per unit area of the surface (symbol H) and is numerically equal to the luminance in foot-lamberts when the surface is uniformly diffusing.

The advantage is that luminous emittance is a more general term. The luminous emittance of a surface is not related to a direction of view, whereas the luminance of a surface is only independent of this direction if the surface produces uniform diffusion.

In Table 3.2 (p. 69), surface distribution factors (D_s) are given for cosine squared and cosine cubed distributions as well as for the more common uniform diffuse cosine distribution. These were introduced to deal with flux transfer from louvered ceilings (see p. 68).

When using these transfer functions, the statement

Flux received by surface a from b $(F_{ab}) = H_b S_b D_s$

is valid for all the distributions, where H_b is the luminous emittance and S_b is the area of the receiving surface; Whereas $F_{ab} = L_b S_b D_s$, where L_b = luminance in foot-lamberts, would apply only in the case of a uniformly diffusing ceiling source.

HELIOS

Moon and Spencer[1] suggested another approach to the problem of specifying brightness. This new approach involves substituting the term helios for luminance and using a more general definition. The definition is expressed in an equation as follows:

$$\mathbf{H} = \pi L \frac{D}{\underset{\omega \to 0}{\omega}}$$

where H is the helios in blondels, D is the flux density in lumens/m², and ω is the solid angle over which the flux is received at the point of measurement (Fig. 2.2).

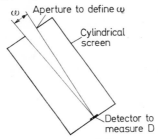

FIG. 2.2. A simple helios meter.

One advantage of the helios concept is that it can deal more satisfactorily with volume sources such as luminous gases and the sky. Moon and Spencer's proposals have not found wide acceptance in this country, but represent an important contribution which will probably have considerable influence on the subject of illumination calculations and photometry in time to come.

UNIFORM DIFFUSE SOURCES

Uniform diffuse sources include secondary sources such as walls reflecting light from primary sources which may or may not in themselves be diffuse sources. The study of this type of source is important since it is the basis of the interreflection theory in current use.

A source is termed uniform diffuse if its luminance, that is, the intensity per unit "apparent" or projected area, is the same from all directions of view.

For this to be true the following relationship must hold:

$$I_\theta = I_m \cos \theta.$$

Proof

$$\text{Luminance } (L) = \frac{I\,(\text{normal})}{\text{projected area in direction of normal}} = \frac{I_m}{\delta a}.$$

When an element of area is viewed at angle θ the projected area δa decreases to

$$\delta a' = \delta a \cos \theta \quad \text{(Fig. 2.1)}.$$

Therefore for a constant value of L,

$$I_\theta = I_m \cos \theta.$$

Thus for a uniform diffuse distribution the polar solid must be a tangent sphere for each element of surface area.

The flux emitted by an element of a uniformly diffusing surface may be determined by reference to a Rousseau diagram.

The diagram given in Fig. 2.3 shows the polar curve, which is a circle, together with the Rousseau construction for the polar curve.

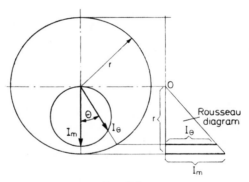

FIG. 2.3.

Since the spacing of the intensity ordinates from point O downwards is proportional to $\cos \theta$, and since each ordinate is itself proportional to $\cos \theta$, a straight-line graph is obtained and the area of the diagram is that of a right-angled triangle.

$$\text{Area of Rousseau diagram} = \frac{I_m r}{2}.$$

$$\text{Flux } (F) = \frac{2\pi}{r} \times \text{area of diagram},$$

giving

$$F = \frac{2\pi}{r} \frac{I_m r}{2}$$

$$= \pi I_m \text{ lumens.}$$

As a check this result will be obtained in a different manner. Consider the element of surface area to part of a sphere as shown in Fig. 2.4.

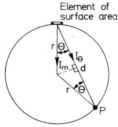

Element of surface area

FIG. 2.4.

The direct illumination at any point P

$$E_p = \frac{I_\theta \cos \theta}{d^2} = \frac{I_m \cos^2\theta}{(2r \cos \theta)^2} = \frac{I_m}{4r^2}.$$

Since θ is absent from this expression, E_p is independent of the position of P on the sphere and so the direct flux received by the inside wall of the sphere is therefore given by

$$F = E_p \times 4\pi r^2 = \frac{I_m}{4r^2} \times 4\pi r^2,$$

and so $F = \pi I_m$ lumens, as before.

THE PRINCIPLE OF EQUIVALENCE

It is an important general principle that two uniform diffuse sources will produce the same illumination at a point P if they

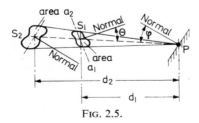

FIG. 2.5.

are of equal luminance and appear to have the same boundary when viewed from P (see Fig. 2.5).

Proof

$$E_{ps_1} = \frac{\delta a_1 L}{d_1^2} \cos \theta_1 \cos \varphi,$$

where L is the luminance in candelas per unit area,

$$E_{ps_2} = \frac{\delta a_2 L}{d_2^2} \cos \theta_2 \cos \varphi.$$

Now

$$\frac{\delta a_1 \cos \theta_1}{d_1^2} = \frac{\delta a_2 \cos \theta_2}{d_2^2},$$

i.e. the same solid angle, therefore

$$E_{ps_1} = E_{ps_2}.$$

THE UNIT HEMISPHERE

We can use the principle of equivalence to establish the unit hemisphere method for calculating direct illumination as follows.

Consider an element of a uniform diffuse source of area δa (Fig. 2.6).

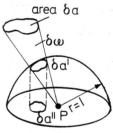

FIG. 2.6.

Let the illumination at P from this element be δE_p, then the illumination δE_p at P produced by δa will be the same as that produced by the element $\delta a'$ formed by the intersection of the solid angle $\delta \omega$ and the unit hemisphere, provided that $\delta a'$ has the same luminance as δa.

And so
$$\delta E_p = \frac{L\delta a' \cos \theta}{1^2}.$$

Also
$$\delta a'' = \delta a' \cos \theta.$$

Therefore
$$\delta E_p = L\delta a''.$$

This argument may be extended to each element of area of the source and so
$$E_p = L \sum \delta a'' = La'',$$

that is, the total illumination at P is given by the product of the source luminance and the area of intersection on the sphere projected on to the base of the unit hemisphere as shown.

To illustrate the value of this method the formulae relating to a number of common forms of source will be derived.

Disc Source

Illumination in the horizontal plane at a point P directly beneath the disc

Referring to Fig. 2.7,
$$E_p = L \sum \delta a'' = La''$$
$$La'' = L\pi x^2$$
$$= L\pi \left(\sin \frac{\alpha}{2}\right)^2$$
$$= L\pi \frac{R^2}{R^2 + h^2} \quad \text{or} \quad L\tfrac{1}{2}\pi (1 - \cos \alpha)$$

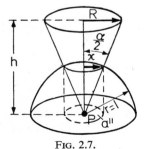

FIG. 2.7.

It will be shown in the section dealing with illumination as a vector quantity that the latter result can be used even when the point is not directly under the centre of the source.

Triangular Source

Illumination on the horizontal plane

The problem is simplified if we consider first the case of the right-angled triangle shown in Fig. 2.8. This triangle has its apex directly above point P. The projection on to the base of the hemisphere of the shaded sector M gives the same value for a'' as the projection of a'.

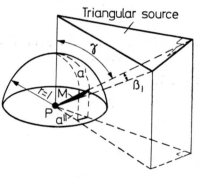

FIG. 2.8.

Area of sector $M = \dfrac{\beta_1 \pi}{2\pi} = \dfrac{\beta_1}{2}$, where β is in radians.

Therefore $a'' = \dfrac{\beta_1}{2} \sin \gamma$ and $E_p = \dfrac{L}{2} \beta_1 \sin \gamma$.

Now the illumination under the apex of any triangle may be obtained by taking the sum or difference of the illumination due to two right-angled triangles as follows.

Case 1. Fig. 2.9(a). Illumination at P from $\triangle DBC$
$\qquad = $ Illumination from $\triangle ABC$
$\qquad - $ Illumination from $\triangle ABD$.
Case 2. Fig. 2.9(b). Illumination at P from $\triangle ABC$
$\qquad = $ Illumination from $\triangle ABD$
$\qquad + $ Illumination from $\triangle DBC$.

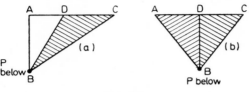

FIG. 2.9.

Rectangular Source (see also Chapter 8)

1. Illumination on the horizontal plane

The illumination under one corner of a rectangular source may readily be obtained by treating the source as two triangular sources (Fig. 2.10).

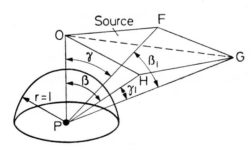

FIG. 2.10.

$$E_p = \text{Illumination from } \triangle OFG$$
$$+ \text{ Illumination from } \triangle OHG$$
$$= \frac{L}{2}(\beta_1 \sin \gamma + \gamma_1 \sin \beta).$$

2*

2. *Illumination in a vertical or perpendicular plane* (Fig. 2.11)

The projection of the solid angle intersection with the hemisphere on to the base of the hemisphere (a'') is equal to the area of the sector subtending angle β, minus the projected area of the shaded sector M.

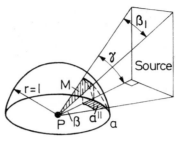

FIG. 2.11.

Area of sector with angle $\beta = \frac{1}{2}\beta$.

Projected area of shaded sector $M = \frac{1}{2}\beta_1 \cos \gamma$.

Therefore $E_p = \dfrac{L}{2}(\beta - \beta_1 \cos \gamma)$.

Narrow Strip Source

1. *Illumination in a parallel plane* (Fig. 2.12)

This may be obtained from the rectangular soure result as follows:

$$E_p = \frac{L}{2}(\beta_1 \sin \gamma + \gamma_1 \sin \beta) \quad \text{(Fig. 2.10)}.$$

Now
$$L = \frac{I}{A} = \frac{I}{l \times W} = \frac{I}{l \times R \tan \beta},$$

giving
$$E_p = \frac{I}{2lR} \frac{(\beta_1 \sin \gamma + \gamma_1 \sin \beta)}{\tan \beta}.$$

Also
$$\tan \beta = \sec \gamma \tan \beta_1.$$

Therefore
$$E_p = \frac{I}{2lR}\left(\frac{\beta_1 \sin \gamma \cos \gamma}{\tan \beta_1} + \gamma_1 \cos \beta\right).$$

Let $W \to 0$, then $\gamma_1 \to \gamma$, $\beta \to 0$, $\beta_1 \to 0$

and $$\frac{\beta_1}{\tan \beta_1} \to 1,$$

so that when I/l is the intensity per unit length of a line source whose width is negligibly small compared with l and R,

$$E_p = \frac{I}{2lR} (\gamma + \sin \gamma \cos \gamma).$$

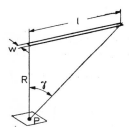

FIG. 2.12.

(Note in the section on "Other Distributions" and for line sources in Chapter 8, $\alpha \equiv \gamma$.)

If, as in Fig. 2.13, the point P is displaced so that R forms an angle θ with the normal to the source, and θ' with the normal at P, the following factors must be taken into account:

(a) the apparent or projected area is reduced by $\cos \theta$;
(b) the light from each element of source reaches the point P with an additional angle of inclination θ'.

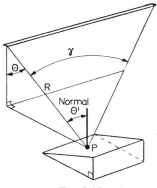

FIG. 2.13.

The equation is therefore modified giving

$$E_p = \frac{I}{2IR} \cos \theta \cos \theta'(\gamma + \sin \gamma \cos \gamma).$$

If P is in the horizontal plane, then $\theta' = \theta$, and

$$E_p = \frac{I}{2IR} \cos^2 \theta(\gamma + \sin \beta \cos \gamma).$$

2. Illumination in a vertical or perpendicular plane normal to the axis of the source (Fig. 2.14)

From the rectangular source equation (Fig. 2.11),

$$E_p = \frac{L}{2}(\beta - B_1 \cos \gamma).$$

Substituting
$$L = \frac{I}{IR \tan \beta},$$

$$E_p = \frac{I}{2IR} \frac{(\beta - \beta_1 \cos \gamma)}{\tan \beta}.$$

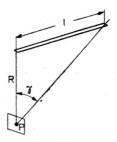

FIG. 2.14.

Also $\tan \beta = \sec \gamma \tan \beta_1$,

$$E_p = \frac{I}{2IR} \left[\frac{\beta}{\tan \beta} - \frac{\beta_1 \cos^2 \gamma}{\tan \beta_1} \right].$$

Let $W \to 0$, then

$$\frac{\beta}{\tan \beta} \to 1 \quad \text{and} \quad \frac{\beta_1}{\tan \beta_1} \to 1.$$

So that for a line source of intensity per unit length I/l and whose width is negligible compared with l and R,

$$E_p = \frac{I}{2lR}(1 - \cos^2 \gamma)$$

$$= \frac{I}{2lR}\sin^2 \gamma.$$

When point P is displaced as in the case of the parallel plane illumination, only the projected area changes for a given value of R and

$$E_p = \frac{I \cos \theta}{2lR}\sin^2 \gamma.$$

Cylindrical Source

If the source is narrow and cylindrical then it may be treated as a strip source of the same value of luminance. However, when point P is displaced the projected area does not alter, and

$$E_p = \frac{I}{2lR}\cos \theta'(\gamma + \sin \gamma \cos \gamma)$$

for the parallel plane, and

$$E_p = \frac{I}{2lR}\sin^2 \gamma$$

for the perpendicular plane.

Note: All the results obtained in this section could also have been obtained by the method used in the section on "Other Distributions" which employs direct integration.

FLUX TRANSFER

In the foregoing sections, illumination at a point from area and line sources has been considered. In this section the flux received by an area from an area or line source will be considered. Before we derive the formulae for the various transfer functions it is convenient to define a general transfer function (f_{ab}). This function has been termed the "form factor" by Phillips and Prokhovnik,[2] since when the sources are uniformly diffuse it is simply a function of the geometry of the surfaces.

$$f_{ab} = \frac{\text{Flux received by surface } b}{\text{Flux emitted by surface } a}.$$

The significance of the order of the subscripts is discussed at the end of this section (p. 38).

RECIPROCITY

When we calculate the flux transfer from one surface to another we often make use of the law of reciprocity. The law states that: if two uniform diffuse light sources illuminate each other the flux transfer from each source to the other is in the same proportion as their luminous emittance values. Thus, if they have the same luminous emittance the flux transfer will be the same in each direction. What is not always realized is that if the sources lie in parallel planes the limitation to uniform diffuse sources is unnecessary.

Proof

1. *Parallel plane reciprocity*

Consider the flux transfer between two parallel surfaces S_1 and S_2 (Fig. 2.15). Let the intensity distribution of each element of area be the same function of angle θ for both surfaces, and let them

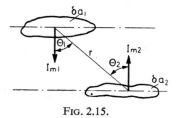

FIG. 2.15.

have luminous emittance H_1 and H_2 respectively, then

$$I_{\theta_1} = I_{m_1} f(\theta), \qquad I_{\theta_2} = I_{m_2} f(\theta).$$

Also,

$$I_{m_1} = MH_1 \delta a_1 \quad \text{and} \quad I_{m_2} = MH_2 \delta a_2 \quad \text{and} \quad \theta_1 = \theta_2$$

where M is a constant relating the intensity normal to the surface to the luminous emittance H.

The flux transferred from 1 to 2

$$F_{12} = \int E_2 da_2 = \int_2 \int_1 \frac{I_{m_1} f(\theta) \cos \theta \, da_2}{r^2} \qquad (2.1)$$

and the flux transferred from 2 to 1,

$$F_{21} = \int E_1 da_1 = \int_1 \int_2 \frac{I_{m_2} f(\theta) \cos \theta \, da_1}{r_2}, \qquad (2.2)$$

substituting for I_m in each case,

(1) becomes $\qquad F_{12} = \int_2 \int_1 \frac{MH_1 da_1 f(\theta) \cos \theta \, da_2}{r^2}, \qquad (2.3)$

(2) becomes $\qquad F_{21} = \int_1 \int_2 \frac{MH_2 da_2 f(\theta) \cos \theta \, da_1}{r^2}. \qquad (2.4)$

Since the order of integration may be reversed,

$$\frac{F_{12}}{H_1} = \frac{F_{21}}{H_2}.$$

Equations (2.3) and (2.4) are true for distributions which are symmetrical about the normal, including a cosine or uniform diffuse distribution.

2. *General reciprocity* (Fig. 2.16)

When the sources have a uniform diffuse distribution,

$$I_{\theta_1} = \frac{H_1}{\pi} da_1 \cos \theta_1 \qquad \text{and} \qquad I_{\theta_2} = \frac{H_2}{\pi} da_2 \cos \theta_2,$$

so that

$$F_{12} = \frac{1}{\pi} \int_2 \int_1 \frac{H_1 da_1 \cos \theta_1 \cos \theta_2 \, da_2}{r^2},$$

$$F_{21} = \frac{1}{\pi} \int_1 \int_2 \frac{H_2 da_2 \cos \theta_2 \cos \theta_1 \, da_1}{r^2},$$

i.e. $\qquad \dfrac{F_{12}}{H_1} = \dfrac{F_{21}}{H_2} \quad$ for any orientation or

$$\frac{S_2 E_2}{H_1} = \frac{S_1 E_1}{H_2}.$$

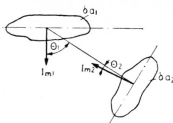

Fig. 2.16.

Infinite Planes

Consider the flux transfer between two infinite planes.
Extension of the illumination equation for a disc source

$$E = \frac{L\pi}{2}(1 - \cos \alpha)$$

or a rectangular source

$$E = 4\frac{L}{2}(\beta_1 \sin \gamma + \gamma_1 \sin \beta)$$

to the cases of infinite radius or infinite sides respectively produces the same result,

$$E = \pi L = H,$$

and since this value of illumination will occur at all points of the receiving plane the flux transfer function must be unity. This result is confirmed by the fact that since a finite distance between the planes must be negligible compared with the size of the planes the result will be the same as if they were placed together, i.e. all the flux from one must reach the other.

Cavities

Flux transfer from aperture to interior: 1 to 2 (Fig. 2.17)

The flux transfer function for the aperture to the interior of a cavity (f_{12}) is unity since all flux entering whether uniformly diffused or not must strike the interior of the cavity.

Flux transfer from interior to aperture: 2 to 1

From the previously established principle that two uniform diffuse sources will produce the same illumination at a point P if they are of equal luminance and appear to have the same boundary when viewed from P, we may conclude that the result will be the same as if the aperture were placed in front of a uniformly diffusing plane of infinite size.

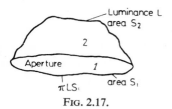

FIG. 2.17.

Hence, the illumination at the aperture due to the luminance of the cavity will be $E = \pi L$.

Let S_2 be the area of the cavity and S_1 the area of the aperture. Then the flux emitted by the cavity $= \pi L S_2$ and the flux received by the aperture $= \pi L S_1$. Therefore the fraction of flux transferred from 2 to 1 is given by

$$\frac{S_1}{S_2} = f_{21}.$$

Flux transfer across the cavity surface: 2 to 2

Surface 2 can "see" itself, and so there must be flux transfer across the cavity surfaces. The transfer function is obtained by subtracting the aperture transfer function from unity.

Thus the fraction of flux transferred from 2 to 2 is

$$1 - \frac{S_1}{S_2} = f_{22}.$$

Within a Cylinder

Flux transferred from 1 to 2 (Fig. 2.18)

In Fig. 2.19 the cylinder is shown within a sphere. The illumination at all points on the inside of the sphere due to the end of

2a*

the cylinder AB must be the same as that which the spherical cap ACB would produce if it had the same luminance (by the principle of equivalence: see p. 23).

FIG. 2.18.

Earlier in the chapter it is shown that the direct illumination on the inside of a sphere from any luminous element of the sphere is the same at all points (Fig. 2.4, p. 23).

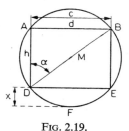

FIG. 2.19.

It follows that the illumination (E) of the spherical cap DFE due to the end of the cylinder AB must be constant.

The flux passing through the disc DE (the opposite end of the cylinder (2)) must be

$$F_{12} = E \times \text{(area of spherical cap } DFE\text{)}.$$

The illumination at point D is given by the disc source formula

$$E = \frac{L\pi}{2} (1 - \cos \alpha)$$

$$= \frac{L\pi}{2} \left[1 - \frac{h}{\sqrt{(h^2 + d^2)}} \right].$$

Since E is a constant,

$$F_{12} = \frac{L\pi}{2} \left[1 - \frac{h}{\sqrt{(h^2 + d^2)}} \right] \times \text{area of the spherical cap } DFE$$

and area of the spherical cap $DFE = \pi \sqrt{(h^2 + d^2)} \, x$.

Substituting
$$x = \frac{\sqrt{(h^2 + d^2)}}{2} - \frac{h}{2}$$

we get
$$\text{area of cap} = \pi \sqrt{(h^2 + d^2)} \left[\frac{\sqrt{(h^2 + d^2)}}{2} - \frac{h}{2} \right].$$

Therefore

$$F_{12} = \frac{L\pi^2}{2} \left[1 - \frac{h}{\sqrt{(h^2 + d^2)}} \right] \sqrt{(h^2 + d^2)} \left[\frac{\sqrt{(h^2 + d^2)}}{2} - \frac{h}{2} \right]$$

$$= L\pi^2 \left[\frac{\sqrt{(h^2 + d^2)} - h}{2} \right] \left[\frac{\sqrt{(h^2 + d^2)} - h}{2} \right]$$

$$= \frac{L\pi^2}{2} \left[\frac{d^2}{2} + h^2 - h\sqrt{(h^2 + d^2)} \right].$$

Also the total flux emitted by $1 = L\pi^2 \dfrac{d^2}{4} = F_1$.

Fraction of total flux transferred from 1 to 2,

$$\frac{F_{12}}{F_1} = 1 + \frac{2h^2}{d^2} - \frac{2h}{d^2}\sqrt{(h^2 + d^2)} = f_{12}.$$

Flux transferred from 1 to 3

The flux which leaves 1 but does not directly reach 2 must be incident on 3, and so the fraction of the total flux emitted by 1 which is received by 3 is given by

$$1 - \frac{F_{12}}{F_1} = \frac{2h}{d^2}\sqrt{(h^2 + d^2)} - \frac{2h^2}{d^2} = f_{13}.$$

Flux transferred from 3 to 1 or 3 to 2

If we use the principle of reciprocity (p. 32) we can obtain the transfer function for surface 1 with respect to surface 3, f_{31}, as follows:

$$\frac{\text{Flux received by 1 from 3}}{\text{Luminous emittance of 3}} = \frac{\text{Flux received by 3 from 1}}{\text{Luminous emittance of 1}},$$

$$\frac{H_3 S_3 f_{31}}{H_3} = \frac{H_1 S_1 f_{13}}{H_1},$$

where S_1 and S_3 are the areas of surfaces 1 and 3 respectively.

Therefore

$$f_{31} = \frac{S_1}{S_3} f_{13}.$$

By symmetry

$$f_{32} = f_{31}.$$

Flux transferred from 3 to 3

The transfer function f_{33} is obtained by subtracting f_{31} and f_{32} from unity, i.e.

$$f_{33} = 1 - f_{31} - f_{32}$$
$$= 1 - 2f_{31}.$$

Within a Square Room (see also Chapter 8)

The flux transfer from surface 1 to surface 2 (Fig. 2.20) is dealt with in the section on zonal multipliers for area sources in Chapter 3. The transfer of flux from 3 to 1, etc., is dealt with in exactly the same way as for the case of the cylinder described above.

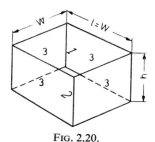

FIG. 2.20.

It can be shown that for equal areas of surfaces 1 and 2, and with the same spacing h, the transfer functions for the cylinder are of the same order as those for the square (within 10%), and may therefore be used as an approximation to the square room transfer functions.

ALTERNATIVE MEANING OF TRANSFER FUNCTION

By definition

$$f_{ab} = \frac{\text{Flux received by surface } b}{\text{Flux emitted by surface } a}$$

so that

$$f_{ab} = \frac{S_b E_b}{S_a H_a} \quad \text{and} \quad f_{ba} = \frac{S_a E_a}{S_b H_b}.$$

Now

$$\frac{S_b E_b}{H_a} = \frac{S_a E_a}{H_b} \quad \text{(reciprocity theorem, see p. 32),}$$

and so

$$f_{ab} = \frac{S_a E_a}{S_a H_b} = \frac{E_a}{H_b},$$

i.e. f_{ab} can also be defined as the illumination of surface a divided by the luminous emittance of surface b.

The relationship between f_{ab} and f_{ba} is also determined since

$$E_a = H_b f_{ab}$$

so that

$$f_{ba} = \frac{S_a}{S_b} \frac{H_b f_{ab}}{H_b}$$

or

$$f_{ba} = \frac{S_a}{S_b} f_{ab}.$$

To sum up, when the transfer functions are considered as ratios between illumination and luminous emittance, the first subscript refers to the receiving surface, but when they are taken as the ratio of two fluxes the first subscript refers to the emitting surface.

OTHER DISTRIBUTIONS

Point Sources

Point sources may be dealt with by means of the inverse-square law regardless of their intensity distribution, provided that this is known.

Linear Sources

Solutions for sources which do not have a simple cosine distribution may be obtained by applying the inverse-square law to each element of the source and integrating.

Consider the illumination at a point P directly opposite one end of the light source (Fig. 2.21).

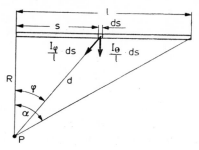

FIG. 2.21.

Fig. 2.22 shows the three basic cases that need to be considered. In this figure a circle of radius R has been drawn normal to the axis of the source, passing through point P.

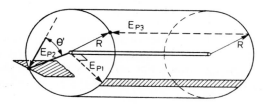

FIG. 2.22.

CASE 1. *On a plane tangential to the circle and parallel with the long axis of the source* (E_{p_1})

$$dE_{p_1} = \frac{\text{Intensity per unit length}}{d^2} \times ds \times \cos \varphi$$

$$= \frac{I_\varphi}{l} \times \frac{ds}{(R \sec \varphi)^2} \times ds \cos \varphi,$$

where I_φ is the intensity of the whole source in direction φ.
And since

$$S = R \tan \varphi,$$
$$ds = R \sec^2 \varphi \, d\varphi,$$

giving
$$dE_{p_1} = \frac{I_\varphi}{l} \times \frac{R \sec^2 \varphi \cos \varphi \, d\varphi}{R^2 \sec^2 \varphi},$$

$$E_{p_1} = \int_0^\alpha \frac{I_\varphi \cos \varphi \, d\varphi}{lR}.$$

The solution depends upon the variation of I_φ over the range of the integral (given by the axial polar curve, Fig. 1.7(b)). This variation may usually be expressed in terms of the intensity at an angle θ normal to the long axis of the source (given by the transverse polar curve) [Fig. 1.7(c)], i.e.

$$I_\varphi = I_\theta f(\varphi) \quad \text{(often of the form } I_\varphi = I_\theta \cos{}^n\varphi\text{)}.$$

Thus
$$E_{p_1} = \frac{I_\theta}{lR} \int_0^\alpha f(\varphi) \cos \varphi \, d\varphi.$$

Holmes [1] calls

$$\int_0^\alpha f(\varphi) \cos \varphi \, d\varphi$$

the parallel plane ASPECT FACTOR and gives it the symbol (AF). This is a convenient notation and will be used in this book. So that

$$E_{p_1} = \frac{I_\theta}{lR} (AF).$$

CASE 2. *On a plane parallel to the long axis of the source but not tangential to the circle (E_{p_2})*

$$E_{p_2} = \frac{I_\theta}{lR} (AF) \cos \theta,$$

since same value of $\cos \theta$ applies for each element of the linear source, and as a constant it may be taken outside the integral sign.

For an alternative approach see the section on illumination as a vector quantity (p. 49).

CASE 3. *On a plane normal to the long axis of the source (E_{p_3})*

$$dE_{p_3} = \frac{\text{Intensity per unit length}}{d^2} \times ds \sin \varphi,$$

giving
$$E_{p_3} = \frac{I_\theta}{lR} (a.f.),$$

where (a.f.) is the perpendicular plane aspect factor, i.e.

$$(a.f.) = \int_0^\alpha f(\varphi) \sin \varphi \, d\varphi.$$

Graphs of AF and a.f. in terms of α for a number of common axial distribution are given in Chapter 8, Figs. 8.5 and 8.6.

The treatment for random orientation is given in the section on illumination as a vector quantity. Where direct integration is not possible, graphical or numerical integration should be used.

CASE 4. *Point not under one end of the source*

If the value of illumination at a point under the end of the source can be calculated, the illumination at any other point may be obtained by the method of component sources. Consider as an example Fig. 2.23. In this case

$$E_{p_a} = E_{AB} + E_{BC},$$
$$E_{p_b} = E_{AD} - E_{CD},$$

where E_{AB}, E_{BC}, E_{AD}, E_{CD} are the illuminations produced at P from sources having the same intensity per unit length as the true source AC but of length indicated by the suffix.

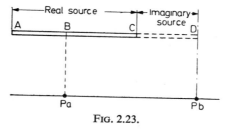

FIG. 2.23.

If the axis of the source is normal to the plane receiving the illumination at P_a, then the illumination would be either E_{AB} or E_{BC} according to which side of the plane was under consideration.

At P_b the illumination would still be given by $E_{p_b} = E_{AD} - E_{CD}$.

FLUX FROM A LINEAR SOURCE ON TO A PARALLEL SURFACE

By using the aspect factor notation an expression may be written for the flux passing through the curved window ($ABCD$) of a sector solid (Fig. 2.24).

The illumination may be taken as constant in value across any arc of the sector window if the mean value of intensity over the angle $\Delta\theta$ is used in its calculation. This is because all other factors in the illumination equation are constant for this arc. However,

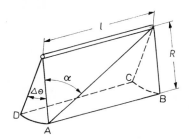

FIG. 2.24.

the value of illumination at a point P will vary with its position along the axis of the sector (Fig. 2.25). This illumination is made up of that from a source of length s subtending an angle φ_1 and that from a source of length $(l - s)$ subtending an angle φ_2.

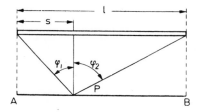

FIG. 2.25.

The flux through the curved window $ABCD$ is therefore given by

$$F_{ABCD} = \int_{s=0}^{s=l} \frac{I_\theta}{lR} R\Delta\theta \, [(AF_{\varphi_1}) + (AF_{\varphi_2})] \, ds \qquad (2.5)$$

$$= \frac{I_\theta}{l} \Delta\theta \int_0^l [(AF_{\varphi_1}) + (AF\varphi_2)] \, ds. \qquad (2.6)$$

Integrating by parts,

$$\int_0^l (\mathrm{AF}_{\varphi_1})\, ds = [s(\mathrm{AF}_{\varphi_1})]_0^l - \int_0^l s\, d(\mathrm{AF}_{\varphi_1})$$

$$= l(\mathrm{AF}_{\varphi}) - \int_0^l s\, d[\int_0^\alpha f(\varphi_1) \cos \varphi_1\, d\varphi].$$

Now

$$s = R \tan \varphi_1.$$

Therefore

$$\int_0^l (\mathrm{AF}_{\varphi_1})\, ds = l(\mathrm{AF}_\alpha) - R \int_0^\alpha f(\varphi_1) \sin \varphi_1\, d\varphi$$

$$= l(\mathrm{AF}_\alpha) - R(\mathrm{a.f.}_\alpha),$$

since when $s = l, \varphi = \alpha.$

By symmetry

$$\int_0^l (\mathrm{AF}_{\varphi_1})\, ds = \int_0^l (\mathrm{AF}_{\varphi_2})\, ds,$$

and so from eq. (2.5)

$$F_{ABCD} = 2I\theta\, \triangle\theta[(\mathrm{AF}_\alpha) - \cot_\alpha (\mathrm{a.f.}_\alpha)]$$

or

$$F_{ABCD} = I_\theta K,$$

where

$$K = 2\triangle\theta[(\mathrm{AF}_\alpha) - \cot_\alpha (\mathrm{a.f.}_\alpha)]. \tag{2.7}$$

Thus for a constant sector angle $\triangle\theta$ (say 10°), and a given axial distribution, K is a function of α only, where $\alpha = \tan^{-1}(l/R)$. A graph giving values of K for 10° sectors plotted against R/l, i.e. $\cot \alpha$, is given in the section on K factors in Chapter 8 (Fig. 8.9).

Use of K Factors

1. The sector solid method may be used to calculate (to a close approximation) the flux received by an area of a parallel plane. For example, it can be used to calculate the flux received by the floor or ceiling or parallel walls from a line of fluorescent tubular lamps or fittings. The procedure is given in Chapter 8.

2. The flux passing through window $ABCD$ when $\cot \alpha = 0$, i.e. $\alpha = 90°$, is the total flux emitted by the source into that sector. By calculating this value for all the sectors contained in an angle

$\theta = 360°$ (Fig. 1.11, p. 16), the total flux emitted by the source may be obtained. The K value for $\alpha = 90°$ is called the limiting value of K and given the symbol K_L.

From eq. (2.7)

$$K_L = 2\triangle\theta \ (AF_{90}).$$

The procedure is given in Chapter 1 and K_L for common axial distributions is given in Table 1.3 (p. 16).

Extension to Cases where the Window is Longer than the Source

In practical installations line sources are frequently terminated short of the walls, and so the K factor method will now be extended to deal with such a case.

Although the distances between the ends of the line source and the walls are assumed to be equal in the treatment given below, the same approach can be used to deal with unequal distances.

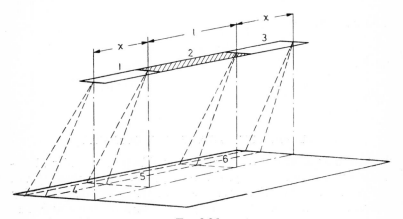

FIG. 2.26.

In Fig. 2.26 let section 2 of length l be the real source and let section 1 of length x and section 3 of length x represent imaginary sources. Let the imaginary sources have the same intensity distribution as the real source. Also let section 1 have the same luminous emittance as section 2.

Now the flux from section 2 to sections 4, 5 and 6 (i.e. $F_{2(4,5,6)}$) can be found as follows:

$$F_{(1,2)(4,5)} - F_{14} = F_{2(4,5)} + F_{15}.$$

By the principle of reciprocity (p. 32),

$$\frac{F_{15}}{H_1} = \frac{F_{51}}{H_5} = \frac{F_{53}}{H_5} = \frac{F_{26}}{H_2} \quad \text{and, since} \quad H_1 = H_2,$$

$$F_{15} = F_{26}.$$

Thus

$$F_{(1,2)(4,5)} - F_{14} = F_{2(4,5,6)},$$

and so for each sector the flux through the sector window

$$F_{2(4,5,6)} = \frac{I_\theta}{l} (x + l) K_{(1,2)} - \frac{I_\theta}{l} x K_1,$$

where $K_{(1,2)}$ is the value of K for

$$\alpha = \tan^{-1} \frac{(x + l)}{R}$$

and K_1 is the value of K for

$$\alpha = \tan^{-1}(x/R),$$

giving

$$F_{2(4,5,6)} = \frac{I_\theta}{l} [(x + l) K_{(1,2)} - x K_1].$$

ILLUMINATION AS A VECTOR QUANTITY

A technique which often proves valuable is to consider illumination as a vector quantity. If S is a point source at the origin of a system of rectangular coordinates and P is a point receiving illumination from this source (Fig. 2.27), then the illumination E_z at P on the plane containing the directions X and Y, is given by

$$E_z = \frac{I}{d^2} \cos \theta_z.$$

Similarly on the plane of X and Z,

$$E_y = \frac{I}{d^2} \cos \theta_y$$

and on the plane of Z and Y

$$E_x = \frac{I}{d^2} \cos \theta_x$$

or

$$E_x = E \cos \theta_x, \quad E_y = E \cos \theta_y, \quad E_z = E \cos \theta_z,$$

where E is the maximum illumination which can be produced at point P by source S. E_x, E_y and E_z can therefore be considered as components of an illumination vector $\mathbf{E}$. Also, since any area source

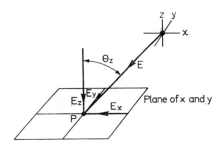

FIG. 2.27.

may be considered to consist of an infinite number of point sources, and the components E_x, E_y and E_z for each of these can be summed, an illumination vector can be obtained for an area or line source.

ILLUMINATION ON AN OBLIQUE PLANE

When the direction and magnitude of $\mathbf{E}$ are known, then the illumination at the point P on any plane is obtained by multiplying by the cosine of the angle (θ_n) between the direction of $\mathbf{E}$ and the normal to the plane at P, i.e.

$$E_p = \mathbf{E} \cos \theta_n.$$

Alternatively,[3] if the component vectors E_x, E_y and E_z are themselves resolved into orthogonal components with one of the components in each case coincident with the normal to the inclined plane, then the other components must be parallel to this plane and contribute zero illumination; so only the components normal to the plane need be considered. Using the notation given in Fig. 2.28 we find

$$E_p = E_z \cos \Phi + E_x \cos \beta \sin \Phi + E_y \sin \beta \sin \Phi.$$

In using this expression, it is found convenient to make the direction of the z-axis to coincide with the normal to the horizontal plane. E_z then becomes the illumination on the horizontal plane. Also E_x and E_y become the illuminations on vertical planes placed at right angles to each other (called E_h, E_{v_1} and E_{v_2} respectively in Chapter 8).

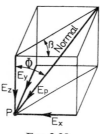

FIG. 2.28.

1. Point Sources

If the y-axis is set parallel to the plane containing the point P (Fig. 2.29), then $\beta = 0°$ and

$$E_p = E_z \cos \Phi + E_x \sin \Phi$$

and, since $E_x = E_z \tan \delta$ (Fig. 2.30),

$$= E_z \frac{x}{h_m},$$

$$E_p = E_z \left(\cos \Phi + \frac{x}{h_m} \sin \Phi \right).$$

Thus the value of illumination occurring on a plane tilted at an angle Φ to the horizontal (called E_t in Chapter 8) can be obtained by multiplying the horizontal plane illumination E_z by a correction factor, i.e.

$$E_p = E_z C_t, \quad \text{where } C_t = \left(\cos \Phi + \frac{x}{h_m} \sin \Phi \right).$$

A graph for obtaining C_t in terms of the angle of tilt Φ and x/h_m is given in Chapter 8 (Fig. 8.18).

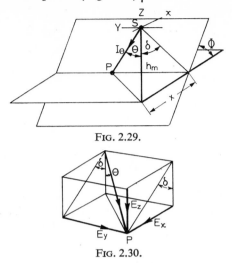

Fig. 2.29.

Fig. 2.30.

2. Line Sources

In this case the y-axis is made to coincide with the axis of the source (Fig. 2.31), and so E_x = Illumination on the vertical plane parallel to the source. E_y = Illumination on the vertical plane normal to the source. E_z = Illumination on the horizontal plane. Now, as before,

$$E_x = E_z \tan \theta$$

$$= E_z \frac{x}{h_m} .$$

(*Note:* θ is used here to be consistent with the other sections on line sources, but it corresponds to angle δ used in the section on point sources.) And so

$$E_p = E_z(\cos \Phi + \frac{h_m}{x} \cos \beta \sin \Phi) + E_y \sin \beta \sin \Phi.$$

When the plane of P is parallel with the axis of the source $\beta = 0$, and

$$E_p = E_z (\cos \Phi + \frac{x}{h_m} \sin \Phi)$$

$$= E_z C_t. \quad \text{(Compare case 2, p.41.)}$$

This is the same result as that obtained for the point source earlier, and the same values for C_t may be used (Fig. 8.18). For some values of β the plane of the point P may cut the source. Under

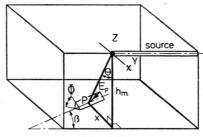

FIG. 2.31.

this condition care must be taken to use only that part of the source which can produce illumination at point P in calculating a value for E_z.

3. Area Sources

The general expression applies to area sources, but since an inclined plane frequently cuts the source and changes not only its size, but also its shape with respect to point P (Fig. 2.32), the calculation is more difficult.

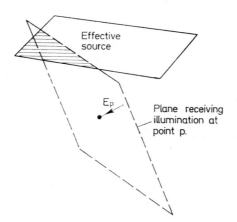

FIG. 2.32.

If the change in size and shape is not taken into account, the value obtained will be the difference in the illumination on the two sides of the plane at P.

EXTENSION OF THE DISC SOURCE FORMULA

In the section on uniform diffuse sources we established the following:

1. The illumination at a point on the inside of a sphere produced by a luminous element of the sphere is independent of the position of the point with respect to the luminous element.
2. That if two sources appear to have the same boundary when viewed from the illuminated point, and also have the same luminance, then the illumination produced is the same in each case.

Thus a luminous disc of diameter AB (Fig. 2.33) will produce the same illumination at P as the spherical cap ACB of the same luminance. The illumination produced by the disc will be the same at every point on the spherical surface denoted by arc AOB.

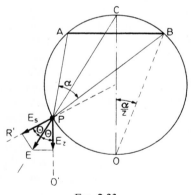

FIG. 2.33.

We have already established an expression for the illumination E_s at one point, namely O (p. 25):

$$E_s = \frac{\pi L}{2}(1 - \cos \alpha).$$

Also it is a property of a circle that angle α is independent of the position of P on the arc AOB and so the equation in this form may be used for any point on the sphere wall. The illumination vector **E** coincides with the direction of the chord CP for the following reason; in Fig. 2.34 distance QC has been chosen to be equal

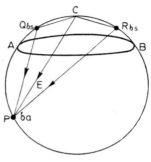

FIG. 2.34.

to CR so that angle QPC = angle CPR (angles subtended by equal chords). We have already established that an element of area δs at Q will produce the same illumination as an element of equal area placed at R. Resolving into a component along CP and at right angles to CP in each case, we find that the components at right angles to CP cancel out. Hence the resultant vector lies along CP. Since this process can be repeated for similar pairs of points until the whole of the cap has been considered, the illumination vector for the cap must lie along CP.

Another property of a circle is that the extension of chord CP (Fig. 2.33) bisects the angle formed by PO' and the extension to the radius PR', i.e. the direction of the illumination vector bisects the angle between the component E_s producing illumination on the sphere wall and the component E_z producing illumination on the parallel plane.

Since the value of each of these components is given by $E \cos \theta$,

$$E_s = E_z.$$

Hence

$$E_p = \frac{\pi L}{2}(1 - \cos \alpha)$$

is the general equation for illumination on the parallel plane from a uniformly diffusing disc source regardless of the position of point P in that plane.

THE SPHERICAL DIFFUSE SOURCE

Using the principle of equivalence established earlier and employed in the previous section, we may treat a diffusing sphere as an equivalent disc source (Fig. 2.35).

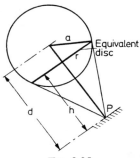

FIG. 2.35.

The disc source equation is

$$E_p = \pi L \frac{r^2}{r^2 + h^2} \quad \text{but} \quad \frac{h^2}{r^2} = \frac{d^2 - a^2}{a^2}.$$

So

$$E_p = \pi L \frac{1}{1 + (d^2 - a^2)/a^2},$$

and since the intensity I_s of the sphere in any direction is given by $\pi L a^2$,

$$E_p = \frac{I_s}{d^2}.$$

Thus a spherical diffuse source obeys the inverse-square law at all distances provided that the measurement of d is taken from the centre of the sphere.

The above result is a consequence of the fact that the illumination vector always acts from the centre of a diffusing sphere. The illumination at a point on a tilted plane for any source is obtained by multiplying by the cosine of the angle between the normal to the illuminated plane and the direction of the illumination vector, giving

$$E_p = \cos \theta_n$$

$$= \frac{I_s}{d^2} \cos \theta_n,$$

and so the cosine law also applies to the diffusing sphere. It should be noted that if the plane of the point P cuts through the source, the above equation will give the difference in the illuminations produced by the sphere on opposite sides of the plane (see "Area Sources").

An alternative and very simple proof that a uniform spherical source obeys the inverse-square law is indicated in Fig. 2.36. The

Fig. 2.36.

flux F received by a sphere of radius r will be the same whatever the value given to r. The illumination at any point on the inside of the enclosing sphere is given by

$$\mathbf{E} = \frac{F}{4\pi r^2}.$$

From this equation it is clear that the illumination varies as the square of the distance of the point of measurement from the centre of the spherical source. Note that this proof does not depend upon the source being uniformly diffusing, but only upon uniform emission per unit area.

VECTOR AND SCALAR ILLUMINATION

Vector Illumination

The previous section has been used to show the advantages of considering illumination as a vector quantity. This has been restricted to its use in solving problems involving the orientation of surfaces with respect to a light source. When more than one light source is involved of which one is behind the surface to be illuminated (Fig. 2.37), a vector calculation applying to both sources

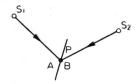

FIG. 2.37. The illumination vector at P for the case shown is $E_A - E_B$.

gives a solution which is the difference between the illuminations. Clearly, for the most common calculation (i.e. the illumination on a particular surface) such calculations are of little value, but it has been suggested that these illumination differences may be used to indicate the directional properties of a lighting installation. The term which has been coined for this work is the "flow" of light.[4]

The method used is to consider the differences of illumination across the diameters of an infinitely small sphere placed at each of the points of interest (Fig. 2.38). Vector illumination at a point

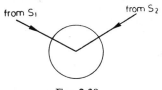

FIG. 2.38.

is defined as the maximum difference of illumination which occurs across the diameters of the sphere. The vector illumination produced at a particular point by each of the sources in an installation can be calculated and combined vectorially to obtain the vector illumination at that point for the whole installation. Vector illumination has both magnitude and direction, and so field diagrams indicating the direction of the vector can be constructed. These are similar in appearance to electric or magnetic field diagrams.

Scalar Illumination

Once the illumination vector is used to denote the difference of illumination on the two sides of a surface (or across the diameters of an infinitely small sphere) it ceases to indicate the quantity of light available at the point of interest. To overcome this difficulty the concept of "scalar" illumination is introduced. The scalar illumination at a point is defined as the average illumination on the surface of an infinitesimally small sphere at that point due to light reaching it from all directions.

The scalar illumination at a point due to a small source (Fig. 2.39)

$$= \frac{\text{Flux intercepted by a disc of the same diameter as the sphere}}{\text{area of the sphere}}$$

$$= \frac{I}{d^2} \times \frac{\pi r^2}{4\pi r^2} = \frac{I}{4d^2}.$$

FIG. 2.39.

When the source is a small element of a uniformly diffusing source (Fig. 2.40) the equation can be rewritten as

$$E_{\text{scalar}} = \frac{L \, ds \cos \theta}{4d^2}.$$

Since $I = L \, ds \cos \theta$,
where L = luminance in candelas/ft^2,

$$E_{\text{scalar}} = \frac{L d\omega}{4}$$

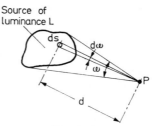

FIG. 2.40.

taking
$$\frac{ds \cos \theta}{d^2} = d\omega.$$

Thus for a uniformly diffusing area source the scalar illumination at a point is given by

$$\frac{L}{4} \int_0^\omega d\omega = \frac{L\omega}{4},$$

where ω is the solid angle subtended by the source at the point of interest (steradians).

Vector and scalar illumination finds use in the study of the "quality" of the light distribution within an enclosed space where it becomes an alternative to studying just the illumination on the various room surfaces.[4]

REFERENCES

1. MOON, P. and SPENCER, D. E., *Lighting Design* (Addison-Wesley Press, 1948).
2. PHILLIPS, R. O. and PROKHOVNIK, S. J., Monograph of I.E.S. (London), No. 3, 1960.
3. BEAN, A. R., Monograph of I.E.S. (London), No. 8, 1964.
4. LYNES, J. A., BURT W., JACKSON, G. K. and CUTTLE, C., *Trans. I.E.S. (London)* **31**, 65 (1966).

CHAPTER 3

DIRECT FLUX AND INTERREFLECTIONS

CLASSIFICATION OF ROOMS

Problems involving the distribution of luminous flux within an interior can be simplified if use is made of the work of Harrison and Anderson, and particularly Hisano, in classifying rooms.

The classification is based on finding the square room which is equivalent to a given rectangular room, so that the calculations need only be made for square rooms.

Hisano[1] has shown that if a rectangular room has the same ratio of horizontal surface area to vertical surface area as a square room, then the results of similar average illumination calculations for the two rooms will agree within 10%. This finding is subject to the following limitations:

(a) the length of the rectangular room must not be greater than four times the width;

(b) the ratio must be equal to or greater than 0·25.

The ratio may be expressed as follows.

$$\frac{2 \times \text{length} \times \text{width}}{2 \times \text{height (length} + \text{width)}}.$$

Two forms of this ratio are used in this book:

$$Room\ Index\ (K_r) = \frac{l \times w}{h_m(l + w)},$$

where h_m is the distance from the working plane to the plane of the lighting fittings (Fig. 3.9),

and $$Room\ Ratio\ (R_r) = \frac{l \times w}{h(l + w)},$$

where h is the distance between the working plane and the ceiling.

Thus for ceiling mounted fittings $h_m = h$ and $K_r = R_r$.
Note: Hisano's equation was

$$K_r = \frac{h_m(w + l)}{2w \times l},$$

but the form given above is that used in British practice.

ZONAL MULTIPLIERS

Interreflection calculations require a knowledge of the direct flux to the floor, walls and ceiling as well as the light output of the sources.

The zonal multiplier method[2] has been devised to solve this problem for rectangular rooms with regular layouts of lighting units. Most of the methods of flux determination already described may be adapted to the calculation of zonal flux, i.e. the flux emitted within certain angular limits. The most useful is the zonal constant method.

Once the zonal flux has been determined it is multiplied by the appropriate zonal multiplier to obtain the flux from that zone which directly reaches the surface in question, usually the working plane or floor.

For example, for a single fitting

$$\text{flux to floor} = \sum_{\theta = 0}^{\theta = 90^\circ} ZM \times \text{zonal flux};$$

for an installation, ZM is the average value for all the fittings and the zonal flux term is the sum of their individual contributions.

Derivation of Zonal Multipliers

The zonal multiplier is the fraction of zonal flux incident on the specified surface. This fraction is approximately equal to the ratio of the unshaded area of the ring shown in Fig. 3.1 to the total area of the ring. The value is exact when the flux distribution across the ring is uniform.

In the majority of cases the zonal multiplier may be obtained to an acceptable accuracy if the ratio of the dotted arc over the

3*

unshaded part of the ring to the complete dotted circle is taken, or

$$ZM = \frac{(360° - 2\varphi)\, r}{360°r}$$

$$= 1 - \frac{2\varphi}{360°},$$

where φ is in degrees.

This may be determined by calculation or by drawing for each source in the installation and the mean value computed. Zonal multipliers are usually calculated for 10° zones, i.e. 0–10°, 10–20°, 20–30°, etc.

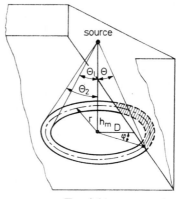

FIG. 3.1.

In a few cases this method may not be sufficiently accurate. For example, in tall, narrow rooms where nearly the whole of the dotted arc may lie inside the room with almost half of the area of the annular ring lying outside the room.

To check doubtful cases of this type an exact calculation of the multiplier can be made if we use the equation for the $2\varphi/360°$ term which is developed below.

$$\frac{\text{Average illumination} \times \text{shaded area of ring}}{\text{Zonal lumens}}$$

$$= \int \frac{(I_\theta \cos^3 \theta / h_m^2) \times \text{length of arc} \times dr}{I_\theta \times \text{zonal constant}},$$

where $r = h_m \tan \theta$,

$$= \frac{1}{\text{zonal constant}} \int_{\theta_1}^{\theta_2} 2\varphi \sin \theta \, d\theta,$$

where
$$\varphi = \cos^{-1}\left(\frac{\theta_1 \, D}{h_m \tan \theta}\right).$$

Integrating by parts gives

$$\frac{1}{\text{zonal constant}} \left[2\varphi(-\cos\theta) - \int 2(-\cos\theta) \frac{d\varphi}{d\theta} \, d\theta \right].$$

Let
$$\left(\frac{D}{h_m}\right)^2 = q \quad \text{and} \quad \frac{q}{\tan^2\theta} = u,$$

then
$$\cos\theta = \sqrt{\left(\frac{u}{u+q}\right)} \quad \text{and} \quad \varphi = \cos^{-1}\sqrt{u},$$

giving

$$\frac{1}{\text{zonal constant}} \left\{ 2\varphi(-\cos\theta) - \int \left[-2\sqrt{\left(\frac{u}{u+q}\right)} \right] \left[\frac{-d\sqrt{u}}{\sqrt{(1-u)}} \right] \right\}$$

$$= \frac{1}{\text{zonal constant}} \times$$

$$\times \left\{ 2\varphi(-\cos\theta) - \int \left[-2\sqrt{\left(\frac{u}{u+q}\right)} \right] \left[-\tfrac{1}{2} \frac{du}{\sqrt{u}\sqrt{(1-\mu)}} \right] \right\}$$

$$= \frac{1}{\text{zonal constant}} \left\{ 2\varphi(-\cos\theta) - \int \frac{du}{\sqrt{[(u+q)(1-u)]}} \right\}$$

$$= \frac{1}{\text{zonal constant}} \times$$

$$\times \left\{ -(2\varphi\cos\theta) - \int \frac{du}{\sqrt{\left[\left(\frac{q+1}{2}\right)^2 - \left(u + \frac{q+1}{2}\right)^2 \right]}} \right\}$$

$$= \frac{1}{\text{zonal constant}} \left[-(2\varphi\cos\theta) - \sin^{-1}\left(\frac{2u+q-1}{q+1}\right) \right]_{\theta_1}^{\theta_2}$$

$$= \frac{1}{\text{zonal constant}} \left[2\varphi\cos\theta + \sin^{-1}\left(\frac{2u+q-1}{q+1}\right) \right]_{\theta_2}^{\theta_1}.$$

Thus the zonal multiplier is obtained from

$$ZM = 1 - \frac{1}{\text{zonal constant}} \left[2\varphi\cos\theta + \sin^{-1}\left(\frac{2u+q-1}{q+1}\right) \right]_{\theta_2}^{\theta_1},$$

where

$$\varphi = \cos^1\left(\frac{D}{h_m \tan \theta}\right), \quad q = \left(\frac{D}{h_m}\right)^2 \quad \text{and} \quad u = \frac{q}{\tan^2\theta}.$$

The zonal multipliers depend upon the position of the sources relative to the wall as well as upon room proportions (room index). Hence in the table of zonal multipliers given in IES Technical Report No. 2, values for $10°$ zones are given for a number of spacing to mounting height ratios.

ZONAL FRACTIONS

One of the problems associated with the calculation of tabulated data for use in routine lighting calculations is the wide range of practical distributions encountered. In practice it has been found that the range can be covered by using a series of mathematically defined distributions of a form such as $I_\theta = I_{max} \cos^n \theta$.

A common problem is to derive the fraction of flux directly incident on the floor, working plane, or ceiling. The first step is to determine the fraction of the total downward flux in each zone.[3]

$$\frac{\text{Zonal fraction}}{(ZF)} = \frac{\text{Flux emitted in zone}}{\text{Total downward flux}}$$

$$= \frac{2\pi \int_{\theta_1}^{\theta_2} I_\theta \sin \theta \, d\theta}{2\pi \int_0^{\frac{1}{2}\pi} I_\theta \sin \theta \, d\theta.}$$

For example, for a distribution of the form $I_\theta = I_{max} \cos^n \theta$

$$ZF = \cos^{(n+1)} \theta_1 - \cos^{(n+1)} \theta_2.$$

In all cases the fraction of flux to the floor or working plane

$$= \sum_0^{\frac{1}{2}\pi} ZM \, ZF.$$

An application of zonal fractions and zonal multipliers is the derivation of the direct ratios used in the BZ method of classification for lighting fittings which is explained in Chapter 8.

ZONAL MULTIPLIERS FOR AREA SOURCES

Croft[4] has shown that the zonal multiplier technique may also be applied to luminous ceilings or to obtaining flux transfer between surfaces. A luminous surface may be considered to be an array of infinitely small sources with each luminous element touching other similar elements.

In the case of sources with a finite spacing, individual zonal multipliers for each source for a particular zonal radius are calculated. These are then added and the mean value obtained.

In the case of area sources integration can be employed since the source forms a continuous surface.

The luminous ceiling represented by *ABCD* (Fig. 3.2) consists of an infinite number of similar elements such as *P*. When we cal-

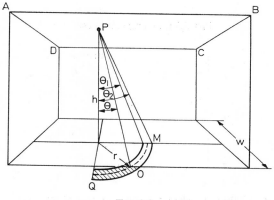

FIG. 3.2.

culate the mean zonal multiplier for a particular zone, with mid-zone angle θ, we need only consider one quadrant as shown. The reason for this simplification is that when the integration is carried out over the whole room the result is the same for each quadrant.

The procedure is similar to that used in the previous section in that the zonal multiplier is taken as the ratio of the part of the mid-zone arc which lies on the floor to the total length of the arc.

For example in the case shown in Fig. 3.2 the zonal multiplier is given by the ratio of arc *MO* to arc *MQ*. The calculation can be further simplified if note is taken of the fact that there are five cases. One case occurs when arc MQ lies entirely outside the room and this gives a zonal multiplier of zero. Figures 3.3(a) and (b) illustrate the other three cases; cases a_1 and a_3 are the same in the that the arc cuts the boundary of the floor at only one point. b_2 is

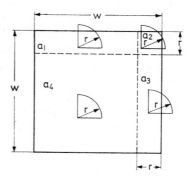

FIG. 3.3.(a) Compound case.

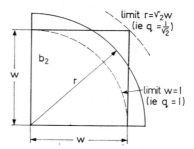

FIG. 3.3.(b) Case where the zonal arc cuts at two points.

the case where the arc cuts at two points. a_2 is a special case of b_2 (i.e. when $w = r$). Case a_4 occurs over the region where the arc does not cut the boundary at all and hence gives a zonal multiplier of unity.

Take the case of b_2 first and refer to Fig. 3.3(b), if

$$W \leqq r < \sqrt{(2)}W \quad \text{and} \quad q = W/r \quad \text{(Fig. 3.4)}.$$

Mean zonal multiplier $\times \sum \text{arc } MQ = \sum \text{arc } NO$, giving

$$ZM_{b_2} \int_0^q \int_0^q \tfrac{1}{2}\pi \, dx \, dy = \int_{\sqrt{(1-q^2)}}^q \int_{\sqrt{(1-y^2)}}^q (\tfrac{1}{2}\pi - \cos^{-1} x - \cos^{-1} y) \, dx \, dy.$$

The smallest permissible value for x occurs when $\cos^{-1} y + \cos^{-1} x = \frac{1}{2}\pi$, i.e. when points N and O are coincident. This is the condition at which the zonal multiplier becomes zero. For a given value of y this point is reached when x is reduced to a value $\sqrt{(1 - y^2)}$,

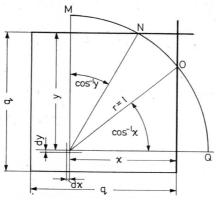

FIG. 3.4. The same case as in Fig. 3.3.(b) but in terms of parameter q.

hence this appears as the lower limit of integration with respect to x. The smallest permissible value for y is obtained by similar reasoning, and occurs when N and O are coincident and the element $dx\, dy$ lies at the boundary $x = q$. So that,

$$ZM_{b_2} = \frac{2}{\pi q^2} \int_{\sqrt{(1-q^2)}}^{q} \int_{\sqrt{(1-y^2)}}^{q} (\sin^{-1} x - \cos^{-1} y)\, dx\, dy.$$

1.
$$\int_{\sqrt{(1-y^2)}}^{q} (\sin^{-1} x - \cos^{-1} y)\, dx,$$

$$\int \sin^{-1} x\, dx = x \sin^{-1} x - \int \frac{x}{\sqrt{(1 - x^2)}}\, dx = x \sin^{-1} x + \sqrt{(1 - x^2)}.$$

Inserting the limits, we obtain

$$\int_{\sqrt{(1-y^2)}}^{q} \sin^{-1} x\, dx = q \sin^{-1} q + \sqrt{(1 - q^2)} - \sqrt{(1 - y^2)} \cos^{-1} y - y.$$

Similarly
$$\int_{\sqrt{(1-y^2)}}^{q} \cos^{-1} y\, dx = [x \cos^{-1} y]_{\sqrt{(1-y^2)}}^{q}$$
$$= q \cos^{-1} y - \sqrt{(1 - y^2)} \cos^{-1} y.$$

3a   LF

Therefore

$$\int_{\sqrt{(1-y^2)}}^{q} (\sin^{-1} x - \cos^{-1} y)\, dx$$
$$= q \sin^{-1} q + \sqrt{(1 - q^2)} - q \cos^{-1} y - y.$$

2. $\quad\displaystyle\int_{\sqrt{(1-q^2)}}^{q} [q \sin^{-1} q + \sqrt{(1 - q^2)} - q \cos^{-1} y - y]\, dy$

$$= \left[yq \sin^{-1} q + y (1 - q^2) - \frac{y^2}{2} - \int q \cos^{-1} y\, dy \right]_{\sqrt{(1-q^2)}}^{q}$$

where

$$\int q \cos^{-1} y\, dy = qy \cos^{-1} y + q \int \frac{u}{\sqrt{(1 - y^2)}}\, dy$$
$$= qy \cos^{-1} y - q \sqrt{(1 - y^2)}$$

giving

$$\int_{\sqrt{(1-q^2)}}^{q} [q \sin^{-1} q + \sqrt{(1 - q^2)} - q \cos^{-1} y - y]\, dy$$

$$= \left[qy \sin^{-1} q + y\sqrt{(1 - q^2)} - \frac{y^2}{2} - qy \cos^{-1} y + q\sqrt{(1 - y^2)} \right]_{\sqrt{(1-q^2)}}^{q}$$

Inserting the limits and simplifying, we obtain

$$ZM_{b_2} = \tfrac{1}{2}\pi \left[2 \sin^{-1} q - \tfrac{1}{2}\pi + \frac{2}{q}\sqrt{(1 - q^2)} - 1 - \tfrac{1}{2}q^2 \right]. \qquad (3.1)$$

To relate q to room ratio R_r:

$$R_r = \frac{w}{2h}, \quad q = \frac{w}{h}, \quad r = h \tan \theta.$$

Therefore

$$q = \frac{ZR_r}{\tan \theta}.$$

Section a_2 is a special case of b_2, where $q = 1$, giving

$$ZM_{a_2} = 1 = \frac{3}{\pi} = 0{\cdot}044.$$

Section a_3 is the case where the arc cuts only one side of the rectangle. Hence the zonal multiplier only varies in the x-direction, and $\cos^{-1} y$ is therefore zero, so

$$ZM_{a_3} \int_0^1 \tfrac{1}{2}\pi\, dx = \int_0^1 (\tfrac{1}{2}\pi - \cos^{-1} x)\, dx;$$

since $q = W/r$ and in this case $W = r$,

$$ZM_{a_3} = \frac{2}{\pi} \int_0^1 \sin^{-1} x \, dx$$

$$= 0{\cdot}363.$$

Section a_1

$$ZM_{a_1} = ZM_{a_3}.$$

In section a_4 the arc does not cut the boundary of the rectangle and the zonal multiplier is unity, i.e.

$$ZM_{a_4} = 1.$$

Equation (3.1) should be used to calculate the zonal multipliers which occur in the range defined by $1/\sqrt{(2)} < q \leqq 1$ (Fig. 3.3(b)), i.e. when $W < r$.

Compound case. When $q > 1(W > r)$, the compound case shown in Fig. 3.3(a) is obtained.

Combining the multipliers for sections a_1, a_2, a_3 and a_4 produces the required zonal multiplier.

Weighting each multiplier according to the proportion of the floor area to which it applies, the true zonal multiplier

$$ZM_a = \frac{\begin{aligned} ZM_{a_1} h \tan \theta(w - h \tan \theta) + ZM_{a_2}(h \tan \theta)^2 \\ + ZM_{a_3} h \tan \theta(w - h \tan \theta) + ZM_{a_4}(w - h \tan \theta)^2 \end{aligned}}{W^2}$$

where

$$h \tan \theta = r.$$

Also, since

$$R_r = W/2h,$$

$$ZM_a = ZM_{a_1}\left[\frac{\tan \theta}{R_r} - \tfrac{1}{2}\left(\frac{\tan \theta}{R_r}\right)^2\right]$$

$$+ ZM_{a_2}\left(\frac{\tan \theta}{2R_r}\right)^2 + ZM_{a_4}\left[1 - \frac{\tan \theta}{R_r} + \left(\frac{\tan \theta}{2R_r}\right)^2\right]$$

$$= 0{\cdot}080\left(\frac{\tan \theta}{R_r}\right)^2 - 0{\cdot}637 \frac{\tan \theta}{R_r} + 1,$$

when $q < 1/\sqrt{(2)}, \sqrt{(2)}W < r$ and the arc lies outside the rectangle so that the zonal multiplier is zero.

Table 3.1 gives a set of zonal multipliers for $10°$ zones for a range of values of room ratio (R_r).

3a*

TABLE 3.1. ZONAL MULTIPLIERS FOR AREA SOURCES

Room ratio R_r zone	0·6	0·8	1·0	1·25	1·5	2·0	2·5	3·0	4·0	5·0
					Zonal multipliers					
0–10°	0·909	0·931	0 945	0·956	0·963	0·972	0·978	0·982	0·986	0·989
10–20°	0·732	0·796	0·835	0·867	0·889	0·916	0·933	0·944	0·958	0·966
20–30°	0·553	0·656	0·720	0·774	0·810	0·856	0·884	0·903	0·927	0·941
30–40°	0·366	0·504	0·593	0·668	0·714	0·787	0·828	0·856	0·891	0·912
40–50°	0·161	0·329	0·443	0·542	0·611	0·702	0·758	0·797	0·846	0·876
50–60°	0·006	0·118	0·253	0·377	0·466	0·586	0·662	0·715	0·783	0·825
60–70°	0	0·000	0·020	0·143	0·253	0·409	0·512	0·586	0·682	0·742
70–80°	0	0	0·000	0·000	0·004	0·090	0·227	0·331	0·475	0·569
80–90°	0	0	0	0	0	0·000	0·000	0·000	0·000	0·010

DIRECT FLUX TO THE WALLS

The zonal multipliers and zonal fractions derived above may be used to determine the direct flux to the floor or to the ceiling. The direct flux to the walls is given by:

Flux to walls = Total flux emitted by the fittings
      − Flux to the floor − Flux to the ceiling.

DIRECT RATIOS AND SURFACE DISTRIBUTION FACTORS

In the earlier sections zonal multipliers have been developed for both individual sources with finite spacing and area sources covering the whole ceiling. If we use these multipliers in conjunction with the zonal fractions derived in the previous section the fraction of the flux emitted in the downward direction which reaches the floor or working plane directly may be determined.

This quantity is called the direct ratio in the Illuminating Engineering Society's Technical Report, No. 2, which deals with the calculation of Utilization Factors (see Chapter 8).

The direct ratios obtained for area sources may be used to calculate flux transfer between surfaces made luminous by reflected light as well as the direct illumination due to self-luminous surfaces. For this reason we will adopt Croft's term surface distribution factor and use the symbol D_s when dealing with area sources.

Thus for a luminous surface, the fraction of flux transferred to a parallel surface which is directly opposite and of the same size

is given by
$$D_s = \sum_0^{\frac{1}{2}\pi} ZM\ ZF.$$

Table 3.2 gives values of D_s for cosine, cosine squared and cosine cubed distributions, for a range of values of R_r.

Note: For a luminous ceiling $R_r = K_r$.

TABLE 3.2. SURFACE DISTRIBUTION FACTOR FOR AREA SOURCES (D_s)

Type of source	Room ratio (R_r) = Room index (K_r) for a luminous ceiling									
	0·6	0·8	1·0	1·25	1·5	2·0	2·5	3·0	4·0	5·0
Uniformly Diffuse (cosine)	0·253	0·343	0·415	0·491	0·547	0·632	0·691	0·733	0·788	0·823
Louvers (cosine squared)	0·341	0·444	0·521	0·597	0·652	0·732	0·778	0·814	0·859	0·887
Deep Louvers (cosine cubed)	0·400	0·505	0·580	0·651	0·701	0·769	0·811	0·841	0·878	0·901

INTERREFLECTIONS

Problems involving interreflections may be solved either by an iterative method, that is, one which considers the successive interreflections, or a steady-state method. The steady-state method based on the conservation of energy principle is used below, since it is easy to apply to a wide range of problems.

The following assumptions are made in the cases dealt with:

1. All reflecting and transmitting surfaces produce uniform diffusion of the redistributed light.
2. All surfaces have uniform reflection and transmission factors.
3. Each surface has a uniform luminance.
4. The initial illumination of each surface is uniform.

Lighting Fittings

Consider a lighting fitting consisting of two surfaces having different reflection and transmission factors and containing a source of luminous flux Q (Fig. 3.5). Such an arrangement is equivalent to two cavities joined by aperture 1. It has already been shown

(Chapter 2) that the fraction of flux emitted by a cavity surface and which emerges from the cavity aperture is given by the ratio of aperture areas (S_1) to cavity area (S_2 or S_3), i.e.,

$$\frac{S_1}{S_2} \quad \text{or} \quad \frac{S_1}{S_3}$$

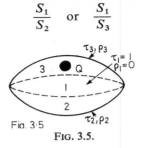

Fig. 3·5

FIG. 3.5.

and that the transfer between the walls of the cavity is given by

$$1 - \frac{S_1}{S_2} \quad \text{or} \quad 1 - \frac{S_1}{S_3}.$$

We will use the notation,[5] as in Chapter 2,

$$\frac{S_1}{S_2} = f_{21}, \quad \frac{S_1}{S_3} = f_{31}, \quad 1 - \frac{S_1}{S_2} = f_{22}, \quad \text{and} \quad 1 - \frac{S_1}{S_3} = f_{33},$$

f_{21} is therefore the fraction of the flux emitted by S_2 which passes through the aperture S_1, and f_{22} is the flux received by S_2 from S_2, and so on.

If we use the conservation of energy principle the following relationship may be established:

Flux received by 2 = Flux received from 3 + Flux received from 2 + Direct flux from the lamp.

Hence

$$E_2 S_2 = E_3 S_3 \varrho_3 f_{32} + E_2 S_2 \varrho_2 f_{22} + D_2 F_1. \tag{3.1}$$

Similarly for surface 3,

$$E_3 S_3 = E_2 S_2 \varrho_2 f_{23} + E_3 S_3 \varrho_3 f_{33} + D_3 F_1, \tag{3.2}$$

where D_x = fraction of source flux received by surface x; F_1 = source flux; E_x = final illumination on surface x; ϱ_x = reflection factor of surface x.

Since all the flux passing through the aperture 1 from 2 strikes 3, and vice versa, $f_{32} = f_{31}$ and $f_{23} = S_{21}$.

Substituting these values in eqns. (3.1) and (3.2) and solving

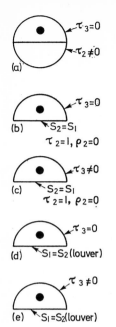

(a) LOR $= \dfrac{[D_2(1 - \varrho_3 f_{33}) + D_3\, \varrho_3 f_{31}]\, \tau_2}{(1 - \varrho_2 f_{22})\,(1 - \varrho_3 f_{33}) - \varrho_2\varrho_3 f_{21}f_{31}}$

(b) LOR $= D_2 + \dfrac{D_3\varrho_3 f_{31}}{1 - \varrho_3 f_{33}}$.

(c) LOR $= D_2 + \dfrac{D_3(\varrho_3 f_{31} + \tau_3)}{1 - \varrho_3 f_{33}}$.

(d) LOR $= \dfrac{[D_2(1 - \varrho_3 f_{33}) + D_3\varrho_3 f_{31}]\tau_2}{(1 - \varrho_3 f_{33}) - \varrho_2\varrho_3 f_{21}f_{31}}$.

ϱ_2 = equivalent reflection factor of louver.

τ_2 = equivalent transmission factor of louver.

(e) LOR $= \dfrac{[D_2(1 - \varrho_3 f_{33}) + D_3\varrho_3 f_{31}]\, \tau_2}{(1 - \varrho_3 f_{33}) - \varrho_2\varrho_3 f_{21}f_{31}}$

$\qquad + \dfrac{[D_3 + D_2\varrho_2 f_{21}]\, \tau_3}{(1 - \varrho_3 f_{33}) - \varrho_2\varrho_3 f_{21}f_{31}}$.

FIG. 3.6.

simultaneously gives

$$E_2 S_2 = \frac{D_2 F_1 (1 - \varrho_3 f_{33}) + D_3 F_1 \varrho_3 f_{31}}{(1 - \varrho_2 f_{22})(1 - \varrho_3 f_{33}) - \varrho_2 \varrho_3 f_{21} f_{31}}$$

and

$$E_3 S_3 = \frac{D_3 F_1 (1 - \varrho_2 f_{22}) + D_2 F_1 \varrho_2 f_{31}}{(1 - \varrho_3 f_{33})(1 - \varrho_2 f_{22}) - \varrho_2 \varrho_3 f_{21} f_{31}} \, .$$

The total light output of fitting is given by:

$$F = E_2 S_2 \tau_2 + E_3 S_3 \tau_3,$$

where τ_2 and τ_3 are the transmission factors of surfaces 2 and 3 respectively. The light output ratio is therefore:

$$\frac{F}{F_1} = \frac{[D_2 (1 - \varrho_3 f_{33}) + D_3 \varrho_3 f_{31}] \tau_2}{(1 - \varrho_2 f_{22})(1 - \varrho_3 f_{33}) - \varrho_2 \varrho_3 f_{21} f_{31}}$$
$$+ \frac{[D_3 (1 - \varrho_2 f_{22}) + D_2 \varrho_2 f_{21}] \tau_3}{(1 - \varrho_2 f_{22})(1 - \varrho_3 f_{33}) - \varrho_2 \varrho_3 f_{21} f_{31}} \, .$$

This formula applies to the general case, and substitution of the appropriate values for τ and ϱ gives the solutions for the special cases shown in Fig. 3.6(a)–(e).

Louvers

It is often necessary to known the transmission and reflection factors of louvers, e.g. case (d) and (e) above, and it is possible to obtain a close estimate for these by means of a similar method. Consider a rectangular or circular louver cell with the dimensions indicated in Fig. 3.7(a) and (b).

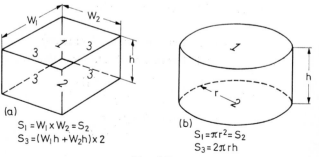

(a)

$S_1 = W_1 \times W_2 = S_2$
$S_3 = (W_1 h + W_2 h) \times 2$

(b)

$S_1 = \pi r^2 = S_2$
$S_3 = 2\pi r h$

FIG. 3.7.

The top (1) and bottom (2) of the cell have zero reflection factor and unity transmission factor. The sides have a reflection factor ϱ_3. The transmission factor of the louver is given by the flux emerging from surface 2 divided by the flux entering surface 1 from above. Assuming that the source above the cell has a uniform luminance and fills the aperture, we obtain

$$\tau = \frac{E_2}{H_1},$$

where H_x is the luminous emittance of surface x in lumens/ft^2.

$$\begin{bmatrix} \text{Now the flux} \\ \text{received by 2} \end{bmatrix} = \begin{bmatrix} \text{Flux received from} \\ 1 \end{bmatrix} + \begin{bmatrix} \text{Flux received from} \\ 3 \end{bmatrix}.$$

Hence

$$E_2 S_2 = H_1 S_1 f_{12} + H_3 S_3 f_{31}. \tag{3.3}$$

Also the flux emitted by 3,

$$H_3 S_3 = (H_1 S_1 f_{13} + H_3 S_3 f_{33}) \varrho_3$$
$$= \frac{H_1 S_1 f_{13} \varrho_3}{(1 - f_{33} \varrho_3)}, \tag{3.4}$$

and substituting in eqn. (3.3) for $H_3 S_3$, we obtain

$$E_2 S_2 = H_1 S_1 f_{12} + \frac{H_1 S_1 f_{13} f_{31} \varrho_3}{(1 - f_{33} \varrho_3)}.$$

Now for most diffusing louvers $S_1 = S_2$.

So

$$\frac{E_2}{H_1} = f_{12} + \frac{f_{13} f_{31}}{[(1/\varrho_3) - f_{33}]}.$$

Since f_{12} represents the fraction of flux transmitted directly through the louver without reflection, the other term must represent the fraction of flux transmitted by reflection.

Now with uniformly diffuse reflection the same fraction of the flux received by 3 would be reflected upwards as downwards and hence the equivalent reflection factor of the louver ϱ is given by inspection, i.e.

$$\varrho = \frac{f_{13} f_{31}}{[(1/\varrho_3) - f_{33}]}.$$

The same result could, of course, have been derived directly. Now the equations developed at this stage apply equally well to rectangular or circular louver cells or any other shape. If we can determine the values of the functions f_{13}, f_{31}, f_{32} we can also find τ and ϱ. The transfer functions or "form factors", as they are often termed, have been derived under the section on flux transfer from uniform diffuse sources for the cases of the square and the circular louver cell (Chapter 2 and Table 3.2).

The method of classification of rectangular enclosures in terms of equivalent square rooms described at the beginning of the chapter can be used to extend the use of the formulae developed above to rectangular louvers.

This method employs the ratio

$$R_r = \frac{S_1 + S_2}{S_3} = \frac{2(W_1 \times W_2)}{2h(W_1 + W_2)},$$

which for a square louver becomes

$$R_r = \frac{W}{2h}.$$

Table 3.2 gives values of surface distribution factor D_s, i.e. the fraction of the transmitted flux transferred from (1) to (2) for a square enclosure, for a range of values of R_r.

Thus for a rectangular louver

$$f_{12} = D_s, \quad f_{13} = 1 - D_s,$$

where D_s is for a cosine distribution.

Also, since by virtue of reciprocity

$$\frac{F_{13}}{H_1} = \frac{F_{31}}{H_3},$$

hence

$$\frac{H_1 S_1 f_{13}}{H_1} = \frac{H_3 S_3 f_{31}}{H_3},$$

giving

$$S_1 f_{13} = S_3 f_{31}.$$

Therefore

$$f_{31} = f_{13} \frac{S_1}{S_3}$$

$$= f_{13} \frac{R_r}{2} = \frac{R_r}{2}(1 - D_s).$$

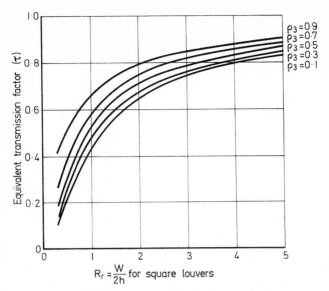

FIG. 3.8.(a) Equivalent transmission factor of a louver.

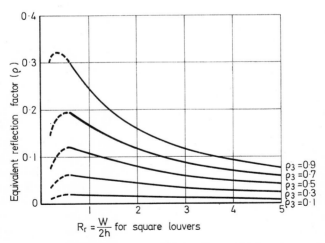

FIG. 3.8.(b). Equivalent reflection factor of a louver.

Also

$$f_{33} = 1 - 2f_{31} \text{ because } f_{31} = f_{32} \text{ and } f_{31} + f_{32} + f_{33} = 1$$
$$= 1 - f_{13}R_r$$
$$= 1 - (1 - D_s) R_r.$$

Substituting these values in the expressions for τ and ϱ, we obtain

and

$$\tau = \frac{(R_r/2)(1 - D_s)^2}{(1/\varrho_3) - 1 + (1 - D_s) R_r} + D_s$$

$$\varrho = \frac{(R_r/2)(1 - D_s)^2}{(1/\varrho_3) - 1 + (1 - D_s) R_r}.$$

Fig. 3.8(a) and (b) gives graphs of τ and ϱ against the ratio R_r, and $W/2h$ (for square louvers).

If the thickness of the cell wall is not negligible then an adjustment may be made as follows:

$\tau = \tau$ (louver cell) × Fraction of total area composed of louver openings

$\varrho = \varrho$ (louver cell) × Fraction of total area composed of louver openings

$+ \varrho$ (louver material) × Fraction of total area composed of louver material.

Translucent Louvers

The results obtained for opaque rectangular louvers can be used for translucent louvers if the transmission factor of the louver material is added to the reflection factor. This can be done because flux emerging from the surface of one louver cell by transmission is balanced by a similar quantity lost by transmission to adjacent cells, and the net result in all but the cells at the extreme edge of the louver is the same as an increase in the reflection factor by an amount equal to the transmission factor.

Thus if the louver material has a transmission factor of 25 % and a reflection factor of 45 %, the louver will have similar characteristics to an opaque louver with a reflection factor of 70 %.

Practical Results

The authors have investigated the accuracy with which the performance of a practical louver can be predicted using the formulae developed in this section. The methods and results of this investigation are fully detailed in Monograph No. 9 published by the Illuminating Engineering Society (London).

The general conclusion is that the accuracy is of the order of 5 %.

The simple treatment given above assumes a uniform distribution of luminous flux on the vertical walls of the louver cell. This assumption is not justified when the cell is deep compared with its width. The point at which this begins to have a serious effect on the results for equivalent louver reflection factor is indicated by the change to the dotted curve in Fig. 3.8(b).

If it is required to do accurate calculations for deep louvers, the same method may be used, but the vertical surfaces must be divided into two or more sections so that uniform illumination of each section may be assumed.

Rooms

The same approach as that used for louvers may be used for solving the interreflection problems encountered in determining the flux utilization and final illumination and luminance values in rectangular enclosures such as rooms.[6]

For simplicity we will consider a three-surface enclosure as in Fig. 3.7(a).

$$\begin{bmatrix} \text{Flux received} \\ \text{by 1} \end{bmatrix} + \begin{bmatrix} \text{Flux received} \\ \text{from 2} \end{bmatrix} = \begin{bmatrix} \text{Flux received} \\ \text{from 3} \end{bmatrix} + \begin{bmatrix} \text{Direct} \\ \text{flux} \end{bmatrix}$$

giving

$$E_1 S_1 = H_2 S_2 f_{21} + H_3 S_3 f_{31} + E_{01} S_1.$$

Similarly, flux received by 2,

$$E_2 S_2 = H_1 S_1 f_{12} + H_3 S_3 f_{32} + E_{02} S_2.$$

and

$$\begin{bmatrix} \text{Flux received} \\ \text{by 3} \end{bmatrix} = \begin{bmatrix} \text{Flux received} \\ \text{from 1} \end{bmatrix} + \begin{bmatrix} \text{Flux received} \\ \text{from 2} \end{bmatrix} + \begin{bmatrix} \text{Flux received} \\ \text{from 3} \end{bmatrix}$$
$$+ \text{ Direct flux},$$

giving

$$E_3 S_3 = H_1 S_1 f_{13} + H_2 S_2 f_{23} + H_3 S_3 f_{33} + E_{03} S_3,$$

where E_{01}, E_{02} and E_{03} are the direct illumination values.

Solution of these equations gives

$$E_2 = \frac{A E_{02} + B E_{01} + C E_{03}}{A - \varrho_2 B f_{12} - \varrho_2 C f_{31}}, \qquad (3.5)$$

$$E_1 = \frac{(1 + \varrho_2 f_{12}) E_2 + E_{01} - E_{02}}{1 + \varrho_1 f_{12}},$$

$$E_3 = \frac{E_1 - f_{12} \varrho_2 E_2 - E_{01}}{\varrho_3 f_{13}},$$

where

$$A = \frac{1}{\varrho_1} \left(\frac{1}{\varrho_3} - f_{33} \right) - f_{13} f_{31};$$

$$B = f_{12} \left(\frac{1}{\varrho_3} - f_{33} \right) + f_{13} f_{31};$$

$$C = f_{13} \left(\frac{1}{\varrho_1} + f_{12} \right); \quad f_{13} = 1 - D_s$$

$$f_{12} = D_s; \quad f_{31} = \frac{R_r}{2} (1 - D_s)$$

$$f_{33} = 1 - (1 - D_s) R_r.$$

Note: Table 3.2 gives values of D_s in terms of R_r for a uniform diffuse distribution (cosine):

$$R_r = \frac{W_1 \times W_2}{h(W_1 + W_2)};$$

or in the notation used in Chapter 2 in the section on Room Classification,

$$R_r = \frac{l \times w}{h(l + w)}.$$

Since the utilization factor (coefficient of utilization) used in the light-flux, or lumen method, is given by

$$\frac{\text{Total flux received by a surface}}{\text{Flux emitted by the lamps}},$$

and since E_1S_1, E_2S_2, E_3S_3 give the total flux received by each surface, this method may be used to obtain utilization factors.

Change of Reflection Factor

Equation (3.5) for E_2 can be rewritten

$$E_2 = [AE_{02} + BE_{01} + CE_{03}]\left[\frac{1}{A - \varrho_2(Bf_{12} - Cf_{31})}\right]$$

and investigation of the constants A, B and C shows that they do not contain ϱ_2. Thus the second factor is the only one dependent upon ϱ_2, the reflection factor of the surface receiving the illumination E_2. This factor is independent of the distribution of the lighting units, since this is denoted by E_{01}, E_{02} and E_{03}.

It follows that the percentage change in illumination E_2 caused by a change of reflection factor ϱ_2 will be independent of the fitting distribution. This means that for a given size of room with fixed wall and ceiling reflection factors the effect on the utilization factor of varying the working plane (or floor) reflection factor will be the same for generally diffusing lighting as for direct lighting, or even as for indirect lighting. Thus a single table of correction factors can be produced in terms of room reflection factors, and room index, to allow for different values of working plane (or floor) reflection factor, for use with the utilization factor tables for all the different types of lighting unit.

Since the equation for the floor (2) could also be used for the ceiling (1) (because of symmetry) the same argument applies to the effect of ceiling reflection factor on ceiling illumination. It is also possible to show that this is true for the walls (3).[6]

Cavities

It is often useful to known what fraction of the flux incident on a cavity or recess is reflected back out of the cavity or recess. This fraction is termed the equivalent reflection factor of the cavity.

We may obtain the required equation by considering the cavity as equivalent to a lighting fitting with all the source output directed on to the interior surface.

Thus if we take the formula for LOR given as case (b) (Fig. 3.6) on p. 71, i.e.

$$\text{LOR} = D_2 + \frac{D_3\varrho_3 f_{31}}{1 - \varrho_3 f_{33}}$$

for a cavity

$$D_2 = 0, \quad D_3 = 1$$

and since

$$f_{31} = \frac{S_1}{S_3} = \frac{\text{Area of aperture}}{\text{Total area of cavity}} \text{ (see Chapter 2)}$$

$$f_{33} = 1 - f_{31},$$

$$\text{LOR} = \varrho \text{ equivalent} = \frac{\varrho_3 S_1}{\varrho_3 S_1 + S_3(1 - \varrho_3)}.$$

The Cavity Method for Utilization Factors

The calculation of utilization factors for suspended fittings may be simplified if the true ceiling is assumed to be replaced by an imaginary ceiling at the height of the lighting fittings (Fig. 3.9). The British Zonal Method described in Chapter 8 incorporates this feature.[1]

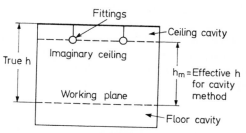

FIG. 3.9. Division of a room into three cavities.

Such an arrangement means that the data calculated for ceiling mounted fittings may be applied to installations of suspended fittings.

The equivalent reflection factor of this ceiling cavity, is calculated using the formula obtained in the previous section. This is an approximate formula since it uses the weighted mean value of the reflection factors of the upper walls and the ceiling. A more accurate solution is provided by Phillips and Prokhovnik.[5]

Since it is the total illumination on the working plane and not the floor that is usually required, a further cavity is introduced with the boundary of the working plane forming the aperture. However, the presence of furniture would modify any equivalent reflection factor calculated for this cavity, and so it is common practice to calculate utilization factors for either of two arbitrarily chosen working plane reflection factors, namely 10% or 30%.

For calculation purposes the room is considered to have an upper surface at the height of the fittings and a lower surface at the level of the working plane. Under this condition $h = h_m$.

One other simplification introduced by this approach is that all the upward flux from the lighting fittings may be assumed to reach the upper surface or ceiling.

REFERENCES

1. HISANO, K. (Edited by P. Moon), *Illum. Engng.* (*N.Y.*) **41**, 232 (1946).
2. JONES, J. R. and NEIDHART, J. J., *Illum. Engng.* (*N.Y.*) **46**, 601 (1951); **48**, 141 (1953).
3. CROFT, R., *Trans. I.E.S.* (*London*) **20**, 259 (1955).
4. CROFT, R. Monograph No. 2 I.E.S. (London), 1959.
5. PHILLIPS, R. O. and PROKHOVNIK, S. J., Monograph No. 3 I.E.S. (London), 1960.
6. LYNES, J. A., Monograph No. 1 I.E.S. (London), 1959.
7. Technical Report No. 2 I.E.S. (London), 1961.

CHAPTER 4

OPTICAL DESIGN

IN THIS chapter the various methods by which the light from a source can be controlled are described and discussed. Nothing more than the basic laws of physics is involved in the redirection of light from a source; the challenge to the designer is to produce a design which is the cheapest possible, has the best possible light distribution, involves the least possible loss of light, is of pleasing appearance, and is practically feasible. Some of these requirements are nearly always conflicting; some, like the best possible light distribution or good appearance, may be the subject of controversy or have to be sacrificed for versatility, but they do provide the questions which the designer has to keep asking.

GENERAL PRINCIPLES

There are three general approaches which are useful in the design of light control systems for fittings.

Firstly, there is what may be called the flux redirection approach. Suppose that both the flux distribution of the source and the flux distribution that is required are known. Then it is possible to redirect the flux from sectors where it is not required into sectors where it is required. This approach is useful for the design of reflector contours and an example will be fully worked out when we deal with them.

Secondly, there is the luminance approach. This makes use of two facts, namely:

(a) The intensity I in any direction of a light control system is equal to the projected area A of the flashed parts multiplied by the luminance L of the system; the flashed area being the area made bright by the source; i.e.

$I = AL$, where A is the projected area (p. 19), or
$I = \int L \, dA$ if L varies across A.

82

(b) If a reflector is specular, the luminance of any part of the reflector is that of the source facing that part multiplied by the reflection factor of the reflector. Similarly the luminance of any part of a flashed lens (or any refractor system) is the luminance of the source facing the part multiplied by the transmission factor of the lens.

The two facts (a) and (b) often enable the feasibility of a problem to be calculated straight away. To take an example, consider the sort of problem which occurs in the design of airfield runway lights. The fitting must not project very much above the level of the runway and the size of window is consequently limited. Suppose we are allowed a window having an area of 1 square inch, and we are required to produce an intensity of 15,000 candelas with a source of luminance 8000 candelas/in². The window luminance required will be 15,000 candelas/in². If the transmission factor of the refractor is 70% and it is assumed that it can be completely flashed, then the source luminance will have to be about 21,000 candelas/in². So obviously the problem cannot be solved unless the window is enlarged or the source luminance increased.

The uninitiated often put forward arguments for trying batteries of lenses and reflectors to concentrate the light and so increase the luminance, but all such arguments must contain fallacies and can be likened to trying to make a perpetual motion machine. A common trap is to consider a point source of light. Such a source must be of infinite luminance so it is not surprising that misleading deductions can be made by considering it. All practical sources are of finite dimensions, and this fact must always be used when considering flashed areas.

Before we deal with the third approach, there is an interesting paradox concerning flashed areas which is worth considering. In this the flashed area concept appears to be at variance with the principle of conservation of energy. Figure 4.1 shows two parabolic reflectors, A and B, illuminated by sources of equal dimensions and luminance. Both reflectors have the same projected area in the direction of the axis but A has a shorter focal length than B. Since both are flashed by sources of equal luminance, their intensities in the direction of the axis will be equal. But because A is of shorter focal length than B, it wraps round the source more and, therefore, collects more flux. Where does this flux go? The answer is that even though the peak intensities of the reflectors will be equal, A will have a wider beam than *B*. It is interesting to note that this conclusion can be confirmed by geometrical considerations. Cones of light reflected off *A* will have a larger apex angle (owing to *A*'s being closer to the source) than cones of light reflected off corre-

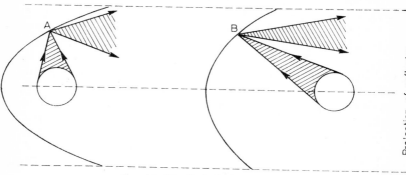

FIG. 4.1. The flashed area paradox.

sponding points of reflector *B*. This argument can be applied to two lenses of different focal lengths but having the same area; the lens of shorter focal length will give the wider beams because it collects more flux, but the peak intensities given by the two lenses will be equal.

The third approach is to think in terms of the magnification of the source. For instance if the system produces a 10 times magnification of the area of the source, then the intensity of the image will be 10 times that of the source multiplied by the losses in the system. This method is only applicable when the source is small compared to the size of the control system so that the image or images are complete.

Which of these three approaches is used is a matter of convenience; they are equivalent to one another as will be shown in the sections dealing with reflector and refractor systems.

REFLECTOR SYSTEMS

In this section we will describe how use can be made of specular or highly polished metallic surfaces in the control of light. Such surfaces are used when a precise or fairly precise form of distribution is required as in floodlights, spotlights and street lanterns.

Light reflected off a specular surface obeys the following two laws:

(1) The incident ray of light, the normal to the reflecting surface at the point of incidence, and reflected ray are all in the same plane.

(2) The angle of reflection is equal to the angle of incidence.

The position of an image can be determined by using these laws. For instance it can be shown that the image formed by a plane mirror is on the normal from the object to the mirror, and is at a distance behind the mirror equal to the distance of the object in front of it. It can also be shown that if such a mirror is rotated through an angle, the reflected rays will be rotated through twice that angle. This fact has obvious importance as regards the accuracy and positioning of mirrors.

Luminance of Image

The luminance of the image has to be known for calculating the intensity to be expected from a flashed area of the mirror. As previously stated, this is equal to the luminance of the source multiplied by the reflection factor. It is not obvious that this law is true for a curved surface, so now we give proof of it.

In Fig. 4.2 PQ is a curved mirror. S is the source. O is the eye

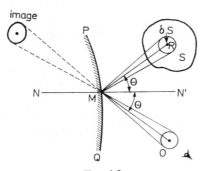

Fig. 4.2.

of the observer, who is looking at the light rays reflected from a small area δA at M. NMN' is the normal at M. The axes of the cones of light which are incident and reflected at M make an angle θ with MN.

Consider a small element of S located at R. Let it have a projected area δS and a luminance L in the direction RM.

Then intensity of $\delta S = L\,\delta S$.

Therefore illumination on $M = \dfrac{L\,\delta S}{d^2}\cos\theta$,   where $d = RM$.

Flux falling on δA at $M = \dfrac{L\,\delta S}{d^2}\cos\theta\,\delta A$.

The reflection factor ϱ is defined as the reflected flux divided by the incident flux. Hence

$$\text{flux leaving } \delta A = \frac{L\,\delta S}{d^2}\cos\theta\,\varrho\,\delta A.$$

Now the solid angle of the incident cone is equal to $\delta S/d^2$ and this is equal to the solid angle of the reflected cone, since all angles of incidence and reflection are equal. Therefore

intensity of $\delta A = L\cos\theta\,\varrho\,\delta A$ (since intensity = flux/solid angle).

The apparent or projected area of δA in the direction of the eye is $\cos\theta\,\delta A$, and since luminance equals intensity divided by projected area,

$$\text{luminance of } \delta A = \varrho L. \tag{4.1}$$

Thus the proof hinges on the fact that the solid angle contained by the reflected cone of light equals that contained by the incident cone. This proof can be repeated for every part of a large source and every point on the mirror from which the source is visible.

Using this relation we can now derive an expression for the intensity of the image, in terms of its magnification.

. Let the projected area of the object in the direction of view be A_1 and that of the image be A_2, also let the corresponding intensities and luminances be I_1 and I_2, and L_1 and L_2.

Luminance L_2 of image $= \varrho L_1$ from eqn. (4.1).
Therefore

$$I_2/I_1 = \varrho A_2/A_1 \text{ since } L_2 = \frac{I_2}{A_2} \text{ and } L_1 = \frac{I_1}{A_1}.$$

If the whole of the image is visible, A_2/A_1 is the area magnification of the optical system, so we can say in this special case that the intensity is proportional to the magnification of the optical system.

Concave Spherical Mirror

Rays emitted from a point object placed at the centre of curvature of a concave mirror will be reflected back onto the object.

An object placed at a distance equal to half the radius of curvature from the mirror will have its rays reflected in the manner shown in Fig. 4.3. Those near the axis will be reflected nearly parallel to the axis.

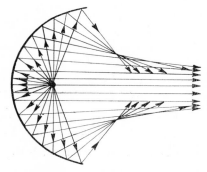

FIG. 4.3. Light reflector by a concave spherical mirror.

The concave spherical mirror will form an image, either real or virtual, of an object placed at any distance from it, but the laws relating to its formation are outside the scope of this book; the parabola, described next, gives a very much more perfect means of control where a narrow beam of high intensity is required.

Parabola

The equation of the parabola is $y^2 = 4ax$, where a is its focal length. Its shape can be obtained by plotting the equation or by cutting a right circular cone in a plane parallel to its surface (this latter method is used to make templates for forming glass parabolic mirrors). It has many interesting geometrical properties and one we shall use concerns the distance of the curve from the directrix, the line running at right angles to the axis at a distance a from the apex of the parabola (Fig. 4.4). The distance FP of the focal point F to any point P on the curve equals the perpendicular distance PA of the point P at (x, y) to the directrix, and is equal to $x + a$.

The most important optical property of the parabolic mirror is that a point source placed at the focus will produce a parallel beam of light as shown in Fig. 4.4. It is interesting to note that if this source is uniform in intensity, the beam will not produce an even

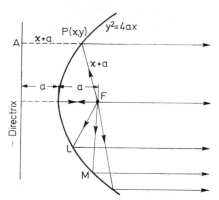

FIG. 4.4. Properties of the parabola.

patch of light, but one which gives the greatest illumination in the centre. This increase of illumination at the centre results from the fact that a cone of light (such as *LFM*) is spread over a smaller area if it is reflected from the centre of the mirror than if it is reflected from the edge of the mirror, since in this second case the mirror cuts the cone at a greater distance from its apex.

In practice we have to consider sources of light which are not points and, therefore, produce a beam of finite divergence. The extent of this divergence will depend on the size of the source and the focal length of the parabola.

Let us consider how we may estimate the polar curve of a trough-shaped reflector used with a cylindrical source having a constant intensity in the transverse plane. Let the radius of the source be r and let its centre be at the focus of the parabola, as shown in Fig. 4.5. Take two points P_1 and P_2 spaced equally either side of the axis. The rays from the centre of the source will be reflected parallel to the axis. Draw lines from the points P_1 and P_2 tangentially to the source. Let these make an angle θ with FP_1 and FP_2. θ will be equal to $\sin^{-1} r/FP_1$, which is equal to $\sin^{-1} r/FP_2$, or $\sin^{-1}[r/(x + a)]$, where (x, y) are the coordinates of any point P. The reflected rays will make an angle θ with the rays parallel to the axis. If the reflector is viewed at an angle θ to the axis the whole of the reflector from P_1 to P_2 will appear flashed. The intensity will be proportional to the projected area of the reflector in that direction, that is LM multiplied by the source length. This procedure can be repeated for a number of points on the reflector so that the light distribution can be determined.

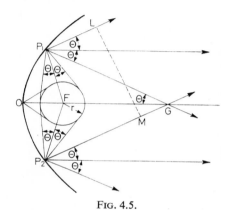

FIG. 4.5.

It will be noticed that the greatest divergence is determined by the angle subtended at O by the lamp.

The rays from the cones diverging from P_1 and P_2 intersect the axis at G. It is only from this point, and beyond, that the whole of the reflector between P_1 and P_2 appears flashed. This is known as the cross-over point for that part of the reflector. Measurements on parabolic reflectors must be taken beyond the cross-over point as determined for the full height of the reflector.

Practical performance

The performance which can be expected from a parabola depends on the accuracy with which it is made and the configuration of the light source. Often it is not essential or even desirable to achieve a tight beam, especially if a large area is to be floodlit. In this case the reflector need not be accurately made. The peak intensity

4 LF

will be reduced, but the beam width will be increased so that the emergent flux will be only a little less than for an accurate reflector, the loss being due to interreflections. A further increase in beam width can be obtained by using a matt or hammered finish for the reflector. Defocusing the lamp only results in a "trouser leg" distribution as shown in Fig. 4.6.

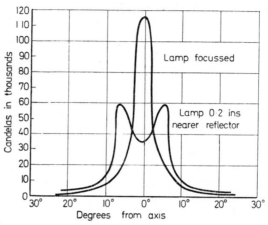

FIG. 4.6. Light distribution curves of 200 W tungsten iodine lamp in parabolic glass reflector of focal length 1·15 in.

Often the uncontrolled direct light from the source itself is a disadvantage since it lies mainly outside the beam and is liable to cause glare. It can be controlled by means of a spherical mirror placed in front of the source. This reflects the light back towards the source. It might seem possible to double the luminance of the main mirror by this method, but, as shown on p. 85, the luminance of the mirror cannot exceed that of the source. For should the spherical mirror reflect the light directly back on to the filament, the result will be to heat this up a little (perhaps damaging it) and give a small increase in luminance. If, on the other hand, it is arranged to form the image to one side of the filament then in essence we are increasing the source size. The result will be to increase the beam spread. Should the flashing of the mirror be incomplete, then it is possible that the larger effective source size will increase the flashed area, and hence the intensity of the beam. Usually the gain that is hoped for by using the spherical mirror is more or less offset by its shading part of the main mirror.

Testing parabolic mirrors

It is often difficult to establish the reasons for the performance of a parabolic mirror not coming up to expectations.

Provided that the source is positioned properly in the focus, the lack of performance must be due to inaccuracy in the mirror contour. The parts in error can be seen by viewing the lighted mirror from a distance and noting where it is unflashed. It is quite useful to photograph the flashing of the mirror. But if the photograph is taken, as it should be, from a great distance, the image may be too small to be of any use. Alternatively, the sun's rays can be reflected on a stiff piece of paper held at right angles to the mirror surface when it can easily be seen what part of the mirror is not true.

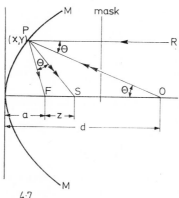

FIG. 4.7. Testing a parabolic reflector.

Determination of the inaccuracy of manufacture in terms of measurements has to be done on a photometric bench. Putting a template in the contour is no good since the high spots hold it off the surface. A plaster cast can be made and a section taken, but this method is messy. The set up for the test on the optical bench is shown in Fig. 4.7. O is a small source on the axis of the mirror MM, the rays from which are brought to a focus found

4*

on a movable screen at S. Interposed between O and MM is a mask which only allows a ring of light to reach MM. Thus the mirror is divided up into concentric rings which are tested one at a time. If the mirror is truly parabolic then all the rings will have their foci in the same position. Allowance is made for the fact that O is not infinitely far away by using a correction derived in the following manner.

In the figure the ray of light OP is reflected off a point on the mirror having coordinates (x, y). PR is a ray of light, parallel to the axis, passing through F, the focal point.

$$\angle FPS = \angle OPR$$
$$= \angle POS.$$

$\triangle FPS$ is similar to $\triangle POF$ since $\angle FPS = \angle POS$, and $\angle PFS$ is common.

Therefore

$$\frac{PF}{FO} = \frac{FS}{PF},$$

$$FS = \frac{PF^2}{FO},$$

giving $\quad z = \frac{(x + a)^2}{d - a}$ (see Fig. 4.4),

where z is the correction FS and d is the distance of the source from the mirror.

The Ellipse

The ellipse (Fig. 4.8) has two foci, marked F_1 and F_2, and if a point source is placed at one the reflected rays of light will pass through the other. The parabola can be regarded as a special case of the ellipse in which one focus is at infinity. The equation of the ellipse is:

$$\frac{x^2}{a^2} + \frac{y^2}{b^2} = 1,$$

where a and b are the half lengths of the major and minor axes.

It also has the property that the sum of F_1P and F_2P is a constant. The most accurate way of producing an elliptical contour or template is by cutting a cylinder at an angle.

This curve is useful where light has to be directed on to a narrow slit or point, or in a floodlight where a specific divergence of beam is required.

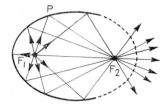

FIG. 4.8. Light reflected from elliptical mirror.

The Hyperbola

Like the ellipse the hyperbola has a second focus but this is behind the mirror and the rays of light diverge from this point. It is sometimes used in place of the ellipse to obtain a specific divergence. But the fact that the rays diverge directly after reflection means that some of them may fall on the casing of the enclosing fitting and would thus be lost as shown in Fig. 4.9.

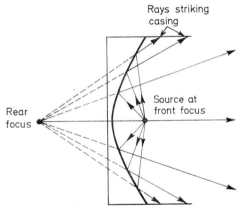

FIG. 4.9. Light reflected from hyperbolic mirror.

The equation of the hyperbola is:

$$\frac{x^2}{a^2} - \frac{y^2}{b^2} = 1,$$

where a and b are constants.

The contour of a hyperbola can be produced by cutting a cone parallel to its axis.

Horned and Peaked Quartics

In order to obtain a beam of greater divergence than given by the parabola, Spencer[1] has developed a family of curves known as horned and peaked quartics. These are obtained by rotating a parabola about an inclined axis passing through the focus.

In Fig. 4.10(a) O is the apex of the parabola LOL', OX its axis, and F its focus. The inclined line about which it is rotated is ZFO'.

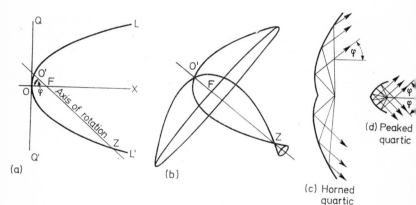

FIG. 4.10. Peaked and horned quartics.

Figure 4.10(b) shows the surfaces generated by the rotation. The upper limb of the parabola, $O'L$, forms a horned quartic, and the lower limb, $O'L'$, a peaked quartic. The peaked quartic closes on itself, but the horned quartic does not. Spencer shows that the equation of these surfaces involves the fourth power of z, the distance along $O'Z$. For this reason she calls the curves peaked and horned quartics.

The optical properties of these surfaces are shown in Fig. 4.10(c) and (d). The peaked quartic reflects the rays back across the axis, and the resultant reflector is compact. In contrast, the horned quartic is more open and is similar to the hyperbola. The spread of light (measured from the axis) with both these surfaces is φ, the inclination of the axis of the parabola to $O'Z$. φ should not be made too great otherwise a dip will be produced in the beam.

Owing to the reflector forming images of the coils of the filament when a tungsten iodine lamp is used, the beam has vertical striations (Fig. 5.35); a fault not confined to horned and peaked quartics. Spencer suggests eliminating these by "modulating the contour". This amounts to rotating small elements of the contour about vertical axes. The angle must be sufficient to fill in the dips between the striations. This procedure is preferable to matting the reflector and so destroying the light control.

The horned quartic has been used with tungsten iodine lamps for photographic floodlights.

Surfaces generated by rotating a parabola[2] about an axis parallel to the true axis, but displaced to one side of it, have been used in motor-car headlights.

Sharp Cut-off Reflectors

In some applications, particularly street lighting, it is essential to have a sharp cut-off of the intensity above a certain angle in order to eliminate glare. If the source can be regarded as point or linear in comparison to the focal length, a parabola can be used with the source itself shielded to stop direct light. A good quality reflector is required otherwise it is necessary to use louvers, which have the drawback of decreasing the efficiency. With tubular fluorescent lamps it is possible to achieve a cut-off by putting a suitable point on the circumference of the lamp at the focus. But only a part of the parabola can be used without rays being reflected above the cut-off.

In order to cope with the problem of achieving a sharp cut-off from a tubular source, Stevens[3] developed a family of curves having the property, shown in Fig. 4.11, that the upper bounding rays of the reflected beams are parallel.

They are defined by the parametric equations (Fig. 4.12)

$$y = \tfrac{1}{2}\left[x\left(p - \frac{1}{p}\right) - a\left(p + \frac{1}{p}\right)\right], \qquad (4.2)$$

$$x = p(c - 2a\varphi) - a, \qquad (4.3)$$

where a is the radius of the tube; $p = dy/dx = \tan \varphi$; and $c = -2y$, when $x = -a$.

c is a constant: as its value is increased a family of curves is obtained passing further and further from the tube.

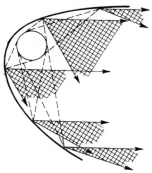

FIG. 4.11. Cones of light reflected by the sharp cut-off reflector.

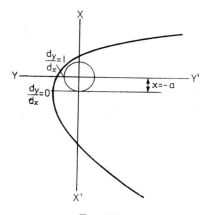

FIG. 4.12.

It is interesting to note that as $a \to 0$ the curves become parabolas of focal length $\tfrac{1}{2}c$.

Should it be desired that the curve go throught a specific point (x, y), the values can be substituted in the equation

$$p = \frac{y + \sqrt{(x^2 + y^2 - a^2)}}{x - a},$$

p can then be substituted in eqn. (4.3) to find the appropriate value of c. Once the value of c is decided upon, points on the curve can be found by substituting appropriate values of p in eqns. (4.2) and (4.3). To do this calculation it is best to set the work out in a table and plot the points as they are calculated so that they can be spaced as evenly as possible.

Involute of Circle

The involute of the circle (Fig. 4.13) has the useful property that if the source is represented by the circle no light is reflected back on to the source. This property ensures a high light output ratio for the minimum width of reflector.

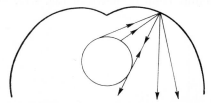

FIG. 4.13. The involute of the circle showing how none of the rays are reflected back to source.

The involute of the circle can be traced by the end of a piece of thread unwound from the circle. It has the equations:

$$x = a(\cos \theta + \theta \sin \theta),$$

$$y = a(\sin \theta + \theta \cos \theta),$$

where the equation of the circle is $x^2 + y^2 = a^2$.

The easiest construction is as follows. The circumference of the circle (Fig. 4.14) representing the source is divided into, say,

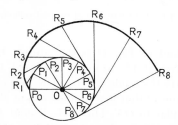

FIG. 4.14. Construction of involute of circle.

12 equal parts, and marked P_1, P_2, P_3, etc. Tangents are drawn at these points and distances equal to 1/12, 2/12, 3/12, etc., of the circumference are marked off along them, giving points R_1, R_2, R_3, etc. These lie on the involute.

Faceted Reflectors

Faceted reflectors,[4] made up of plane elements, have the advantage over curved reflectors that they give a distribution free of striations. Unfortunately they are difficult to manufacture economically though there is a possibility that they could be manufactured by the extrusion of aluminium.

One type for giving a flat-topped beam from a linear source such as a tungsten iodine lamp is shown in Fig. 4.15. Suppose we re-

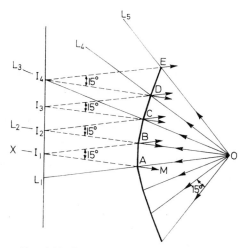

FIG. 4.15. Construction of faceted reflector.

quire a beam spread of 15°. O is the source. Lines OL_1, OL_2, OL_3, etc., are drawn at 15° to each other. OX is the axis of the reflector and bisects the angle L_2OL_1. The first element AB is put at any distance from O that gives a convenient size of drawing. It is made perpendicular to OX. The next element BC is put at such an angle that the ray OB is reflected parallel to AM. OC will then be reflected at 15° to $A\dot{M}$. CD and the succeeding elements are put in a similar manner. It will be found that the elements are tangental to a parabola of focal length equal to the perpendicular distance of AB from O. The images I_1, I_2, I_3, etc., lie on the directrix.

The size of the drawing can be scaled to suit the desired reflector dimensions, which are partly dictated by lamp size.

Figure 4.16 shows the performance of a faceted reflector compared to that of a parabolic reflector. The beam is nearly square topped, but with a source of larger diameter such as a fluorescent tube, the corners would become more rounded.

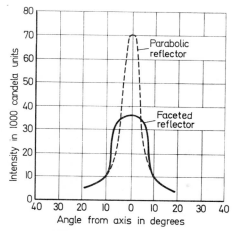

FIG. 4.16. Transverse distribution curves of parabolic and faceted reflectors using 1500 W tungsten iodine lamp.

Non-mathematically Defined Contours

When the required distribution cannot be obtained by one of the contours already described the following method in which the contour is tailored to the polar curve can be used. It only applies to point and linear sources of light. If large sources such as GLS lamps are used, a good degree of accuracy cannot be expected.

In the case of point sources the reflector will be a surface of revolution (i.e. symmetrical about the main axis). But in the case of linear sources the reflector will be trough-shaped.

4 a*

In outline, the method consists in determining the flux available in each angular zone from the bare lamp. It is then directed into the zones where there is a deficit between the direct bare lamp flux

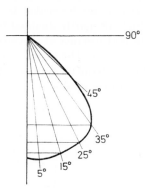

FIG. 4.17. Required polar curve showing horizontal lines proportional to zonal flux.

and the required flux. The calculation is rather tedious, but Lynes[5] has devised an elegant geometrical construction which reduces the work and will be described here. It will be assumed that the curve required is as shown in Fig. 4.17. The procedure can be split down into six parts.

1. *Selection of reflector system*

Jolley, Waldram and Wilson[6] have described four possible reflector systems (Fig. 4.18) from which the most suitable one has to be selected. In (a) and (b) the reflectors reflect the light back over the axis, whereas in (c) and (d) the light is reflected away from the axis of the contour. In (a) and (c) the bottom of the reflectors reflects light into the zones nearest the downward vertical whereas the opposite is true in (b) and (d). (b) and (c) give the most compact reflectors. (a) has the disadvantage, besides large size, that the reflected rays from the top of the reflector pass through the lamp envelope and may be obstructed by the internal structure of the lamp. (b) and (c) are the most used types; (b) where a fairly concentrated distribution is required and (c) where a flat surface such as a chalk board has to be illuminated as evenly as possible from one side by a linear source. (b) will therefore be the most suitable for our purpose.

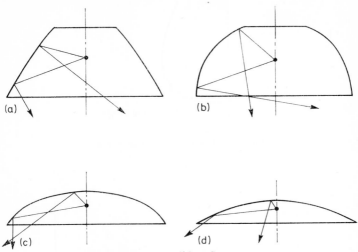

FIG. 4.18. Four possible reflector systems.

2. *Determination of flux available in each angular zone from bare lamp*

We make use of the fact that the flux in each zone of the polar curve is proportional to the horizontal distance from the mid-zone intensity point to the vertical axis. This fact was proved in Chapter 1 for a point source (see Wohlauer's method). These lines are drawn on the polar curve of the bare lamp as shown in Fig. 4.19.

We have to find the flux available from the bare lamp taking into account the absorption by the reflector and the bare lamp. Draw a horizontal line *AB* (Fig. 4.20). From *A* step off, end-to-end, the lengths of the horizontal lines drawn in Fig. 4.19. Mark the limits of the zones as shown until the cut-off angle of 50° is reached at *D*.

Above this angle we have to allow for the absorption of the reflector, and in cases where the light is reflected through the lamp, the additional losses must be allowed for. If the reflection factor of the reflector is 0·8 and the transmission factor of the lamp is 0·8 the

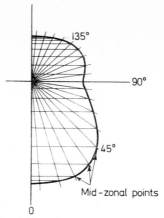

FIG. 4.19. Polar curve of bare lamp.

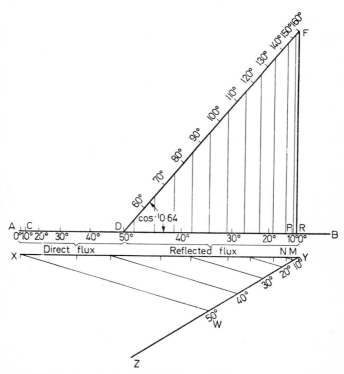

FIG. 4.20. Construction for finding flux available and flux required in each zone.

net fraction of flux emitted from the reflector will be 0·64. We therefore mark off the remaining zones along a line *DF* inclined to *AB* at an angle of which the cosine is 0·64. Perpendiculars are then dropped from mid-point of each zone on to *AB*. These mark off cumulative totals of the flux from the bare lamp, the distance *AR* representing the total flux available.

3. *Determination of the flux required in each angular zone*

Before the flux required in each angular zone can be found, it is necessary to make the total flux required equal to that available. This process amounts to multiplying the polar curve of the required distribution by a scale factor so that it represents the same amount of flux as is available for redistribution.

In Fig. 4.20 we have to make the required flux equivalent to *AR*. Beneath *AR*, therefore, draw a line *XY*, equal in length and parallel to it. From *Y* draw a line *YW* inclined at an angle of about 30°. From *Y* step-off distances corresponding to the flux required (shown in Fig. 4.17) in each zone in a similar manner as was done for the available flux. We step off the distances from the right-hand side because in reflector type (b) rays from the top of the reflector are reflected nearest the vertical. For reflectors (a) and (c) the sloping line would be drawn under *A*. The limit of the last zone is at *W*. Join *WX* and draw lines parallel to it through the zonal limits as shown.

The flux required in each zone has now been marked off along *XY*. But to find the amount which has to be reflected into each zone we must first subtract the direct flux. For instance, in the 0–10° zone we step-off a distance *MY* equal to *AC*. The remainder *MN* is equivalent to the flux required by reflection. If more flux is available than is required in any particular zone, then it is impossible to achieve the required distribution without using a more complicated reflector system or, perhaps, inverting the lamp.

4. *Relating the reflected flux to the required flux*

The flux required by reflection is marked off along *DR*. For instance *PR* is made equal to *NM* is marked 10°. The positions of 20°, 30° and 40° are found in a similar manner. We can now draw up the first three columns in Table 4.1. θ, the mid-zone angle, is the average of the zonal limits. δ, the angle into which light must be redirected, is estimated from the position of the various perpendiculars on the angular scale along DR. For instance, for the 50–60° zone, we estimate how the mid-zone perpendicular divides the distance between 40° and 50°. It is at about 48°. This procedure is then repeated for the other zones.

Interpolation is sometimes not easy, in which case smaller zones should be used.

5. *Determination of the angles of the contour elements*

Table 4.1 has now to be completed to determine the inclination of each reflector element to the vertical.

The inclination of the reflector element to the vertical can then be found by using the formula

$$\varphi = \tfrac{1}{2}(\theta - \delta),$$

where the symbols are defined in Table 4.1 (p. 106).

This can be derived as follows.

In Fig. 4.21 A is the centre of the light source and XX' an element of the reflector surface. φ, δ and θ have the same meanings as in Table 4.1. β is the angle of incidence, equal to the angle of reflection.

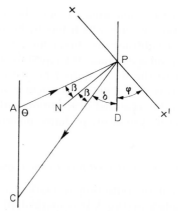

FIG. 4.21. Diagram for showing $\varphi = \tfrac{1}{2}(\theta - \delta)$.

Since $\angle\ NPX' = 90°$,

$$\beta + \delta + \varphi = 90°.$$

In the triangle APC,

$$\theta + \delta + 2\beta = 180°.$$

$$\theta + \delta + 2(90° - \delta - \varphi) = 180°.$$

Therefore

$$\varphi = \tfrac{1}{2}(\theta - \delta).$$

In the forms of reflector (Fig. 4.18 c and d) where the reflected ray goes to the right of PD, δ will be positive in the formula.

6. *Drawing the reflector contour*

The centre of the light source is marked, and radial lines are drawn emanating from it at 10° intervals to mark the zonal limits, as shown in Fig. 4.22. The first element, between the 150° and 160°

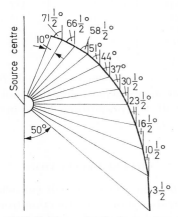

FIG. 4.22. Setting out reflector contour.

radial lines, is drawn inclined at angle of $71\tfrac{1}{2}°$ to the vertical as derived in Table 4.1. The process is continued for the rest of the elements. The curved contour is then drawn smoothly tangential to all the elements.

The distance of the first element from the centre of the source governs the size of the reflector and should be chosen to allow adequate ventilation and easy relamping.

Steps (1), (2) and (3) could have been done by calculation using zonal constants (solid angles) but this is a much longer and more tedious process than the geometrical construction.

TABLE 4.1. DETERMINATION OF THE INCLINATION OF THE CONTOUR ELEMENTS TO THE UPWARD VERTICAL (all angles in degrees)

Limits of zone	θ Mid-zone angle	δ Angle into which light must be redirected	$\theta - \delta$	φ $\frac{1}{2}(\theta - \delta)$ Inclination of element to vertical
50–60°	55			
		48	7	$3\frac{1}{2}$
60–70°	65			
		45	20	10
70–80°	75			
		42	33	$16\frac{1}{2}$
80–90°	85			
		38	47	$23\frac{1}{2}$
90–100°	95			
		34	61	$30\frac{1}{2}$
100–110°	105			
		31	74	37
110–120°	115			
		27	88	44
120–130°	125			
		23	102	51
130–140°	135			
		18	117	$58\frac{1}{2}$
140–150°	145			
		12	133	$66\frac{1}{2}$
150–160°	155			
		8	143	$71\frac{1}{2}$
160–170°	165			

Trough reflectors can be designed to give a desired distribution in the transverse (non-axial) plane using the above procedure, but instead of marking off steps proportional to $I_\theta \sin \theta$, they are marked off proportional to I_θ.

DIFFUSE REFLECTION

The kind of reflection which we will consider here is that in which the light is scattered in every direction from the surface. We have already mentioned that metals can be given a matt finish, but we now want to discuss the optical properties of white paint finishes. The distribution of light from such finishes approximates to the cosine law for uniform diffusers, though when their surface is glossy then there will be a small specular component superimposed on this. The specular component has been found by experiment to have a negligible effect on the light distribution from fittings; the purpose of the glossy finish being to make cleaning easier rather than to control the light distribution. It is also worth noting that even the most matt finish will reflect light specularly at grazing angles of incidence.

One of the most important properties of diffuse finishes is the reflection factor. This should be as high as possible to achieve a high light output ratio.

The polar curves of fittings using diffusing finishes can be predicted by adopting the following procedure. The light output ratio is found by using the method given in Chapter 3, p. 71. The shape of the polar curve due to reflected light is found by determining the projected areas at the appropriate angles of elevation. This is multiplied by a factor so that it represents the flux output of the fitting less any bare lamp flux emerging directly from the fitting. The polar curve representing this directly emerging flux is added to the polar curve of the reflected light to give the final curve. The opposite process of working out the reflector shape to achieve a required distribution is not usually undertaken as a mathematical procedure. Reflectors are usually designed to give a certain shielding angle from the lamp, and the size made large enough to give a reasonable light output ratio and prevent overheating.

REFRACTOR SYSTEMS

In designing refractor systems for controlling the distribution of light, we make use of the fact that when a ray of light passes through a boundary between two media of different optical density it changes its direction of travel. The following two laws enable the direction to be found.

(1) The refracted ray lies in the same plane as the normal to the boundary and the incident ray, and is on the opposite side of the normal to the incident ray (Fig. 4.23a).

(2) The sine of the angle of incidence (i) bears a constant ratio to the sine of the angle of refraction (r) for light of a given wavelength, that is

$$\sin i = \mu \sin r,$$

when μ is the constant of proportionality and is known as the refractive index of the medium in which the ray is refracted with respect to the first medium. If the incident ray is in air it is usual to refer to μ as being the refractive index of the other more optically dense medium. The refractive indices of some common substances are shown in Table 4.2.

TABLE 4.2. REFRACTIVE INDICES OF SOME TRANSPARENT MEDIA

Substance	Refractive Index	Critical angle (Degrees)
Water	1·33	49
Acrylic	1·49	42
Soda glass	1·52	41
Polystyrene	1·59	39
Flint glass	1·62	38

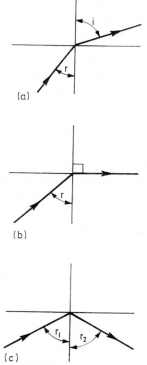

FIG. 4.23. Three possibilities at a boundary between two media. (a) Ray travelling into less dense medium; $\sin i = \mu \sin r$. (b) Ray emerging parallel to surface; $\sin r = 1/\mu$ (r is the critical angle). (c) Ray totally internally reflected; $r_1 = r_2$, both being greater than critical angle.

Light paths are reversible, that is if a ray of light takes a certain path through a refractor system, a ray in the opposite direction will follow the same path.

Internal Reflection and the Critical Angle

A consequence of the second law is that a ray of light is bent towards the normal when passing into an optically dense medium, but when emerging it is bent away from the normal. If the angle of refraction is increased until the emergent ray is parallel to the boundary, it, the angle of refraction, is known as the critical angle (Fig. 4.23 b). In this case the angle of emergence (i) is 90°, so that

$$\text{critical angle} = \sin^{-1} \frac{1}{\mu}.$$

Values of this for some common substances are tabulated in Table 4.2.

When the angle of refraction is increased to values greater than the critical angle total internal reflection takes place (Fig. 4.23 c) and the normal laws of reflection are obeyed.

Reflection at Boundaries

We have stated that reflection occurs when the critical angle is exceeded, but in actual fact a certain proportion of the light is always reflected when passing through a boundary between two media. The proportion depends on the plane of polarization of the light (i.e. the plane at right angles to the plane in which the light is vibrating) with regard to the plane of incidence (the plane of the normal and the incident ray), and on the angles of reflection and refraction.

If the plane of polarization is at right angles to the plane of incidence, Fresnel has shown that the reflection factor ϱ_1 is given by

$$\varrho_1 = \tan^2(i - r)/\tan^2(i + r). \tag{4.4}$$

He has also shown that when the plane of polarization is parallel to the plane of incidence, the reflection factor ϱ_2 is given by

$$\varrho_2 = \sin^2(i - r)/\sin^2(i + r). \tag{4.5}$$

When the light is unpolarized the light vibrates equally in all planes, so that the reflection factor is given by

$$\varrho = \tfrac{1}{2}(\varrho_2 + \varrho_1).$$

Figure 4.24 shows how the reflection factor varies with the angles of incidence and refraction for a medium of refractive index of 1·5 in air. The full line is for rays reflected in the less dense medium and the dotted line is for rays reflected in the more dense medium.

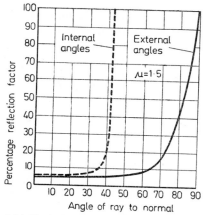

FIG. 4.24. Variation of reflection factor with angle.

This phenomenon of reflection at boundaries is important to the designer who must be careful not to make his angles of incidence so great that the losses, or the scattering, become significant.

Polarization by Reflection and Transmission

It is interesting to note that if the light is incident at an angle (known as Brewster's angle) such that

$$i + r = 90°,$$

then

$$\sin i = \mu \sin (90° - i)$$

so that

and

$$\tan i = \mu$$

$$\varrho_1 = 0 \quad \text{from eqn. (4.4).}$$

Hence at every angle of incidence the reflected light is partially polarized in the plane of incidence and is completely polarized if the angle of incidence is at Brewster's angle. The refracted light is partially polarized in a plane perpendicular to the plane of incidence, and the degree of polarization can be increased by using a number of plates. Diffusers for fittings which produce a significant amount of polarized light at Brewster's angle have been made by embedding glass flakes in a resin. These polarizing materials are known as multilayer polarizers[7]. Their application will be discussed on p. 163. They are claimed to reduce glare caused by light reflected from non-electrically conducting materials.

Luminance of an Image Formed by a Refractor System

As stated at the beginning of this chapter the luminance L of an image formed by a refractor system is given by

$$L = \tau L_0,$$

where L_0 is the luminance of the object and τ is the transmission factor of the system defined as the flux transmitted divided by that incident.

As the truth of this equation is far from obvious it will be proved for a lens system.

In Fig. 4.25 O is the object of luminance L_0 distant u from the lens of area A. The image I is formed at a distance v from the lens, and is viewed beyond I.

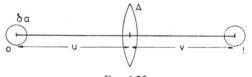

FIG. 4.25.

If the lens is small, the solid angle subtended by it at O is A/u^2.

Consider a small area of the object δa; its intensity will be $\delta a\, L_0$ (since luminance is measured in intensity per unit area).

The flux reaching the lens is given by intensity multiplied by solid angle, i.e.,

$$\delta a\, L_0 \times \frac{A}{u^2} = \delta a\, L_0 \frac{A}{u^2}.$$

(This could have also been arrived at by using the inverse-square law of illumination.)

If τ is the transmission factor of the lens then the flux emerging will be

$$\delta a \, L_0 \, \frac{A}{u^2} \, \tau. \tag{4.6}$$

Let L_1 be the luminance of the image.

The area of the image will be $\delta a \, v^2/u^2$, so that its intensity will be $L_1 \, \delta a \, v^2/u^2$ (intensity = luminance $\times$ area).

Any cone of light leaving the image will subtend the same solid angle as the lens subtends at the image point, i.e. A_2/v^2 (for points near the axis), so that the total flux leaving the image will be

$$\frac{A}{v^2} \times L_1 \, \delta a \times \frac{v^2}{u^2}$$

(since flux = solid angle $\times$ intensity). This is equal to the flux leaving the lens, so

$$\frac{A}{v^2} L_1 \, \delta a \, \frac{v^2}{u^2} = \delta a \, L_0 \, \frac{A}{u^2} \, \tau \quad \text{from eqn. (4.6).}$$

Therefore

$$L_1 = \tau L_0.$$

This is the luminance of the image as viewed in air. It is difficult at first sight to see why this differs from the luminance of an image produced on a screen, which as photographers know depends on the aperture of the lens in relation to v.

When we view the aerial image the light remains concentrated into the solid angle A/v^2, but when we view the image formed on a screen it is scattered in all directions. To find the luminance of the image on a screen, therefore, we have to determine the illumination. We then multiply this by the reflection or transmission factor, as appropriate.

The illumination of the image is given by the flux falling on it divided by its area.

From eqn. (4.6) the flux reaching the image is $\delta a_0 \, L_0 \, (A/u^2)\tau$. The size of the image is $\delta a \, (v^2/u^2)$. Therefore illumination of image is

$$\left(\delta a_0 \, L_0 \, \frac{A}{u^2} \, \tau \right) \div \left(\delta a_0 \, \frac{v^2}{u^2} \right)$$

or

$$L_0 \, \frac{A}{v^2} \, \tau. \tag{4.7}$$

It is interesting to note that in a camera the image is usually formed near the focal plane, so that v is approximately equal to f, the focal length, and the formula becomes $L_0(A/f^2)\,\tau$. The f number is the diameter of the aperture divided into the focal length, that is, it is proportional to the reciprocal of the square root of A/f^2. From eqn. (4.7) it is obvious that the illumination of the image can be increased by making the lens larger. But in the case of the aerial image the effect of the larger lens is simply to increase the divergence of the cones of light leaving the image. The additional flux collected would not enter the eye providing the original cone of light was sufficiently large to cover the pupil. Hence there would not be any increase of image luminance with lens size.

Deviation of a Ray at a Boundary

In the calculation of prism angles, the deviation $(i - r)$ of a ray at one of the faces is often known and the angle of incidence (i) has to be found. A formula for this purpose can be derived as follows:

$$\sin i = \mu \sin r$$
$$= \mu \sin [i - (i - r)]$$
$$= \mu [\sin i \cos (i - r) - \sin (i - r) \cos i],$$
$$\tan i = \mu [\tan i \cos (i - r) - \sin (i - r)];$$

therefore
$$\tan i = \frac{\mu \sin (i - r)}{\mu \cos (i - r) - 1}.$$

A nomogram, given in Appendix B, enables i and r to be determined for known values of the deviation.

Prism Systems

Prisms are classed as refracting or reflecting according to whether they make use solely of refraction or make use of total internal reflection as well as refraction.

Figure 4.26 shows some common forms,[8] but in making use of prisms for the control of light it is usually necessary to calculate the prism angles specially for the job. These calculations involve nothing more than the relation $\sin i = \mu \sin r$ and simple geometry, but they tend to be somewhat complicated. It is easy to make mistakes unless the work is properly laid out.

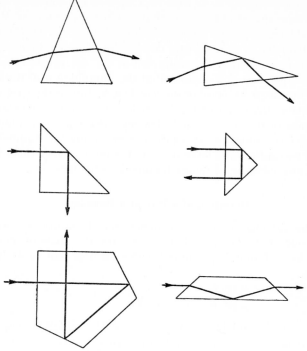

FIG. 4.26. Some common prism forms.

Refracting Prisms

The trace of a ray through a refracting prism is shown in Fig. 4.27. XX' and the Y ordinates are put in for reference. The ray of light is shown leaving the source at an angle P to $Y_1 Y_1$. Suppose it is required to determine B and C such that the ray is deviated through an angle D to emerge at angle Q to $Y_4 Y_4$; the following useful relations can be used:

  (1) $D = (i - r) + (i' - r')$.

  (2) $D = 180° - (P + Q)$.

  (3) $A = B + C$.   (4.8)

  (4) $A = r + r'$.

  (5) $i' = 90° + C - Q$.

  (6) $i = 90° + B - P$.

It is also helpful to remember that the light is always deviated towards the base of the prism.

If the angle of incidence, and therefore refraction, lies on the other side of the normal to that shown on the diagram (that is, towards the refracting angle), then it and the angle of refraction are taken to be negative. D can never be negative since the light is always deviated towards the base of the prism.

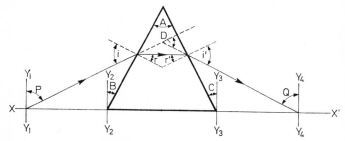

FIG. 4.27. Trace of a ray through a prism.

To show how these relationships are used and what sort of decisions have to be made we will give an actual example of the calculation of a prism bank for a street lantern in Chapter 5.

Geometrical Construction

The following is an ingenious geometrical construction that can be used for finding prism angles very quickly.[9]

Method

Two concentric circles centre O are drawn, one of unit radius and the other of radius μ, as shown in Fig. 4.28(a). Axis $X'OX$ is put in for reference.

Using the same notation as previously, we draw a line at an angle i to OX to cut the inner circle in R.

RC is drawn parallel to $X'OX$.

Finally, OB is drawn at an angle D to OR, and CB is joined.

$\angle RCB = A$, the prism angle.

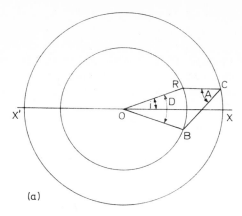

FIG. 4.28 (a).

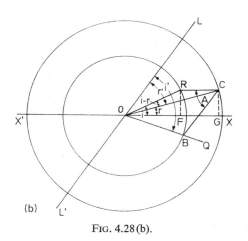

FIG. 4.28 (b).

Proof

In Fig. 4.28(b) make the angle ROX equal to i and draw RC parallel to OX as in Fig. 4.28(a). Join OC and drop the perpendiculars RF and CG on to OX.

Then

$$\sin i = \frac{RF}{RO}$$

and
$$\sin \angle COX = \frac{CG}{CO}.$$

But
$$CO = \mu\, RO, \quad \text{by construction}$$

and
$$CG = RF, \quad \text{by construction}.$$

Therefore
$$\sin \angle COX = \frac{RF}{\mu RO}$$
$$= \frac{1}{\mu}\sin i$$
$$= \sin r$$

Therefore
$$\angle COX = r \quad \text{and} \quad \angle COR = i - r.$$

Draw CB at an angle A to RC and make LOL' parallel to CB. The angle XOL is then equal to A. Hence the angle COL is equal to $A - r$, and is, therefore, also equal to r', from eqn. (4.8).

By dropping perpendiculars from B and C on to LOL', and by proceeding in the same way as above, it can be shown that the angle BOL is equal to i', and the angle COB is equal to $i' - r'$.

Hence $D = \angle COR + \angle COB$, since $D = (i - r) + (i' - r')$,
$$= \angle ROB.$$

Hence if the angle XOR is made equal to i, and the angle RCB is made equal to A, the angle BOR will be equal to D. It also follows that if the angle BOR is made equal to D, the angle RCB will be equal to A. Hence the proposition is proved.

If OB is produced to Q, the angle QBC equals i'. It can also be seen that the angle OCR equals r and the angle OCB equals r'. Hence all angles of incidence and refraction can be found in Fig. 4.28(a) by joining OC and producing OB.

Graphical Calculator

This is given in Appendix C and enables the prism angles to be read off directly. It is calculated for a refractive index of 1·49.

Reflecting Prisms

We now turn to the calculation of reflecting prisms. These have the advantage of being able to bend the light rays through a greater angle than refracting prisms but suffer from the drawback that they are liable to give inaccurate control since their functioning depends on the accuracy of all three faces, and not just two.

Figure 4.29 shows the trace of a ray through the reflecting prism *UVW*. *XX'* and the *Y* ordinates are put in for reference in the same way as for the refracting prism. The ray leaves the source

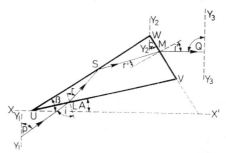

FIG. 4.29. Trace of a ray through a reflecting prism.

at an angle P to Y_1Y_1 and enters the face UV at the point L. It is reflected from the face UW at the point S and leaves the prism through the face WV at the point M, making an angle Q with Y_3Y_3.

Making use of the fact that the angles LSU and WSM are equal, we can find the following relations between the various marked angles:

(1) $i = A + P$,

(2) $i' = C - Q + 90°$,

(3) $B = \frac{1}{2}(A + C + 90° - r - r')$,
     since $\angle SUL + \angle SLU = \angle SWM + \angle SMW$,
    and acute angle $SWY_2 = 90° - B$.

These relations enable B to be found once C and A have been set. The work can be most conveniently set out in a table.

Usually the face UV is sloped below XX' to avoid under-cutting the prisms and to make manufacture easier. The formulae given above still apply but A is negative.

To achieve complete flashing of the face WV in the direction of the emergent rays, UV must either be parallel to SM or converge towards SM (to a point on the right-hand side of the figure). If UV is made parallel to SM, MV will be completely flashed for rays making a smaller angle than P with $Y_1 Y_1$, and will be incompletely flashed for rays making a larger angle than P with $Y_1 Y_1$. The condition for UV to be parallel with SM can be found quite easily.

$\angle MSW = B - A$, since UV is parallel to SM.

In the triangle SMW,

$$\angle MSW + \angle SMW + \angle SWM = 180°.$$
Therefore

$$(B - A) + (90° - r') + (90° - B + C) = 180°, \quad \text{giving}$$

(4) $A = C - r'$.

Thus if C is fixed, A can be found by using expressions (2) and (4). Then B can be found by using expressions (1) and (3).

In all these calculations, it should be checked that the angle of incidence of the reflected ray $(B - A + r)$, is in fact equal to or greater than the critical angle; the condition that it does not pass through the face UW.

The prisms mask each other when made into a bank. It is very useful, as in all prism design, to draw the prisms to find the extent of the masking. At the same time, the effect of light interreflected from parts of the optical system other than the light source can be found.

Tracing Rays Through a Refracting Prism in Planes other than the Principal Plane

So far we have discussed the trace a ray makes in passing through the principal plane of a prism (the plane passing through the normals to the surfaces) but very often we want to know what happens to rays which enter the prism in other planes.[10]

To solve this problem we have to consider how to project the trace of a ray, when it is passing into a medium of refractive index μ, on to an inclined plane passing through the normal to the ray. In Fig. 4.30 $ACFE$ is the plane in which the ray COE is travelling. $X'OX$ is the boundary between the air and the lower medium, which has a refractive index μ. AOF is a normal to the boundary.

The inclined plane *ABFD* passes through *AOF*. *BOD* is the projection of the ray on the inclined plane, so that the angles *ABC* and *EDF* are right angles.

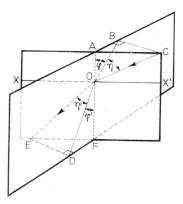

Fɪɢ. 4.30.

Let $\angle BOC = \eta$, $\angle EOD = \eta'$, $\angle BOA = \varphi$ and $\angle DOF = \varphi'$.

By construction make

$$\mu\, CO = OE, \tag{4.9}$$

so $\sin \angle COA = \mu \sin \angle EOF.$

Therefore

$$\frac{AC}{CO} = \mu\,\frac{EF}{OE}$$

$$= \frac{EF}{CO} \quad \text{from eqn. (4.9)}$$

giving $AC = EF.$

In the triangles *ABC* and *EFD*,

$$\angle CAB = \angle EFD,$$

$$\angle ABC = \angle EDF\,(=90°),$$

$$AC = EF.$$

Therefore the triangles are equal in all respects, so $AB = DF$ and $BC = ED$.

$$\sin \eta = \frac{BC}{CO}$$

$$= \mu \frac{ED}{OE}$$

$$= \mu \sin \eta'.$$

Hence the sine of the angle between the ray and its projection before refraction is equal to μ times that after refraction.

Also

$$\sin \varphi \cos \eta = \frac{AB}{BO} \times \frac{BO}{CO}$$

$$= \mu \frac{AB}{OE}$$

$$= \mu \frac{DF}{OD} \times \frac{OD}{OE}$$

$$= \mu \sin \varphi' \cos \eta'.$$

Let us now consider what happens when a ray passes into a prism in an inclined plane (Fig. 4.31 a). Let η and η' be the angles the entering ray makes with its projections on the principal plane before and after refraction. Let the corresponding angles be ξ', ξ for the emergent ray. Since the ray in the prism has a constant inclination to its projection, η' and ξ' will be equal, so that η and ξ must also be equal. Thus the incident and emergent rays make the same angle with the principal plane. The equations are

$$\sin \eta = \mu \sin \eta',$$

$$\sin \xi = \mu \sin \xi',$$

$$\eta' = \xi' \quad \text{and} \quad \eta = \xi.$$

Let φ and φ' be the angles the projections of the entering ray make with the normal before and after refraction (Fig. 4.31 b). And let ψ' and ψ be the angles the projections of the emergent ray make with the normal before and after refraction.

Then

$$\sin \varphi \cos \eta = \mu \sin \varphi' \cos \xi'$$

and

$$\sin \psi \cos \eta = \mu \sin \psi' \cos \xi'.$$

Also

$$A = \varphi' + \psi'.$$

These equations enable the path of any ray to be traced through a prism.

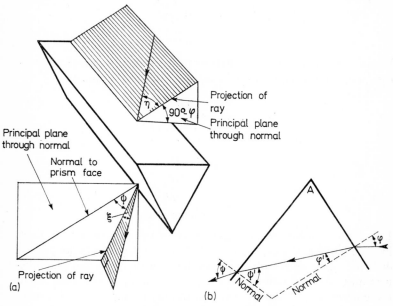

FIG. 4.31(a). Oblique ray passing through prism.
FIG. 4.31(b). Projection of an oblique ray on the principal plane.

Concluding Notes on Prism Design

We have given the basic formulae and procedures for designing prism banks, but all the possibilities and tricks of the trade have been far from explored here. New ideas are being brought out all the time and one of the best ways of keeping really abreast of developments is by consulting patents.

Lenses

We will not give proofs of the various lens formulae, but we give a summary of them as they apply to thin lenses, for reference.

These formulae are only really applicable to rays near the axis. More complicated formulae have to be used in other cases.

Let u be the distance of the object from the lens, v the distance of the image from the lens, and f the focal length of the lens. Then

$$\frac{1}{u} + \frac{1}{v} = \frac{1}{f},$$

$$(\mu - 1)\left(\frac{1}{r_1} + \frac{1}{r_2}\right) = 1/f,$$

where μ is the refractive index of the lens material and r_1 and r_2 are the radii of curvature of the lens;

$$\frac{1}{f} = \frac{1}{f_1} + \frac{1}{f_2},$$

where f is the equivalent focal length of two lenses of focal lengths f_1 and f_2 placed together.

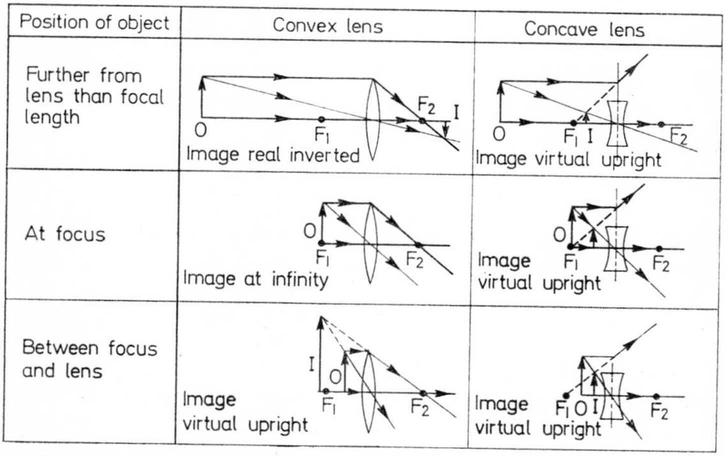

Position of object	Convex lens	Concave lens
Further from lens than focal length	Image real inverted	Image virtual upright
At focus	Image at infinity	Image virtual upright
Between focus and lens	Image virtual upright	Image virtual upright

FIG. 4.32. Formation of images by thin lenses for rays near the axis.

Linear magnification $= v/u$.

To make these formulae universally applicable the following sign convention can be used:

All distances to real points are reckoned as positive, and all distances to virtual points negative.

5*

The focal length of a converging lens is positive, that of a diverging lens negative.

A convex (converging) surface has a positive radius of curvature, and a concave (diverging) surface a negative radius of curvature.

The following are the rules for tracing rays through a lens:

Rays parallel to the axis and passing through the lens are brought to focus (real) on the far side of a converging lens, or diverge from the near side focus (virtual) of a diverging lens. Also rays through the centre of the lens are undeviated.

Figure 4.32 shows some ways in which an image may be formed by a lens. O is the object, I the image, and f_1 and f_2 the foci.

Flashing of Lenses

It is important for the designer to know what intensity he can expect from a lens system or to be able to solve the problem of designing a lens system to give a specified intensity and beam spread. The calculations involved consist of finding the flashed area of the lens in the important directions and multiplying by the luminance of the lens in those directions. There are three cases we must consider for finding the flashed area.

1. *Image of source smaller than lens*

In Fig. 4.33 the lens forms an image I at R of the source, which is not shown. The position of the image is found by using the formula $\dfrac{1}{u} + \dfrac{1}{v} = \dfrac{1}{f}$ and the size of the image by using magnification $= v/u$.

Each point on the lens emits a cone of light on to the image. Five such points, A_1, A_2, A_3, A_4 and A_5, are shown. The bounding rays from these points are drawn to the image. Let us consider how the flashing of the lens changes as we move back from A_3 along the axis.

At A_3 only the point A_3 itself will appear flashed since none of the other cones of light would enter the eye. As we move back the disc of flashed area would grow larger, and at B, for instance, A_2 to A_4 would appear flashed because the bounding rays from these points cross over at this point.

At C the inner bounding rays from A_1 and A_5 cross over, so that the whole of the lens would appear flashed, and illumination calculations could be done by regarding the lens as a disc of the luminance of the source multiplied by the transmission factor of

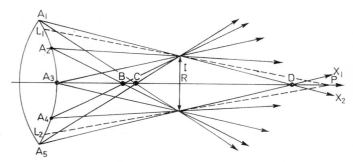

FIG. 4.33. Flashing of lens when image is smaller than lens.

the optical system. The whole of the lens will continue to appear flashed until we reach D, where the outer bounding rays from A_1 and A_5 cross over. Past this point the edges of the lens will gradually become unflashed. At the point P, for instance, only the part of the lens lying between L_1 and L_2 will be flashed, L_1 and L_2 being found by drawing the dotted lines through P and the top and the bottom of the image to meet the lens in L_1 and L_2.

Past the point D the optical system behaves, therefore, as though the lens were flashed and there were a pupil in front of it, at the position of the image, having the same size as the image. This pupil acts as the equivalent light source for points beyond D, and is known as the exit pupil. The lens is the exit pupil between C and D.

Only in the cone X_1DX_2 will the pupil appear completely flashed. If we go outside the cone X_1DX_2 we can estimate the size of the exit pupil by finding how much of the flashed lens would be visible through the pupil.

2. *Image of source equal in size to that of lens*

In this case (Fig. 4.34) the outer bounding rays from A_1 and A_5 are parallel so that the lens is the exit pupil for all points on the axis beyond C, where the inner bounding rays from the edge of the lens cross over.

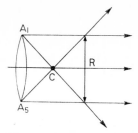

FIG. 4.34. Flashing of lens when image is the same size as lens.

3. Image of source greater in size to that of lens

This is similar to the previous case except that the rays demarcating the zone in which the whole of the lens is flashed are diverging, as shown in Fig. 4.35.

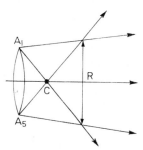

FIG. 4.35. Flashing of lens when image is larger than lens.

Spherical Aberration

Parallel rays of light passing through a lens near its rim will meet the axis nearer to the lens than more central rays. This effect by which the rays fail to come to a point focus is known as spherical aberration. Its degree varies with the configuration of the lens as is shown in Fig. 4.36. The first lens, a meniscus with its concave surface facing the parallel beam, gives the worst aberration.[11] The biconvex shown gives the least where spherical surfaces are employed. The hyperbolic and the elliptical give none.

Spherical aberration becomes important to the designer when a large area of lens has to be flashed to obtain the required intensity, and a large beam spread is needed so that the source has to be placed as close as possible to the lens. In other words it is important when the maximum amount of flux from the source has to be used.

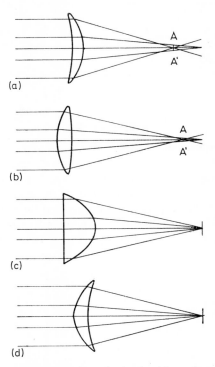

FIG. 4.36. Spherical aberration obtained with various lens shapes. (a) Concavo-convex. (b) Front radius one-sixth of rear radius. (c) Rear surface hyperbolic. (d) Front surface elliptical rear surface spherical with centre at focus.

If the source is smaller than AA in Fig. 4.36(a) and (b) then only part of the lens will be flashed when viewed from the left-hand side of the figure. Unfortunately, the hyperbolical and the elliptical lenses shown have rather a long focus compared to their area, so they collect only a small proportion of flux. Figure 4.37 shows two arrangements employing lenses with parabolic surfaces. These both give a very good performance.

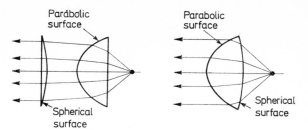

FIG. 3.37. Lens systems with parabolic surfaces.

Stepped Lenses

In certain applications such as lighthouses and theatre spotlights it is convenient to use lenses, sometimes with back reflectors, for controlling the light. Owing to their short focal length in comparison with their diameter, such lenses would be thick and heavy.[12] To overcome this disadvantage, it was suggested by Buffon that they could be considerably reduced in thickness by stepping them in concentric zones as shown in Fig. 4.38(a). However, because of

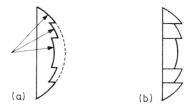

FIG. 4.38. (a) Buffon lens. (b) Fresnel lens.

their large diameter in comparison to their focal length, they suffered from spherical aberration. Fresnel conceived the idea of overcoming this by calculating the curvature on each of the separate rings such that the rays emerging from the top and bottom of the faces were parallel, as shown in Fig. 4.38(b). Modern developments include stepped lenses which give approximations to parabolic surfaces for use as condensers in enlargers and projectors.

We will now give the derivation of the formulae for calculating a Fresnel lens.[13]

In Fig. 4.39 *ABJF* is a section of a ring. The source is positioned at *S*. *SLFG* and *SBEKH* are the traces of the extreme rays, which emerge parallel to the axis of the lens. *D* is the centre of curvature of the curved surface *FJ*.

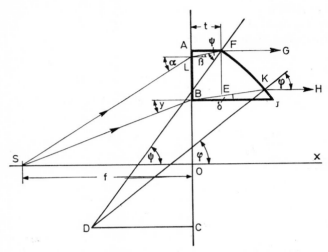

FIG. 4.39. Construction of Fresnel lens.

Let *DF* and *DK* make angles of ψ and φ with the axis.

Also let the angles of incidence and emergence at *L* and *B* be as marked in the figure.

Therefore

$$\sin \alpha = \mu \sin \beta$$

and

$$\sin \gamma = \mu \sin \delta.$$

Also the angles of incidence and emergence at *F* and *K* are $(\psi - \beta, \psi)$ and $(\varphi - \delta, \varphi)$ respectively, so that

$$\sin \psi = \mu \sin (\psi - \beta)$$

and

$$\sin \varphi = \mu \sin (\varphi - \delta).$$

Therefore

$$\tan \psi = \frac{\mu \sin \beta}{\mu \cos \beta - 1} \quad \text{(see p. 113)}$$

and
$$\tan \varphi = \frac{\mu \sin \delta}{\mu \cos \delta - 1},$$

from which ψ and φ can be determined.

Let $\qquad AB = b, \quad SO = f, \quad$ and $\quad AF = t,$

then $b = f(\tan \alpha - \tan \gamma) + t \tan \beta$.

Draw FE parallel to AO to meet BK in E.

Consider the triangle FEK:

$$\angle FEK = 90° - \delta]$$

$$\angle FKE = \angle FKD - \angle BKD$$
$$= 90° - \tfrac{1}{2}(\psi - \varphi) - (\varphi - \delta)$$
$$= 90° - \tfrac{1}{2}(\psi + \varphi) + \delta$$

$$\frac{\sin \angle FKE}{FE} = \frac{\sin \angle FEK}{\text{chord } FK}.$$

Therefore

$$\text{chord } FK = \frac{FE \cos \delta}{\cos (\tfrac{1}{2}(\psi + \varphi) - \delta)}$$
$$= \frac{(b - t \tan \delta) \cos \delta}{\cos [\tfrac{1}{2}(\psi + \varphi) - \delta]}.$$

Let $r = DF = DJ$: the radius of curvature of FK, then chord $FK = 2r \sin \tfrac{1}{2}(\psi - \varphi)$.

Also the coordinates of D referred to O are given by

$$DC = r \cos \psi - t,$$
$$OC = r \sin \psi - f \tan \alpha - t \tan \delta,$$

and, therefore, the radius and centre of curvature are determined.

Having found the form of the section of the lens, we may use it in two ways. It may be rotated about the vertical axis through the lamp to generate a system for controlling the light in the vertical plane only, or it may be rotated about a horizontal axis through the lamp to control a cone of light from the lamp.

DIFFUSE TRANSMISSION

Opal glass and plastics are designed to scatter the light and so hide the source from view. They are used to reduce the luminance that would otherwise be obtained from the bare source, and hence confer a reduction in glare.

Usually they are used as close to the lamps as is consistent with maintaining an even luminance and not creating heating problems. To achieve an even luminance near the lamps it is necessary to use an opal with a comparatively low transmission factor, and a high reflection factor, so that little light is transmitted directly from the lamps, most of it being transmitted after interreflection. The use of an opal with a low transmission factor will, of course, reduce the light output ratio, and some figures taken from a fluorescent fitting are given in Table 4.3 to show the extent of the reduction.

TABLE 4.3. VARIATION OF LIGHT OUTPUT RATIO WITH CHARACTERISTICS OF DIFFUSER MATERIAL FOR A SINGLE TUBE 5 ft 80 W FLUORESCENT FITTING

Type of diffuser material	Transmission factor	Reflection factor	Light output ratio
Clear Acrylic	0·94	0·06	80%
Opal Acrylic	0·77	0·19	77%
Opal Acrylic	0·55	0·42	71%
Opal Acrylic	0·28	0·67	69%
No diffuser	1·00	0·00	90%

As with diffuse reflection, it is not possible to effect precise control with diffuse transmission. The best that can be done is to ensure the greatest projected area is obtained in the direction in which the greatest intensity is required.

REFERENCES

1. SPENCER, D. E., *Illum. Engng.* (*N.Y.*) **57**, 166 (1962).
2. ANON., *The Engineer* **219**, 318 (1965).
3. STEVENS, R. W., *Trans. I.E.S.* (*London*) **18**, 243 (1953).
4. KEITZ, H. A. E., *Light Calculations and Measurements*, Philips Technical Library, 1955.
5. LYNES, J. A., *Light and Lighting* **48**, 239 (1955).
6. JOLLEY, L. B. W., WALDRAM, J. M. and WILSON, G. H., *The Theory and Design of Illuminating Engineering Equipment*, Chapman & Hall, 1930.
7. MARKS, A. M., *Illum. Engng.* (*N.Y.*) **54**, 123 (1959).
8. EMSLEY, H. H., *Reflecting Prisms*, U.K., Bausch & Lomb.
9. MACH, E., *The Principles of Physical Optics*, Methuen, 1926.
   GORDIGN, M. J., *Illum. Engng.* (*N.Y.*) **45**, 405 (1960).

10. HEATH, R. S., *A Treatise on Geometrical Optics*, Cambridge, 1887.
    HERMAN, R. A., *A Treatise on Geometrical Optics*, Cambridge, 1900.
11. VAN ALBADA, L.E.W., *Graphical Design of Optical Systems*, Pitman, 1955.
    MARTIN, L. C., *Technical Optics*, Vol. II, Pitman, 1950.
12. HAMPTON, W. M., *Trans. I.E.S.* (*London*) **17**, 63 (1952).
13. HEATH, R. S., *A Treatise on Geometrical Optics*, Cambridge, 1887.

CHAPTER 5

APPLICATIONS OF THE PRINCIPLES OF OPTICAL DESIGN

IN CHAPTER 4 we have shown how the laws of optics can be used in the design of light control systems. In this chapter we will consider the subject of optical design from a different, if more practical standpoint. We will discuss the problems set to the designer by various common applications of lighting, and how the tools of optical control can be used to solve them.

However, it must be said at the outset that optical design very often involves practical work as well as theoretical work. It is very difficult to calculate the effect of such factors as the scattering of light in the optical system, the obstruction of the image by the lamp in reflector systems, the non-uniformity of the luminance of discharge lamps (particularly MBF/U lamps), and the rounding of the edges of prisms. To find the effect of these uncertainties, a mock-up of the optical system should be made and photometrically tested. Besides allowing the feasibility of a design to be tested, this procedure enables final adjustments to be made to the lamp position, reflector angle and other optical components. Also the effect of lamp tolerances and manufacturing tolerances in the optical system can be estimated. Hence the designing of a successful optical system depends as much on sound practical work as on a good knowledge of optics.

STREET LIGHTING

The broad requirements of the light distribution from a street lighting lantern can be derived once the mechanism of street lighting is understood.

In a well-lighted street objects are shown up in silhouette by the bright background of the road surface. This statement gives the gist of Waldram's silhouette principle, which replaced the older ideas about achieving even illumination over the road surface.[1] It has governed the thinking on street lighting since it was first propounded in the early 1930's, and the present Code of Practice CP 1004: 1963 is based on it. However, it should not be accepted uncritically. In today's crowded traffic conditions the driver is lucky if he can see much of the road surface and it may be that illumination levels, on the vertical rather than horizontal, are important in these conditions. Nevertheless, we will describe the mechanism of silhouette vision since this governs lantern design at the present time.

Each lantern produces a bright patch of light on the road as shown in Fig. 5.1. Objects are revealed in silhouette against the pattern of bright patches.

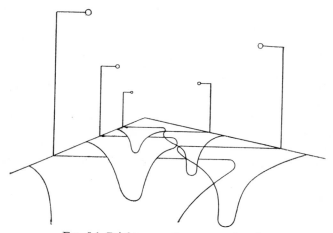

FIG. 5.1. Brightness pattern on road surface.

Ideally the lanterns should be so spaced that these patches combine to give a sufficiently high level of luminance to reveal objects anywhere on the road surface. In practice some dark areas are unavoidable as may be seen from the figure. But most objects have sufficient height for part of their surface, at least, to be revealed against a bright part of the road.

The reason for the patch from an individual lantern being T-shaped may be understood by considering two extremes—the wet road surface and the very matt road surface.

When the road surface is wet the reflection of light is specular or at least highly preferential. Each lantern gives a streak of light in the direction of the observer. If the road were exactly flat an image of the lantern would be formed. It is the irregularities of the road surface, the undulations and the surface markings, which elongate the image up and down the road and spread it sideways.

A very rough matt surface will give a pool of light under the lantern. The brightness of the pool and its extent depend on the reflection factor of the surface. The rough surface will trap light incident at large angles so a tail of the T will not be formed.

Most surfaces lie between these two extremes. There is usually a certain amount of preferential reflection, especially at large angles of incidence. This is mainly responsible for the formation of the tail of the T. The pool under the lantern forms the top of the T.

From this brief explanation it can be seen that there are three main requirements for the light distribution. Firstly, the lantern should give a peak of intensity at a sufficiently high angle to make best use of the reflecting properties of the surface of the road. Secondly, the intensities below the peak should gradually become smaller in order that the luminance of the road close to the lamp-post should not be so great as to cause a patchy appearance.

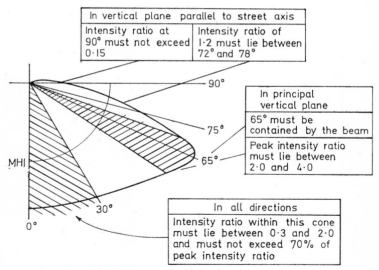

In vertical plane parallel to street axis	
Intensity ratio at 90° must not exceed 0·15	Intensity ratio of 1·2 must lie between 72° and 78°

In principal vertical plane
65° must be contained by the beam
Peak intensity ratio must lie between 2·0 and 4·0

In all directions
Intensity ratio within this cone must lie between 0·3 and 2·0 and must not exceed 70% of peak intensity ratio

FIG. 5.2(a). Distribution limits for cut-off lanterns.

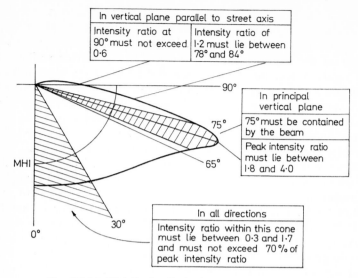

In vertical plane parallel to street axis	
Intensity ratio at 90° must not exceed 0·6	Intensity ratio of 1·2 must lie between 78° and 84°

In principal vertical plane

75° must be contained by the beam

Peak intensity ratio must lie between 1·8 and 4·0

In all directions

Intensity ratio within this cone must lie between 0·3 and 1·7 and must not exceed 70% of peak intensity ratio

FIG. 5.2(b). Distribution limits for semi-cut-off lanterns.

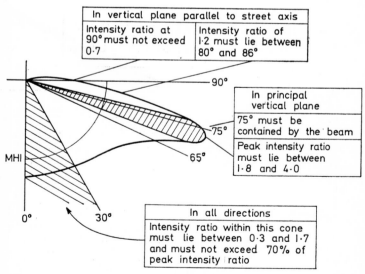

In vertical plane parallel to street axis	
Intensity ratio at 90° must not exceed 0·7	Intensity ratio of 1·2 must lie between 80° and 86°

In principal vertical plane

75° must be contained by the beam

Peak intensity ratio must lie between 1·8 and 4·0

In all directions

Intensity ratio within this cone must lie between 0·3 and 1·7 and must not exceed 70% of peak intensity ratio

FIG. 5.2(c). Distribution limits for semi-cut-off (sodium) lanterns.

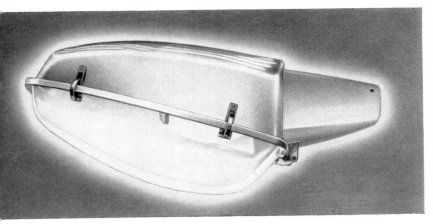

FIG. 5.5. A Group A street lantern for the 400 or 250 W MBF/U lamp with a pressed aluminium canopy using the reflector principle shown in Fig. 5.4. (*By courtesy of Atlas Lighting Ltd.*)

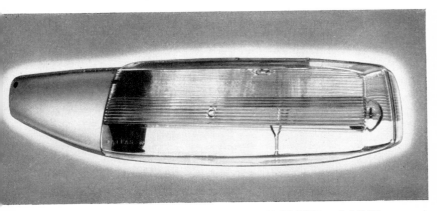

FIG. 5.6. A Group A street lantern for the 100 W SOX and 140 W SOI/H lamps using refractor control with prisms facing the lamp. (*By courtesy of Atlas Lighting Ltd.*)

FIG. 5.11. A Group A street lantern for the 150 W SOX and 200 W SLI/H lamps using the refractor and reflector control shown in Fig. 5.10. (*By courtesy of AEI Lamp & Lighting Co. Ltd.*)

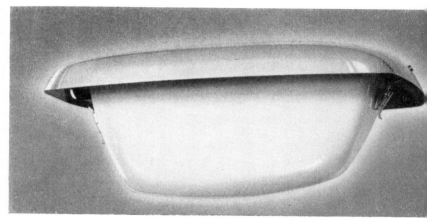

FIG. 5.15. A Group B street lantern for low wattage SOI/H lamps using an opal dish shaped to give the maximum projected area in the direction of the peak. (*By courtesy of Atlas Lighting Ltd.*)

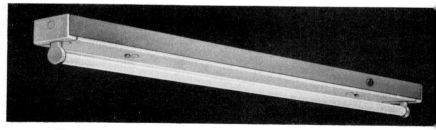

FIG. 5.16. A batten fitting for a single fluorescent tube. (*By courtesy of Atlas Lighting Ltd.*)

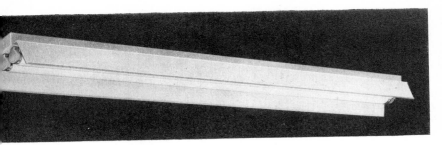

FIG. 5.17. A metal reflector fitting for two fluorescent tubes. Note that the bottom edges of the reflector are turned out to give strength and create the impression of increasing the thickness of the material. (*By courtesy of Atlas Lighting Ltd.*)

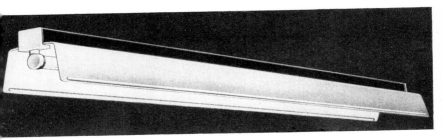

FIG. 5.18. A plastic reflector fitting for a single fluorescent tube. Note the shallow channel along the bottom edges of the reflector to impart strength and create the impression of increasing the thickness of the material. (*By courtesy of Atlas Lighting Ltd.*)

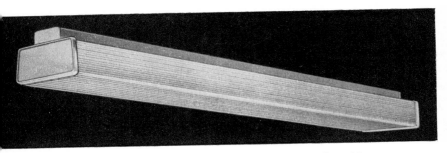

FIG. 5.19. A totally enclosed fitting for two fluorescent tubes with an opal reeded diffuser. (*By courtesy of Atlas Lighting Ltd.*)

FIG. 5.20. A totally enclosed fitting for four fluorescent tubes with prismatic control. This fitting is designed to fit in the modules of the ceiling. (*By courtesy of Atlas Lighting Ltd.*)

FIG. 5.30. An opal shade suitable for use in schools. (*By courtesy of Atlas Lighting Ltd.*)

FIG. 5.31. A fitting with circular louvers designed to be recessed into the ceiling. (*By courtesy of Atlas Lighting Ltd.*)

FIG. 5.32. A decorative fitting with a faceted glass bowl. (*By courtesy of Atlas Lighting Ltd.*)

Fig. 5.34. A tungsten iodine floodlight with a dimpled reflector to spread the beam. (*By courtesy of Atlas Lighting Ltd.*)

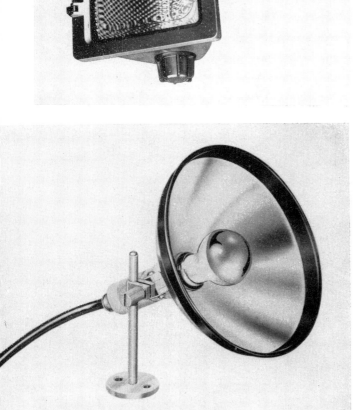

Fig. 5.33. A spotlight fitting. Note that the front of the lamp is silvered and the skirt is black to reduce stray light. (*By courtesy of Atlas Lighting Ltd.*)

FIG. 5.36. A floodlight for use with a 1000 W or 1500 W projector or GLS lamp. Note the patterned front glass. (*By courtesy of Atlas Lighting Ltd.*)

Thirdly, the reduction in intensity above the peak (that is the run-back) should be sharp in order to reduce glare, but not so sharp as to limit flexibility in the spacing of the lanterns.

In the part of the Code of Practice,[2] *Street Lighting*, relating to Group A Traffic Routes, these requirements have been taken into consideration in specifying suitable light distributions.

The Code of Practice is backed up by BS 1788: 1964, which lays down the light distribution requirements more precisely. Figure 5.2(a), (b) and (c) show these requirements graphically.[3] They are relaxed for sources having a luminance of less than 10 candelas/in^2.

Intensities are specified in terms of intensity ratios. The intensity ratio (IR) in any given direction is defined as the ratio of the intensity in that direction to the mean intensity below the horizontal (mean hemispherical intensity or MHI for short), i.e.

$$IR = \frac{\text{Intensity}}{\text{MHI}}$$

$$= \frac{\text{Intensity} \times 2\pi}{\text{Flux below horizontal}} \cdot$$

Some other essential definitions are given below.

Beam centre (*azimuth*)

The direction midway between the directions at which the intensity is 90% of the maximum intensity, these intensities being measured at the angle of elevation of maximum intensity.

Principal vertical polar curve

The polar curve of the light distribution in the vertical plane through the beam centre in azimuth.

Peak intensity

The maximum intensity in the plane of the principal polar curve.

Beam

The cone of light from the lantern that contains the maximum intensity and is bounded by the surface that passes through intensities that are 90% of the peak intensity. For example if the peak intensity were 800 candelas, the beam would be bounded by a surface surrounding this peak and joining intensity values of 720 candelas.

Whilst the light output ratio of the lantern below the horizontal is not specified, the Code does relate spacing of the lantern on the roadway to the flux below the horizontal. It is therefore advantageous to make the lantern as efficient as possible.

Referring back to Fig. 5.2 we can see that two main types of distribution are recognized—the cut-off and the semi-cut-off. The essential differences between these are (1) that in the cut-off lanterns the beam must include 65° whereas in the semi-cut-off it must include 75°, and (2) that the intensity ratio allowed at the horizontal in the plane parallel to the road axis is much smaller in the cut-off lantern than in the semi-cut-off lantern. The cut-off distribution produces less glare but the spacing of the lanterns has to be closer because of the lower beam elevation. A summary of the relative merits of these two distributions is given in the Code.

A consequence of the low permissible IR at the horizontal for cut-off lanterns is that the use of prism banks is precluded, though it may be possible to use them on the bottom of the bowl. The scattered light has been found in practice to give too high an intensity ratio at the horizontal. It is, however, possible to use them with some sort of louvering so that they are not visible from the horizontal. But this solution tends to be inelegant and costly. It is worth mentioning, however, that louvering is often used for lanterns complying with the Ministry of Transport aeroscreen specification for lanterns in the vicinity of airports, which allows very little light above the horizontal. All cut-off lanterns so far produced are of reflector design. If we want to design a lantern which can be converted from one type to the other by moving the lamp or some such simple adjustment, it seems, therefore, that we have to use a reflector design. Let us now have a look at some control systems.

Reflector Systems

Figure 5.3 shows a typical construction that we can adopt. A section of the lamp is drawn and a horizontal line $X'OX$ is drawn touching the bottom of the lamp at O. Suppose we are considering a cut-off lantern, we must make the reflectors come down to this line so that the lamp is not visible from the horizontal. *AB* is drawn at 65° to the vertical and tangentially to the lamp to cut *X'OX* in *B*. The right-hand reflector must not be put closer to the lamp than *B* if the whole of it is to be visible at the angle of the peak.

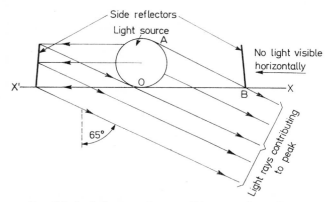

FIG. 5.3. Optical system for cut-off lantern using reflectors.

The reflectors are inclined so that they appear flashed at the peak angle. With a small source it may be necessary to give them a parabolic or circular curvature in vertical section to ensure complete flashing.

It will be noticed that the peak intensity cannot be increased by extending the reflectors higher than indicated since they would be masked by the lamp. If a greater peak intensity is required it is necessary to widen the lantern.

In semi-cut-off lanterns it is permissible to allow some of the lamp to protrude below *X'OX*, since an intensity ratio of 0·6 is allowed at the horizontal. Although this relaxation allows the lantern to be narrower than otherwise, it will usually be wider than the cut-off version since *AB* will be inclined at 75° to the vertical.

Reflector control is usually used for the 400 W MBF/U fluorescent mercury vapour lamp. This lamp is used horizontally in most lanterns, but owing to its large diameter the construction given above would lead to an impracticably wide lantern. To overcome this difficulty the reflectors are curved in plan as shown in Fig. 5.4 and Fig. 5.5 (*inset Plate section*) so that they are flashed in front of and behind the lamp. They also have to be inclined to the vertical so that they are flashed at the peak angle.

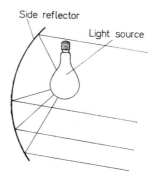

FIG. 5.4. Curvature of one side reflector in plan.

Owing to the arc tube being visible through the phosphor of a 400 W MBF/U lamp, the axis of the lamp is brighter than the edges. This fact enables the reflectors to be made smaller than would be anticipated by considering the lamp to be of uniform luminance. In order to take advantage of it, the reflectors have to be curved in vertical section as well as plan.

If the top of the canopy is not carefully constructed it will reflect light on to the side reflectors and cause a secondary peak at a low angle, about 45°. Control by means of flutes or facets is needed to avoid this.

Most lanterns for the 400 W MBF/U lamp direct too much light into the 0–30° zone, and a white patch on the bowl is used to reduce this. A case can be made for using the lamp vertically to avoid this subtractive form of light control.

It is usually possible to convert the lantern from semi-cut-off to cut-off by raising the lamp.

The control of light from sodium lamps presents different problems. Sodium lamps are long, and it is therefore impracticable to curve the reflectors in plan to obtain flashing in front of the lamp as for the 400 W MBF/U lamp. Hence unless the lantern is made sufficiently wide, the lamp will obstruct the reflectors. For this reason nearly all semi-cut-off lanterns for sodium lamps rely on prismatic control (Fig. 5.6, *Plate section*, and Fig. 6.4), though some have specular reflectors as well (Fig. 5.11). Because of the lower peak angle, width is not such a problem with the cut-off lanterns of reflector design and these have been made for the linear sodium lamp.

Refractor Systems

We will start this section by giving an example of the calculation of a prism bank for a Group A sodium lantern. If preferred the geometrical construction described in Chapter 4 for the determination of prism angles or Appendixes A, B, or C could be used instead of the purely calculational method given here.

Suppose the lantern is to be for a 140 W SOI/H sodium lamp, a cross-section of which is shown in Fig. 5.7 and the light distri-

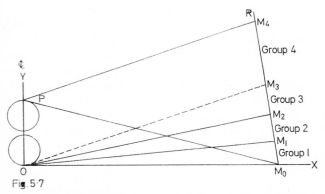

Fig. 5.7

FIG. 5.7. Cross-section of lantern for SOI/H lamp.

bution is to comply with the specification for semi-cut-off [SCO(S)] sodium lamps discussed earlier in this chapter. Essentially these objectives require us to have a peak of light at 75° and a rapid cut-off above this. Before starting, the polar curves of the lamp must be examined in relation to the required light distribution. We have then to make the following decisions, though not necessarily in the order given.

1. *Orientation of Lamp*

The 140 W SOI/H lamp has to be run within 20° of the horizontal, but with some lamps such as the MBF/U and incandescent lamps we would have to decide whether to run the lamp with its axis horizontal or vertical.

We do have to decide whether to run the arc tubes one above the other or side by side. The first arrangement gives the greatest intensity sideways. With the side by side arrangement, it is possible to design a narrower lantern, as may be seen by following the construction given in the next section. But the intensity in the 0–30° zone would be too great so we have to reject this alternative.

2. *Width of lantern*

This is governed by the angle of peak and the height of the source. A line OX is drawn out horizontally (Fig. 5.7) from the bottom of the lamp. Another line PM_0 cutting OX in M_0 is drawn tangentially to the top of the lamp, at 75° to the downward vertical.

The prism bank is put in so that its lower edge touches M_0. The bank itself is designed so that it is flashed at 75° (or slightly higher to give a margin of safety) to the downward vertical. These two design features mean that if the lantern were viewed at 75° the bare lamp would be visible, and above this there would be the flashed prisms. Both these combine to give a large flashed area, and therefore intensity, in the required direction. If the lantern were viewed at 90° the prisms would block the view of the lamp, and providing that the prisms were designed to emit no light at 90°, they would appear dark. Thus by positioning the prism bank as we have done, we can achieve a good peak intensity and a very small intensity at 90°. Actually, there is always some intensity at 90° because of light being scattered in the prisms. The scattering may be due to inaccuracy of manufacture of the prism angles, rounding off the prism edges, the prism surfaces not being highly polished, or the impossibility of allowing for interreflections within the lantern.

3. *Attitude of prisms*

We have now to decide whether to form the prisms on the outside or inside of the lantern.

The outside position has two disadvantages. Firstly, the prisms will inevitably get dirty in time, a serious disadvantage, since prisms are difficult to clean. Secondly, from Fig.5.8 it is apparent that it is impossible to have the whole area of the prism bank flashed,

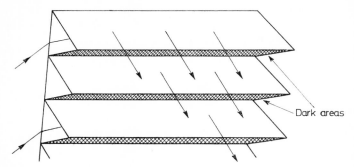

FIG. 5.8. Dark areas in the direction of the peak caused by the non-working or return faces of outwardly facing prisms.

since the non-working faces of the prisms cannot refract direct light from the source into the beam. To overcome the first disadvantage they can be impressed on a separate panel. This can then be stuck on the inside of the lantern bowl to form an airtight seal (Fig. 5.10). This design has the advantage, besides forming an airtight seal with the bowl, that the same panels can be used in different lanterns for different lamps. If necessary a number can be stuck end to end where the lantern is long. An economy can thus be effected on tool charges.

If the prisms are made to face the lamp (Fig. 5.10, and Fig. 5.11, *Plate section*) the whole of the prism bank can be flashed at the peak angle. And providing the lantern design is such that it does not allow ingress of dirt they should stay clean. The light falling on the non-working, nearly horizontal, faces will be refracted upwards and be therefore lost, but the amount can be kept small.

It should be noted that here we have a paradox. The outwardly facing prisms direct all the light into the emergent beam providing that the non-working faces are parallel to the rays of light in the prism. The inwardly facing prisms direct upwards that part of the beam which falls onto the non-working faces. Hence we can say that the outwardly facing prisms are more efficient since they direct all the flux into the beam. Yet, and this is the paradox, there are dark spaces in the emergent beam.

The paradox may be resolved as follows. In Fig. 5.9 AB is a bank of outwardly facing prisms and AC is a bank of the same prisms facing inwards. Let a be the projected area of the outward face of a prism in the direction of the peak. Then it is evident that the flashed area of AB is $7a$ and from AC it is $4a$. Hence the intensity from AC will be less than from AB.

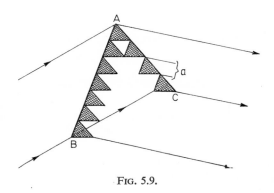

FIG. 5.9.

Thus if we are concerned with redirecting a parallel or near parallel beam it is better to use outwardly facing prisms. In street lighting the problem is different. Light is diverging in all directions from the lamp. The limitation is not the amount of flux available but the height we can make the prism bank; this height is limited by the angle through which the prisms can turn the light. Hence, if we want the greatest peak intensity possible we must use inwardly facing prisms.

For the purposes of the example let us decide to have the prisms facing inwards.

4. *Angle of lantern face*

One of the prism angles B or C (Fig. 4.26) will be fixed according to the choice of angle of the side face of the bowl. If the prisms are facing outwards it will be found most convenient to make the bowl narrow towards the bottom so that the face of the bowl bends the light rays downwards. For prisms facing inwards the bowl should widen towards the bottom.

In the lantern we are designing we will make the face of the bowl slope at 8° (that is we will make C equal to 8°) to conform with aesthetic considerations governing the overall shape of the lantern. We therefore draw a line RM_0 at 82° to OM_0 in Fig. 5.7.

5. Calculation of prism angles

The work is best set out as in Table 5.1. The procedure is to make rays from the bottom of the lamp emerge at 75°, so that rays from the rest of the lamp will emerge at lower angles. The calculation is shown in the table; which makes use of the relationships given in Chapter 4. P will be 90°, Q 75° and C 8° and these figures are written in the first three columns. A and B can then be worked out by following the columns through and using the nomograms and graphs given in Appendixes A, B and C. μ is taken to be 1·49. (Alternatively the graphical method given on p. 115 could be used; most people find this more straightforward than the other methods.)

6. Size of prism groups

The prisms in a bank can be calculated separately so that they will all differ from each other. But to save tool costs they can be repeated so as to form groups each comprising prisms having the same angles.

The effect of the first method is to form repeated images of one part of the lamp in the direction of the peak. Brighter flashing results if this part is brighter than the rest of the light source. The second method (which we shall use) produces an image of an extended part of the source. If the source is of substantially even luminance, the peak intensity will be reduced only a little by using this method.

The next question is how far up can we continue the prism bank upwards using the group 1 prisms without the light from the bottom of the lamp emerging at too high an angle. To answer this we have to decide what is the greatest angle of elevation we can afford to allow light rays to emerge. We know from BS 1788 that an IR of 1·2 must occur between 80° and 86° and the intensity at 90° must

TABLE 5.1. DETERMINATION OF PRISM ANGLES A AND B. (All figures in degrees)

Prism group	P	Q	C	i' $90°+C-Q$	r'	$i'-r'$	D $180°-P-Q$	$i-r$ $D-(i-r)$	i	r	A $r+r'$	B $A-C$
1	90	75	8	23	15·2	7·8	15	7·2	20·8	13·6	28·8	20·8
2	84·3	75	8	23	15·2	7·8	20·7	12·9	36·5	23·6	38·8	30·8
3	77·8	75	8	23	15·2	7·8	27·2	19·4	51·0	31·6	46·8	38·8
4	71·3	75	8	23	15·2	7·8	33·7	25·9	62·3	36·4	51·6	43·6

TABLE 5.2. DETERMINATION OF EXTENT OF PRISM GROUPS. (All figures in degrees)

Prism group	Q	A	B	C	i' $90°+C-Q$	r'	$i'-r'$	r $A-r'$	i	$i-r$	D $(i-r)+(i'-r')$	P $180°-D-Q$
1	81	28·8	20·8	8	17	11·5	5·5	17·3	26·5	9·2	14·7	84·3
2	81	38·8	30·8	8	17	11·5	5·5	27·3	43·0	15·7	21·2	77·8
3	81	46·8	38·8	8	17	11·5	5·5	35·3	59·5	24·2	29·7	69·3
4	81	51·6	43·6	8	17	11·5	5·5	40·1	73·5	33·4	38·9	60·1

be below an IR of 0·7. It has been found from experience that if we do not allow light to emerge above 81° we can comply with these requirements. Previous experience is necessary because we have to take into account manufacturing tolerances as explained in the section on deciding the width of the lantern, and simply to rely on calculations based on the flashed area required might give misleading results.

It follows that we have to find at what angle a light ray must leave the lamp to emerge at 81°. Or to express the question in symbols, we have to find the value of P when Q is 81°, and A and B are 28·8° and 20·8° respectively. For this purpose we could use Table 5.1, but it will be found more convenient to use Table 5.2 specially drawn up for the purpose. P is found in the last column to be 84·3°. In Fig. 5.7 a line OM_1 cutting the prism bank at M_1 is drawn at 84·3° to the vertical. M_1M_0 represents the size of the first group of prisms. We check that M_1M_0 is smaller than the diameter of the limb of the arc tube, so that the whole group of prisms is flashed at 75°. If it were greater we would have to reduce the size of the prism bank to make it equal to the arc tube diameter. We now calculate the angles of the next group of prisms, using Table 5.1 again. P is now 84·3° (as found in Table 5.2), but Q and C are the same as before so that the answers in the next four columns are also the same as before. We find that the prism angles are 38·8° and 30·8° and using these values in Table 5.2 we find P to be 77·8°.

The angle YOM_2 is then made equal to this so determining the position of M_2. M_3 is found to be 2 cm from M_2, but since this is at a greater distance than the diameter of the arc tubes, it is actually positioned at 1·6 cm from M_2. By measurement P (angle YOM_3) is found to be 71·3° and this entered in Table 5.1. The values of A and B, 51·6° and 43·6°, are used in Table 5.2 to find the new value of P. This works out to be 60·1°.

It will be noted that i is 73·5°. It can be seen from Fig. 4.24 that at this angle of incidence the loss of luminance is about 25%. Whilst this is not prohibitive we would not want to use a larger value of i than this. We therefore find M_4 by drawing a line parallel to OM_3 and tangential to the top of the top arc tube. In the middle of this prism group there would be a small strip, corresponding to the gap between the arc tubes, which would not be flashed. From the last row in Table 5.2 it is evident that it is impossible for rays to emerge from this prism bank horizontally owing to total internal reflection taking place ($r = 40 \cdot 1°$).

7. Use of reflecting prisms

We have now to consider whether it would be worth extending the prism bank further by means of reflecting prisms. We can calculate the intensity in the peak direction if we know either the intensity or the luminance of the lamp in the relevant direction. It will be equal to:

$$\left[\begin{array}{c} \text{(Lamp intensity at 75°} \\ \times \text{ transmission losses)} \end{array}\right] + \left[\begin{array}{l} \text{(Area of flashed prisms projected} \\ \text{in the 75° direction} \times \text{lamp luminance} \\ \times \text{ transmission losses)} \end{array}\right]$$

In actual practice it was found that the prism bank was sufficiently large without resorting to reflecting prisms; it gave an IR of 2·2 whereas only 1·8 is required by BS 1788.

However, if we had needed to use reflecting prisms, we would have made use of the relations given in Chapter 4. It will be noticed by referring to Fig. 4.29 that as P is increased so is Q. Consequently, we would have adopted the opposite procedure than that used for refracting prisms (refer back to § 5); we would have needed to start by considering rays from the top of the lamp to the top of the prism bank.

8. Angle of the non-working faces

It remains to calculate the angles of non-working faces of the prisms. These can all be made parallel to the ray of light emerging at 75° (that is at 90° + 15·2° to the outer face). In this way the whole of the prism bank will be flashed at 75°, but it must be checked that no light is refracted into the run-back zone.

9. Concluding comments on design

It is worth noting that when the angle of deviation D is a minimum, $i = i'$, and it can be shown that the losses due to reflection are a minimum. Hence, it is best to work as close to this condition as possible. In the example we have worked through, this was nearly achieved in the first group of prisms, but in subsequent groups the departure has become greater and greater.

Let us now consider some other designs.

It is possible to make the lantern narrower than the above approach signified. In one ingenious design, shown in Figs. 5.10 and 5.11, suitable for SOI/H, SO/H, SOX and SLI/H lamps, a

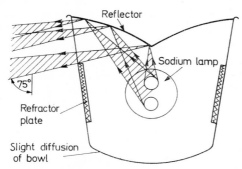

FIG. 5.10. Combined refractor and reflector control system for sodium lamp.

reflector above the lamp is used to supplement the peak intensity. Below the peak angle the prisms gradually become unflashed and so give a gradual reduction of the intensity. Care has to be taken that all the prisms do not become unflashed at the same time otherwise a serious dip in intensity at about 50° may result.

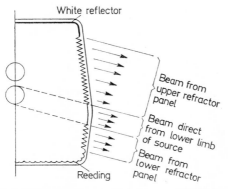

FIG. 5.12. Optical system for sodium lamp (SOX) featuring clear window in refractor panel.

In a variation of this design the V-shaped reflector is positioned beneath the lamp with the V pointing upwards. So as not to cut off the downward light unduly, the reflector runs only part of the length of the lamp.

In another design[4] for the SOX lamp (Fig. 5.12) the refractor system is interrupted by a clear portion running horizontally. At the peak angle, part of the lamp is visible together with flashed areas of the refractor plate beneath and above it. At the horizontal the lamp is obscured except for a small part of it visible through the clear portion. This system does give a dip in the polar curve at about 50°. But it is possible to fill this in by using a diffusing pattern on the part of the bowl beneath the lamp. It has the advantage that the lantern width is halved compared with the conventional design.

Group B Lanterns

Group B lanterns tend to look like small versions of their Group A counterparts. However, there is, as yet, nothing laid down as to what their distribution should be. Probably, their most important function is to provide light for pedestrians rather than motorists, who should be using their dipped headlights. They should also provide sufficient light to give the motorist advance warning of bends and junctions.

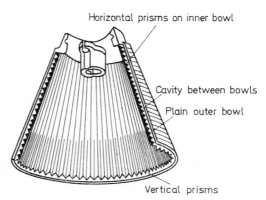

FIG. 5.13. Group B street lantern.

Many lanterns use GLS and low wattage mercury vapour lamps burning in a vertical position. These have vertical prisms (as well as the usual horizontal ones), to direct the light up and down the road axis.

In some lanterns the vertical prisms are formed on the exposed surface (since these have a smaller tendency to hold dirt than horizontal ones) and the horizontal ones on the enclosed surface. The lantern shown in Fig. 5.13 comprises two bowls which are sealed together with a cavity between. Both sets of prisms are formed on the inner bowl but the horizontal ones are sealed into the cavity.

Figure 5.14 shows a lantern that relies entirely on internal prisms for control both in elevation and azimuth.

Some lanterns, more of a decorative nature, rely on an opal dish which may be shaped to give maximum intensity in the peak direction (Fig. 5.15, *Plate section*).

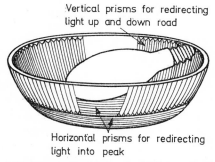

Vertical prisms for redirecting light up and down road

Horizontal prisms for redirecting light into peak

FIG. 5.14. Glass refractor bowl with internal prisms.

INDOOR FITTINGS

The factors which must be considered in the design of optical systems of general purpose indoor fittings are as follows:

(a) Efficient use of bare lamp flux.

(b) Control of glare.

(c) Ease of maintenance.

We must also consider appearance. This is governed to some extent by the materials to be used, the processes available for shaping these, and the necessity of making the fitting harmonize with its surroundings. Fashion also plays a large part.

(a) *Efficient use of bare lamp flux*

The most important function of a lighting fitting is the provision of illumination on the working plane, or more specifically, on the visual task. The more efficiently it can perform this the lower will be the running costs.

There is no one figure that will grade a fitting according to this criterion and be valid in every circumstance. The light output ratio (LOR) is misleading since it does not take account of light distribution. Utilization factors do take account of the light distribution from the fitting but vary according to the dimensions of the room and the reflection factors of its surfaces. Table 5.3 com-

TABLE 5.3. COMPARISON OF THE PERFORMANCE OF A BATTEN AND REFLECTOR
FITTING

	% LOR			Utilization factors	
	Up	Down	Total	75% ceiling RF	30% ceiling RF
Batten fitting	22	67	89	0·61	0·46
Reflector fitting	0	73	73	0·58	0·55

pares the performance of a batten and a reflector fitting. The utilization factors are for a room ratio of 3, wall reflection factor of 50%, and floor reflection factor of 10%. The order of merit in terms of LOR or utilization factor for a room having a ceiling reflection factor of 75% places the batten fitting first. Owing to the batten fitting having a high upward LOR, the order is reversed when the ceiling reflection factor is only 30%. Hence, in comparing fittings, figures must be used that relate to the situation in which the fittings are to be installed.

(b) *Control of glare*

Glare from a fitting can be calculated by using the following formula, derived experimentally by the Building Research Station.[5]

$$\text{Glare index} = 10 \log \frac{B_s^{1·6} \, \omega^{0·8}}{B_b \, P^{1·6}},$$

where B_s is the source luminance in foot-lamberts, ω is the solid angle subtended by the source at the eye, B_b is luminance of the whole background in foot-lamberts (it is numerically equal to the vertical illumination in lumens per square foot at the eye), P is the position index for each individual source, based on the data of Luckiesh and Guth (it takes into account the fact that glare varies according to the position of the source in the visual field).

The glare index for each fitting in an installation could be found by using this formula, and the results summed up to give the index for the whole installation. This would be a tedious calculation. Fortunately it has been done by the IES for installations in which the fittings are arranged in symmetrical arrays, and the results given in convenient tabular form in the IES Code.[6] A study of the tables in this reveals that the factors which the designer must control in order to limit glare are as follows.

(1) BZ classification in which the downward distribution of the fitting is matched against the 10 canonical distributions given in Chapter 8. These are numbered from 1 to 10, 1 being the most concentrated downwards and 10 the least concentrated. Generally, the higher the BZ number the more glaring the fitting will be. There are cases, however, where the higher BZ rating increases the background luminance and so decreases the glare.

(2) Flux in the lower hemisphere. This increases the glare index. But it would be unwise to control glare by reducing it, since more fittings would be needed to produce a given illumination.

(3) The upward and downward flux fractions. These are the fractions of the flux emitted in the upper and lower hemisphere respectively. They are expressed as a percentage of the flux emitted from the fitting. A high upper flux fraction helps to reduce the glare index by decreasing the contrast between the fitting and its background, that is, it increases B_b in the formula for glare index.

As would be expected the advantage of a high upward flux fraction is not so pronounced with a ceiling of low reflection factor.

(4) Luminous area, defined as follows:

> BZ 1 to BZ 8: The orthogonally projected luminous area as seen vertically beneath the fitting, that is at 0°.
> BZ 9 and BZ 10: The maximum orthogonally projected luminous area as seen from 90°.
> The glare index decreases with projected area since B_s is reduced for a given intensity.

(c) *Maintenance*

Deposition of dust and grime on the light controlling surfaces fitting will, of course, reduce its LOR. There is little the designer can do to control it, except to provide through ventilation. The following figures indicate the extent to which through ventilation (as indicated by upward LOR) reduces depreciation:

Closed top reflector	(0% upward LOR)	100	Depreciation as
Slotted reflector	(11% upward LOR)	88	a percentage of
Louvered	(30% upward LOR)	72	closed top
Slotted reflector	(27% upward LOR)	56	reflector

Plastic is liable to become electrostatically charged and attract a thick coat of dust. It is usual to treat it with an anti-static compound.

Fluorescent Fittings

Fluorescent fittings present special problems. Because the output of the tube varies with temperature, they must be designed to run as cool as possible. And because of their length, it is difficult to control the distribution of light in the vertical axial plane.

In the course of discussing the various design problems, it will be necessary to refer to some of the different types of fluorescent fittings. Some typical ones are shown in Figs. 5.16–5.20, *Plate section.*

Let us first of all look at the problem of keeping the temperature of the tubes as close as possible to the optimum.

The loss[7] due to heating depends on the type of fitting, the number of tubes, and the power they dissipate per unit length.

In a batten fitting having one tube, the loss is about 5%. But in an enclosed diffuser fitting it is about 20%; the exact figure depends on the cross-sectional area of the diffuser. The addition of a second tube may increase the loss of light output by 8%, and there will be a further loss of about 5% due to mutual obstruction. The figures have been taken from experimental work carried out on fittings using 5 ft 80 W tubes. Where the power dissipated per foot is less, the loss is lower, as in the case of the 5 ft 65 W and 4 ft 40 W tubes. The difference is 10% for diffuser fittings.

There are many ways of reducing the loss. The provision of
good ventilation is the obvious one. Slots in the metal reflector
fitting have been shown to increase the output of a twin 80 W
fitting by 3%, but produce no change in the single tube version. In
the case of enclosed diffuser fittings the ventilation produced
by a gap between the diffuser and the spine gives a significant
increase. The cross-sectional area of enclosed diffusers should
be as great as economically and aesthetically possible. Tube
centres should not be closer than $2\frac{1}{2}$ in. otherwise losses due to
mutual obstruction and heating may be unnecessarily high.

The light output of the tube is governed by the pressure of
the mercury vapour. This pressure in turn depends on the coolest
part of the tube. Thus if one part of the tube is cooled, the whole
tube behaves as though it were at the reduced temperature. Initially
it takes about 36 operating hours for the cooling effect to be
completed, and at the end of this period small globules of mercury
will have condensed at the cool spot. These globules do not dis-
perse when the lamp is switched off, and the improvement in
light output is permanent unless the lamp is moved.

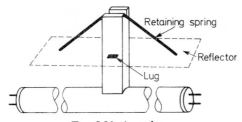

FIG. 5.21. A cooler.

A cool spot on the tube can be produced by a draught of cool
air. It is preferable that this should be underneath the tube, for
here the tube is already cooler than the top or sides. The draught
can be produced by a small hole in the diffuser, under the centre
of each tube. Some provision must be made in the top of the diffuser to allow the current of air an uninterrupted flow, either by
holes or gaps between the diffuser and the metalwork.

In another method a bar of metal, the "cooler", is used to
conduct the heat away from the tube. In the usual arrangement,
shown in Fig. 5.21, the cooler is held on to the top of the tube by
means of a spring, and lugs prevent it falling out when the tube

6*

is removed. It protrudes into the control gear channel into which it conducts the heat. Since it conducts heat away from the top of the tube, the hottest part, it suffers from an initial disadvantage com-pared with the hole method.

Circuits making use of the Peltier effect have been devised. In these a direct current is passed through a junction between two different metals, and a cooling effect is produced at the junc-tion. In order to produce direct current it is necessary to use a transformer and a rectifier, which increase the cost of the fitting as well as its bulk.

Glare

One method of reducing glare is by shielding the lamp from view with a reflector or louver. The degree of shielding is measured by the cut-off or the shielding angle.

The cut-off angle is the angle between the downward vertical and the direction at which the lamps just cease to be visible (Fig. 5.22).

The shielding angle is the angle complementary to the cut-off angle.

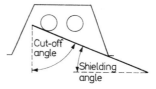

Fig. 5.22. Cut-off and shielding angle.

Commonly, the shielding angle for reflector fittings is made between 30° and 45°. But the reflector does not give any control down the length of the fitting. Consequently the BZ classification will not be any better than 4, and may be 5 for some room sizes. Slots in reflector fittings decrease the glare by reducing the contrast with ceiling.

Louvers (Fig. 5.23) in the form of cells give control both trans-versely and axially. They are commonly made of transluscent plastic and are made $\frac{1}{2}$ in. square by $\frac{1}{2}$ in. deep. White painted metal ones have been nearly completely superseded by plastic ones.

Where very strict control of glare is required black painted metal louvers can be used, but these absorb a lot of light.

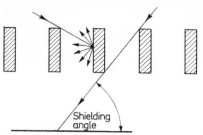

FIG. 5.23. Action of diffusing louvers. Light is emitted above the shielding angle owing to diffuse reflection.

Figure 5.24 shows a specular louver that is curved in section.[8] The effect of the curve, which is parabolic, is to reflect light below the shielding angle. The large obstruction caused by the top of the wedge makes this form of light control inefficient. The louver is made of plastic coated with a metallic film. Figure 5.25 shows a stepped louver using the same principle. This is made of aluminium.

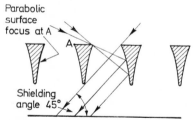

FIG. 5.24. Specular louvers shaped to reflect light below the cut-off.

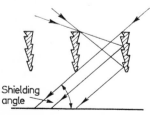

FIG. 5.25. Specular louvers stepped to give the same action as wedge louvers in Fig. 5.24.

Both these types of louver are considered by many people to give a "dead" effect.

Diffusers with dense opal sides and a clear base, plain or reeded, give a certain amount of glare control and can be extruded.

More precise control may be obtained by means of prismatic diffusers. These are most cheaply made by extrusion. This process does not give the designed shape very accurately, but is much more commonly used than injection moulding, which is accurate but expensive.

If the diffuser is totally enclosing, the side prisms can be designed to deviate a certain amount of light up, so increasing the ceiling brightness. The remainder of the light can be deviated downwards out of the glare zone.

The base of the diffuser can be designed to control the glare by means of prisms running longitudinally. Figure 5.26 shows the

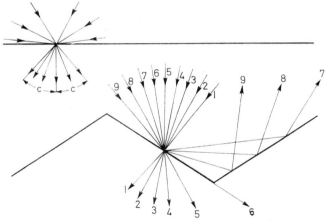

FIG. 5.26. Transverse section of base prism showing reflection and refraction of rays.

action of a base prism. Rays entering the panel from all directions are concentrated into a cone having an apical angle equal to twice the critical angle. The angle of the prism is made such that ray 9 is reflected off the second face at the critical angle. If the prism angle were made any larger, ray 9 would pass through this face. If it were made any smaller, ray 1 would leave the first face at a higher angle than necessary.

Figure 5.27 shows the path of ray 9 alone. Let us use this to find x, the half prism angle. LM and MN are the two faces of the prism. $ABCD$ is the path of the ray. N_1N_2 and N_3N_4 are the normals at B and C respectively. XB and RM are vertical construction lines.

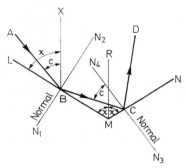

Fig. 5.27.

$$\angle\ XBA\ =\ c, \text{the critical angle (see Fig. 5.27 in relation}$$
$$\text{to Fig. 5.26)}$$

$$\text{now}\ \angle\ XBL\ =\ \angle RMB = x.$$

$$\text{Therefore}\ \angle\ MBC\ =\ \angle\ ABL$$

$$=\ x\ -\ c.$$

$$\angle\ BCM = 90° - c, \text{since}\ \angle\ N_4CB = c.$$

Therefore in the triangle BCM,

$$(x - c) + (90° - c) + 2x = 180°.$$

$$x = 30° + \frac{2}{3}c.$$

If $\mu = 1\cdot49$, then $c = 43°$, so $x = 58°$.

We have now to find how the polar curve is modified in the vertical axial plane. Surprisingly, the prisms do produce a run-back in this plane. It needs some thought to see how this is achieved since the rays of light that produce the axial polar curve enter the prism at an angle to the vertical axial plane. (It is a mistake to think that because a section along the length of the prisms would be shown as two parallel lines, the rays will behave as though they are passing through a parallel-sided block.)

To find how the angle of run-back varies with the prism angle, we need to use the equations given on p. 121.

In Fig. 5.28 *AB* is the incident ray. It makes an angle η with its projection *A'B* on the principal plane. *A'B* makes an angle of φ with the normal.

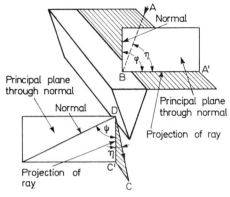

FIG. 5.28. A horizontal ray of light travelling obliquely through a prism.

CD is the emergent ray. This is in the axial plane. It also makes an angle η with its projection, *C'D*, on the principal plane. η is the cut-off angle we want to find. *C'D* makes an angle ψ with the normal.

The highest value of η will be produced when *AB* is parallel to the prism base. That is, φ will be a right angle.

Figure 5.29 shows the rays projected on to the principal plane.

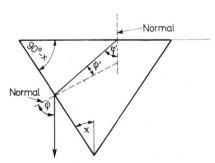

FIG. 5.29. Projection of an oblique ray on to principal plane.

Since the emergent ray is in the axial plane, its projection will be directly downwards.

Therefore

$$\psi = 90° - x \tag{5.1}$$

and

$$90° - x = \varphi' + \psi'. \tag{5.2}$$

Now

but

$$\sin \varphi \cos \eta = \mu \sin \varphi' \cos \eta',$$

$$\varphi = 90°.$$

Therefore

Therefore

$$\cos \eta = \mu \sin \varphi' \cos \eta'.$$

$$1 - \cos^2 \eta' = 1 - \frac{\cos^2 \eta}{\mu^2 \sin^2 \varphi'}.$$

Since

$$\sin \eta = \mu \sin \eta',$$

$$\frac{\sin^2 \eta}{\mu^2} = 1 - \frac{\cos^2 \eta}{\mu^2 \sin^2 \varphi'}.$$

Therefore

$$1 - \cos^2 \eta = \mu^2 - \frac{\cos^2 \eta}{\sin^2 \varphi'}.$$

Therefore

$$\cos^2 \eta = (\mu^2 - 1) \tan^2 \varphi'. \tag{5.3}$$

We must now relate φ' to x.

and

$$\cos \eta = \mu \sin \varphi' \cos \eta'$$

$$\sin \psi \cos \eta = \mu \sin \psi' \cos \eta'.$$

Therefore

$$\sin \psi \sin \varphi' = \sin \psi'$$

by division and rearrangement of the terms.

Now

and

Now $\psi = 90° - x$ (from eqn. (5.1))

$$\psi' = 90° - x - \varphi'$$ (from eqn. (5.2)).

Therefore

by substitution,

$$\cos x \sin \varphi' = \cos (x + \varphi'),$$

$$= \cos x \cos \varphi' - \sin x \sin \varphi'.$$

Therefore

$$\tan \varphi' = \frac{\cos x}{\cos x + \sin x}$$

$$= \frac{1}{1 + \tan x}.$$

Therefore

$$\cos^2 \eta = (\mu^2 - 1)\left(\frac{1}{1 + \tan x}\right)^2$$

by substitution in eqn. (5.3) or

$$\cos \eta = \sqrt{(\mu^2 - 1)}\frac{1}{1 + \tan x}.$$

If x equals 58° and μ equals 1·49 as in the previous example, η works out to be 66°. Hence at this angle the luminance is zero in the axial plane. The run-back, however, will not be abrupt at this angle owing to the fact that at angles somewhat smaller than 66° the luminance of the prism will be reduced because the incident rays will have a large angle of incidence. In other words, there is a gradual reduction in luminance in a zone before the cut-off angle is reached. It will be remembered that in the transverse plane the run-back was complete at 58°. Thus good control has been obtained in both planes. By making the prism angle smaller, control in the axial plane is better but it deteriorates in the transverse plane. And it is possible to find the compromise angle that gives the best BZ classification, either by calculation or by means of mock-up panels.

Although longitudinal prisms are easy to produce by extrusion, they are not greatly favoured in wide fittings owing to the fact that it is possible to see the position of the tubes through them. Pyramids and cones overcome this disadvantage and are claimed by some to provide sparkle. They can be produced during the extrusion process by rollers.

So far we have only considered direct glare from the fitting. Very often reflected glare, or more precisely glare by reflection, can have an adverse effect. It is more easily controlled by the avoidance of shiny surfaces and careful positioning of the fitting than by any special design features of the fittings.

However, reflected glare can be reduced by polarized light. Ordinary polarizers only transmit 50% of the light at the most and are expensive. The multilayer polarizers, referred to in Chapter 4, have a good transmission factor, but the fraction of light that is polarized is not very great, even at Brewster's angle. According to Blackwell,[9] a 1% increase in contrast is equivalent to a 15% increase in illumination level. So that if we only manage to increase the contrast by as little as 6% by using multilayer polarizers, we have gained the equivalent to a 90% increase in illumination level. That is, our visual performance will be as though we were working at nearly twice the illumination level. Needless to say a lot of controversy surrounds this work. Some workers doubt that a 1% increase in contrast is equivalent to a 15% increase in illumination level at supra-threshold levels of illumination (that is at illumination levels well above those at which objects are just visible). They have also pointed out that most of our viewing is done at quite different angles from Brewster's, where the maximum polarization effect occurs.

A cautionary note—polarization cannot control reflected glare from metallic surfaces unless the viewer wears polarizing glasses.

Incandescent Fittings

Fittings using incandescent lamps do not present the optical problems encountered with fluorescent fittings; they are compact and the light output of the lamps does not vary with temperature. Therefore our treatment of these fittings need only be short compared with that of fluorescent fittings, especially as many of the principles applicable to fluorescent fittings apply to incandescent.

Opal bowls provide the most common form of light control. These are made of sufficient optical density to be of reasonably even luminance. They are made in different shapes mainly to provide different decorative effects but also to give some variation in light distribution. The one shown in Fig. 5.30, Plate section, has been designed to meet the Ministry of Education specification (Statutory Instrument No. 890, 1959) for lighting in classrooms. (This stipulates that the luminance of any part of the fitting must not exceed 1500 foot-lamberts, these luminances being measured between 45° and 90° to the downward vertical. Also there must be sufficient upward light to prevent excessive contrast between the fitting and its surroundings.)

Circular louvers can be used to reduce glare and these are sometimes used in the bottom opening of opal bowls. Figure 5.31, Plate section, shows a circular louver used on a display fitting.

Decorative effects can be achieved by using coloured glasses. Bubbles produce an effect akin to sparkle. Some elaborate bowls and chandeliers have faceted glass geometrical figures which produce sparkle (Fig. 5.32, Plate section).

Metal reflectors finished white on the inside, the light reflecting surface, are commonly used in industrial situations. Desk lamps are usually of this type.

Spotlights

Spotlights should provide a narrow beam of high intensity. The small width of the beam is important for eliminating glare.

Fluorescent tubes are unsuitable for spotlights because of their large size and low luminance. Incandescent lamps are therefore used. It is necessary that these should have a small filament to produce a tight beam, and hence they are usually of low voltage, say 12 V.

A spotlight fitting is shown in Fig. 5.33, Plate section. The reflector, which is 6 in. in diameter, is made of spun aluminium. Its shape is parabolic, and is finished with a black skirt to prevent reflections off the turned edge. The protruding half of the lamp is internally coated to eliminate glare and reduce waste of light. The model illustrated gives an intensity of 25,000 candelas and a beam width of 10°, with a 50 W 12 V lamp.

FLOODLIGHTING

Floodlighting at Close Offset

Buildings very often have to be lighted by floodlights close to their base, that is at close offset, owing to space limitations. In order to achieve reasonable uniformity from side to side, the floodlights should have a wide lateral distribution, and to achieve a reasonable brightness high up the building, the peak intensity should be high. Also the beam should be narrow in elevation so that the base of the building is not too bright.

Long sources such as fluorescent tungsten iodine, and sodium are ideal for this purpose when their light is controlled by a trough-shaped parabolic reflector. This gives a good sideways spread.

In order to broaden the beam in elevation a matt reflector is often used. However, in the case of the tungsten iodine lamp this has been found to increase the temperature of the pinch of the lamp excessively. A dimpled specular reflector is, therefore, used in its place.

Figure 5.34, Plate section, shows a tungsten iodine floodlight with a dimpled reflector, and Fig. 5.35 the distribution curve for one fitted with a specular reflector. It will be noticed that the horizontal distribution curve has three peaks. These are formed by the coils of the filament masking and unmasking each other.

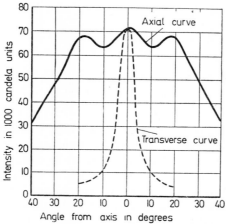

Fig. 5.35. Light distribution of floodlighting fitting illustrated in Fig. 5.34 using 1500 W tungsten iodine lamp.

The reflectors are made in anodized aluminium and are held in position by a template at each end. The contour is not accurate by optical standards but is adequate for the needs of floodlighting.

Area Floodlighting

Large areas such as football fields and railway yards are normally lit from a number of towers carrying the floodlight projectors. These towers may be as high as 150 ft so that a large area can be lit from one tower and glare avoided.

Tungsten iodine floodlights as described for close offset lighting are to some extent replacing floodlights using GLS or projector lamps because of their smaller size and wide lateral spread.

Figure 5.36, Plate section, shows a floodlight for use with 1000 or 1500 W projector or GLS lamps. Its performance is shown in Fig. 5.37. Compared with the tungsten iodine floodlight, a smaller

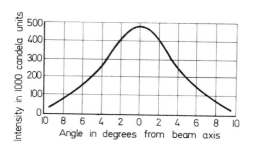

FIG. 5.37. Light distribution of floodlighting fitting illustrated in Fig. 5.36 using 1500 W GLS lamp.

proportion of lamp flux is controlled owing to the larger focal length of the parabola. This is 5 in. compared to $\frac{1}{2}$ in. for the TI floodlight. The greater length is necessary because of the larger filament size. In the particular floodlight illustrated a glass reflector is used; this is much more accurate than the metal reflectors used in the standard TI floodlight. A slightly patterned front glass is used to even out striations.

Floodlighting in Aerodromes

Very accurate control of light is needed when using floodlighting on aerodromes, especially on the aprons, to avoid distracting the pilots. This can be achieved by using a tungsten iodine lamp, but with an accurate glass parabolic reflector. Adjustment has to be provided for focusing the lamp accurately. A baffle is used to stop direct light from the lamp. An apron floodlight might have an intensity of 220,000 candelas running back to 5000 candelas in $2\frac{1}{2}$ degrees when used with a 1500 W tungsten iodine lamp.

PIPED LIGHT

One of the most fascinating phenomena occurring in optics is the way in which light can be piped along a rod, block, or sheet of transparent medium such as glass or acrylic plastic.

Consider Fig. 5.38. *RSTU* is a section through a sheet of glass. Light enters the face *RU* from all directions. The light entering at

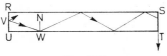

FIG. 5.38.

the point *V*, for instance, will form a cone of rays, the cone having an apex angle equal to twice the critical angle *c*. An extreme ray *VW* is shown reaching the face *UT* at *W*. It makes an angle 90°–*c* with the normal *NW*. If *c* is 43°, as it is for glass having a refractive index of 1·5, the angle of incidence, *NWV*, at *W* will be 47°. This is greater than the critical angle so that the ray will be reflected, and it will zigzag down the sheet leaving parallel to *ST*. Less extreme rays will also be reflected (unless they travel straight through), and leave at smaller angles of emergence.

The sheet can be bent (Fig. 5.39) provided that the bend is not

FIG. 5.39.

so sharp that the rays are incident at less than the critical angle at the bend.

The piped light principle has many applications.

It is used in aircraft instrument panels.[10] Figure 5.40 shows a section through such a panel. Light is provided by the midget lamp and its light is transmitted through the clear plastic after passing through the red filter. It is overlaid with a layer of white plastic, and finished with a layer of black plastic. This final layer is machined away to give the desired legend, which is seen red by transmitted light and white by reflected light. Figure 5.41 shows how the edge can be finished at an angle so as to direct the light on to an instrument face.

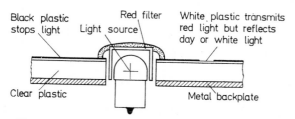

FIG. 5.40. Section through aircraft instrument panel.

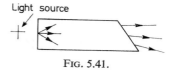

FIG. 5.41.

It can by used as a form of blackboard or indicator-board lighting. A sheet of white glass (difficult to obtain and very expensive) or plastic is illuminated round its edges by fluorescent tubes; reflector tubes can be used for increased light utilization. When the sheet is written on with a wax crayon or other suitable pencil, the writing appears self-luminescent. What happens is shown in Fig. 5.42. The light travels into the wax and is scattered by the

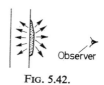

FIG. 5.42.

coloured particles. The roughness of the surface also plays a part in allowing the light to escape. The ambient light level has to be adjusted to a suitably low level otherwise the effect is lost. A dark background is also important.

To produce a decorative effect the plastic or glass sheet can be surface frosted to scatter the light.

This account cannot be ended without mentioning fibre optics.[11] The fibres consist of glass drawn out into fibres and packed together in bundles. To prevent the light from crossing into adjacent fibres at points of contact, each fibre is coated with glass of a low refractive index. The bundles can be used for illuminating inaccessible parts, in the body for instance, and for transmitting an image.

CONTROL BY OBSTRUCTION—THE VASI UNIT

Obstruction is a wasteful method of light control if the obstructing shields are black. Yet there is one device which uses just such a method. It is a visual landing aid for pilots and is known as the visual approach slope indicator—VASI for short.[12] It gives the pilot the correct glide path for landing; it gives the angle of approach and the point of touch-down.

The principle can be understood from Fig. 5.43. This shows a section through two of the indicators, which are set behind each

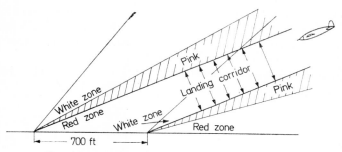

Fig. 5.43. Landing corridor formed by VASI units.

other facing down the runway. Each indicator gives a zone of white light and a zone of red light separated by a narrow zone of pink light subtending an angle of only $\frac{1}{2}°$. The pink zones of the two indicators are set with their inner boundaries parallel. These boundaries form a corridor down which the pilot lands his plane. When he is between the pink zones he sees red from the rear indicator and white from the near one. If he is too high both indicators show white; if he is too low both show red.

The problem to the designer is to produce an indicator with a red and white zone separated by a pink zone of only $\frac{1}{2}°$. The obvious solution is to use two parabolic reflectors one above the other, one giving white the other giving red light. But this is not a workable solution owing to the difficulty of getting a beam that is wide on one side of its axis and provides the necessary sharp run-back on the other.

The solution is shown in Fig. 5.44. The light source focuses a beam of light on the slot. A filter covers the top half of the light

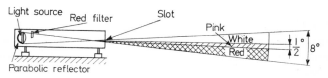

FIG. 5.44. The production of the white, pink, and red zones by VASI unit.

source and it is this that produces the red half of the beam. The pink zone is produced by the white and red zones being visible together and merging at a distance. The height of the slot is 2 in. and the indicator is 48 in. long so the pink zone should extend over $\tan^{-1} 2/48$ or $2\frac{1}{2}°$. However, owing to the white zone being brighter than the red zone, this becomes swamped. The result is that the pink zone is only visible as such over $\frac{1}{2}°$.

Three 200 W lamps are used in each indicator, 12 indicators being used in a complete installation as shown in Fig. 5.45.

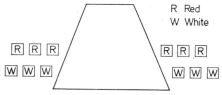

FIG. 5.45. Appearance of VASI units at correct approach.

An important manufacturing consideration is that the optical accuracy of the system simply depends on the position and width of the slot in relation to filter. Since these are easy to control the indicator does not have to be made to the small tolerances associated with optical instruments. Misalignment of the filament in its reflector will result in a decrease of brightness of the indicator, not in a decrease of accuracy of indication.

CONTROL BY OBSTRUCTION—THE LIGHTING CHANNEL

The lighting channel is another example of the use of obstruction as a method of control, though unlike the VASI unit just described the light shields are not necessarily black. Such a channel may give either direct or indirect illumination, or it may give both. Figure 5.46 illustrates these three forms.

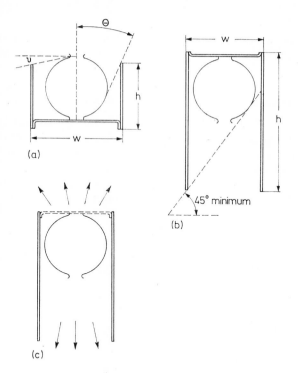

Fig. 5.46

(a) Indirect. (b) Direct. (c) Direct/indirect.

A common use for these channels is to provide a high level of
illumination and at the same time create the impression of a ceiling
level which is lower than the true ceiling. They are most effective
when mounted 8–10 ft. above the floor and 3–4 ft. apart.

The values of the width W and the height H must be chosen
to meet a number of requirements:

1. The channel must have the correct proportions relative to the
   area in which it is employed.
2. The fluorescent tube must not be visible at normal angles of
   view. It is common practice to make angle v zero or even
   negative.
3. To avoid excessive glare the shielding angle of a downward
   channel should be at least 45° as shown, but angles greater
   than 60° are to be avoided, as the channel then becomes very
   inefficient.

Lighting channels are often constructed in timber, and, like
coves, to be described next, are part of the fabric of the building.

CONTROL BY OBSTRUCTION—THE LIGHTING COVE

The purpose of a lighting cove is to provide indirect lighting
by supporting, and concealing, light sources which illuminate the
ceiling. The efficiency depends upon the ceiling reflection factor,
the type of light source, and the dimensions of the cove.

Although the efficiency of cove lighting is low, the advent of
tubular fluorescent lamps has made this form of lighting more

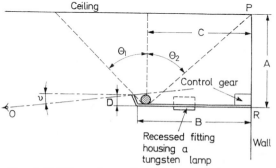

Fig. 5.47. Effect of cove dimensions on performance.

economic. It is frequently used where appearance is an important factor in the design, e.g. restaurants, showrooms, etc.

Lighting coves are part of the fabric of the building and are usually part of a design scheme co-ordinated by an architect. The architect would be concerned to see that the coves had the correct proportions in relation to the rest of the interior, and this places some restriction on the lighting designer.

Figure 5.47 shows a cross-section of a typical cove.

The influence of cove dimensions and material on the efficiency of the cove and the appearance of the ceiling is considered below.

1. The uniformity of ceiling illumination increases as dimension A is increased.

2. Increase in dimension B allows more light to reach the ceiling but the soffit or shelf traps more of the reflected light.

3. The sight screen height D is governed by angle v for fixed values of B and C. This angle should be determined for the farthest position of the observer O from the cove, which may be on a room diagonal or even outside the room, e.g. at the other end of a corridor opening into the room. D should be as small as possible to obtain the maximum cove efficiency.

4. With a long cove of length greater than $5A$, the angles θ_1 and θ_2 may be taken as proportional to the light received directly from the lamp by the ceiling. θ_1 increases with decrease in C for a given value of B, but this change leads to a greater obstruction of reflected light.

5. Reflectors can be used to direct the light out of the cove and improve the uniformity of ceiling illumination, but the problems of maintenance and increased capital cost usually rule this method out. However, reflector fluorescent tubes are often used, and they give a worthwhile increase in efficiency. When reflector tubes are replaced they must be adjusted until the maximum intensity from each tube is in the same direction as before, otherwise a change in cove performance will occur.

6. Wall surface PR is sometimes painted in a dark colour since with the correct ratios of dimensions A, B and C it has the effect of making the ceiling appear to "float". To produce a satisfactory effect A must be large compared with B, and C large compared with the tube diameter.

7. It is unusual for a cove system to be used alone; because it produces soft illumination of low value with very little shadow definition or modelling, and lack of modelling can make the visual scene uninteresting. Additional lighting is frequently employed in the form of tungsten filament spot lights to provide interest and to increase the illumination level locally. These spotlights are sometimes recessed into the cove shelf or soffit, and the backs of the spotlights project into the cove. Care must be taken to ensure that these projections cannot be seen by an observer at O.

8. Instead of using an opaque sight screen, a transluscent screen of opal glass or acrylic plastic is sometimes used to increase the efficiency of the cove.

Interreflection theory could be used to predict the light output ratios of both coves and channels, but in most cases it is sufficient to determine the flux emitted directly by the lamp.

The K factor method (Chapters 1, 2 and 8) can be used for this purpose. It can also be used to calculate the direct flux to the ceiling from a cove or the direct flux to the ceiling or floor from a channel. The flux received by the ceiling having been determined the amount reflected to the floor or working plane can be calculated by using the transfer functions for uniformly diffusing surfaces. e.g. cosine surface distribution factors (Chapter 3).

DISTRIBUTED LIGHT CONTROL

This type of light control was devised by R. W. Stevens.[13] It has been used for the lighting of staircases and landings from a single projector lamp. Figure 5.48 shows the principle. Light is beamed down the well of a staircase by a parabolic mirror. It is intercepted at appropriate intervals by annular diffusers which spread the light on to the landings and stairs.

FLUORESCENT PARAPET LIGHTING

There are two main requirements of parapet lighting. Firstly, it should provide a beam of light of sufficient intensity and at a sufficiently high angle of elevation to reveal objects right across the road. This requirement is easier to meet if there are parapet

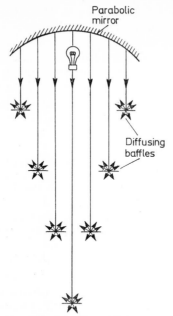

FIG. 5.48. Distributed light control.

fittings on both sides of the road. And secondly, it should be glare free. This is especially important if the line of fittings is not continous as the flicker is distracting.

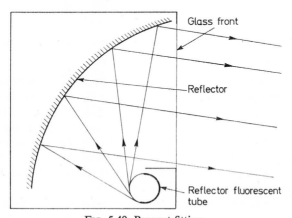

FIG. 5.49. Parapet fitting.

Where fluorescent tubes are used, the sharp cut-off reflector described in Chapter 4 has an obvious application.[14]

Figure 5.49 shows how it can be made up into a fitting. It will be noted that the tube is shielded from view, and to obtain a greater reflector brightness a reflector tube (or aperture tube) is used. Owing to gradual accumulation of dirt on the glass some of the light will be scattered. The effect of this is minimized by using black vertical louvers outside the glass.

UNIFORM BACKGROUND LUMINANCE

A background of uniform luminance is required in tracing boxes and for examining objects by transmitted light. One solution to its provision is the use of a number of fluorescent tubes, suitably spaced, behind an opal screen. Another is a cylindrical reflector, having a diffuse white finish, with a line filament or fluorescent lamp in its axis. But this requires a housing as deep as it is wide. An elegant solution is provided by a cylindrical reflector that passes as close to the lamp as possible (theoretically it should go through the lamp centre) as in Fig. 5.50. The finish of the reflector is

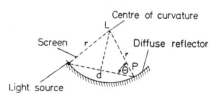

Fig. 5.50. Section of cylindrical reflector for providing uniform luminance.

matt white as in the previous solution. Mirrors are put at both ends of the lamp, facing each other and normal to its axis, in order to give, in effect, an infinitely long source. The illumination from this falls off inversely as the distance—an essential requirement. For in Fig. 5.50, let the distances be as marked. Let I be the intensity per unit length of the source, normal to its surface.

Then the illumination at any point P is proportional to $I \cos \theta / d$. This is equal to $I/2r$, since $\frac{1}{2}d = r \cos \theta$.

Since $I/2r$ is a constant, the direct illumination is uniform. Also the interreflected light provides nearly uniform illumination.

In practice a screen is needed in front of the lamp to shield the user from direct light.

SOME APPLICATIONS OF LENSES

Lens systems are mainly used in preference to reflector systems where more than one beam is required from a single light source or where it is required to vary the width of the beam.

Stepped lenses are used in lighthouses and beacons on aerodromes, where a number of beams have to be transmitted simultaneously from the same unit. They are also used in theatre spotlights and floodlights, where they have the advantage over simple reflector systems that the beam width can be altered by focusing. The lens has to be specially computed to eliminate "trouser legging" and like most dual purpose designs is a compromise; the spot is not as good as it could be if the optical system were solely designed to give a spot, and similarly some performance is lost in the flood position. The inner surface of the lens is usually patterned to even out striations. Reflectors are used to project as much light as possible through the lens.

Reflectors are also often combined with stepped lenses in automobile lights and in traffic signs and signals.

Stepped lenses in acrylic plastic can be made with a very fine pitch (in the order of a hundredth of an inch), injection moulding or compression moulding being used to achieve this.[15] These are used as components in projector systems.

Parabolic lenses find an application in airfield runway lights. The bi-directional runway insert fitting, as its name implies, is fitted into a hole in the runway, and it produces two beams of light at 180° to each other in azimuth and at 3° above the horizontal. So that it does not constitute a hazard to aircraft running over it, it must not project more than $\frac{5}{8}$ in. above the surface. This limitation on size makes it important that the optical system is fully flashed to obtain a beam of sufficient intensity to be effective. Stepped lenses are inefficient in this respect because the curved surfaces between the faces of the prisms result in a loss of flashed area. Spherical lenses do not flash right to the edge owing to spherical aberration unless more than one lens is used. Parabolic surfaced lenses, however, give a very good performance and are, in fact, used.

REFERENCES

1. WALDRAM, J. M., *Street Lighting*, Edward Arnold, 1952.
2. *Street Lighting*, British Standard Code of Practice CP 1004: Parts 1 and 2: 1963.
3. HEWITT, H., *Public Lighting* **28**, 284 (1963).
4. ICI Information Service Note 1124, "*Perspex*" *Refractor Plate Designs for Street Lighting Lanterns using Sodium Lamps*.
5. HOPKINSON, R. G., *Trans. I.E.S.* (*London*) **25**, 135 (1963).
6. *Recommendations for Good Interior Lighting*, The I.E.S. Code, I.E.S., London, 1961.
7. SIMONS, R. H., I.E.S. Monograph No. 5, I.E.S., London, 1962.
8. DOBRAS, Q. D., and PHILLIPS, D. A., *Illum. Engng.* (*N.Y.*) **46**, 627 (1959).
9. BLACKWELL, H. R., *Illum. Engng.* (*N.Y.*) **58**, 161 (1963).
10. STRANGE, J. W., and STEVENS, B., *Trans. I.E.S.* (*London*) **23**, 65 (1958).
11. KAPANY, N. S., *Scientific American* **23**, 72 (1960).
12. CALVERT, E. S., *Trans. I.E.S.* (*London*) **22**, 271 (1957).
13. STEVENS, R. W., *Trans. I.E.S.* (*London*) **25**, 149 (1960).
14. SPENCER, D. E., *Illum. Engng.* (*N.Y.*) **54**, 167 (1959).
15. ICI Technical Service Note G 107, *Plastics in Lighting*, Part 1.

CHAPTER 6

MECHANICAL, THERMAL AND ELECTRICAL DESIGN AND TESTING

A DETAILED knowledge of the mechanical design of lighting fittings cannot be obtained just from a textbook. Equipment must be examined and manufacturers catalogue descriptions consulted. This section is intended to supplement such studies.

The final form a lighting fitting depends upon the following: optical performance required; materials available; manufacturing techniques used; and safety requirements, both thermal and electrical.

All the foregoing factors must be considered and related to the cost and appearance of the fitting.

In some fittings such as industrial reflector units for fluorescent lamps, the light control consists simply of reflecting most of the light towards the working plane by means of a diffusing reflector. This reflector is also formed to give the desired cut-off to reduce direct glare.

The main design effort is directed to solving the thermal problems created by housing the control gear in an enclosure close to the lamp and to details such as: standardization of parts for a range of fittings; simplification of assembly, wiring and maintenance.

In other fittings, such as special projectors, the optical performance, lamp life and fitting size might be the most important design factors. However, in all lighting fittings some or all of the following must be designed:

1. Lampholders and wiring.
2. Reflector and housing.
3. Refractor or diffuser or screen or louver, and housing.
4. Control gear and housing.

LAMPHOLDERS

Wherever possible standard lampholders are used. Up to 150 W the bayonet cap (BC) holder is common for tungsten filament lamps and this is made of bakelite, or of brass with a porcelain insert to carry the brass plungers which connect the supply to the lamp contacts. Trouble is often experienced when a shade ring is used with a bakelite holder since it distorts when heated and frequently cannot be removed after use. The low cost of bakelite was the reason for the continued use of lampholders with this unsatisfactory feature. A recent British Standard (BC 52: 1963) has introduced a coarser thread and specified tests for these lampholders which should overcome this problem. A supplement to this standard is in preparation which deals with lampholders made from heat resisting materials.

Edison Screw (ES) lampholders may be used for lamp sizes up to 200 W and Goliath Screws (GES) for higher wattages. The screw-type holders are made from brass with porcelain insulation and are used with centre contact lamps, the circuit being completed via the screw thread.

One of the big problems experienced in recent years is the overheating of lampholders and associated wiring caused by the use of smaller envelopes for tungsten filament lamps, since these have a higher temperature at the lamp cap when burnt cap up. Failure of plunger springs and lampholder mouldings may occur if care is not taken to avoid rises in temperature greater than the limiting values given below:

Phosphor bronze	135°C	⎫ Plunger
Ordinary steel	170°C	⎬ springs
Special spring steel	200°C	⎭
Urea based	80°C	⎫
Phenolic based	150°C	⎬ Mouldings
Special heat resisting material	200°C	⎭

The British Standard specifies a maximum temperature for moulded lampholders of 135°C and 220°C for heat-resisting materials, measured at the shade ring (BS 52: 1963 and Supplement No. 1).

Deterioration of Lampholder Wiring

Deterioration of the cable insulation is usually discovered when the fitting is moved and the insulation material disintegrates. The region where insulation failure is most common is where the two cores separate to be joined to the individual lampholder terminals. This is usually the hottest region, and the point where the core sheaths are touching is therefore the most likely place for a short circuit to occur.

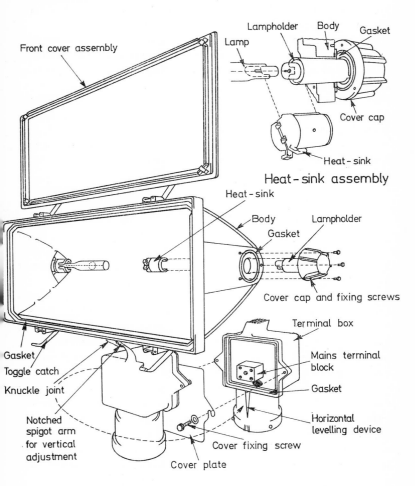

FIG. 6.1. Exploded view of tungsten iodine floodlight (Fig. 5.34) but incorporating a terminal box. Also shown is the heat sink for conducting heat away from the lamp pinch. (*By courtesy of Atlas Lighting Ltd.*)

PVC and rubber insulated cables are generally used for the wiring of lighting fittings. Keen and Stephenson[1] have suggested 85°C as the maximum temperature for these where the insulation has no mechanical load to bear. The manufacturers specify limits of 60°C for vulcanized rubber and 70°C for PVC. High temperature grade PVC may be used up to 105°C and silicone rubber up to 150°C.

As with many other types of electrical equipment satisfactory heat dissipation requires careful consideration in the design of a lighting fitting (see heat sink, Fig. 6.1, but note that in the latest design of lamp this is no longer necessary).

For example, large industrial reflector fittings often terminate the cable away from the lampholder and make the final connections by solid copper rods or strips well separated in air and shrouded by a metal canopy. Alternatively, a terminal box is incorporated and the final connection made with asbestos covered leads (Fig. 6.1).

Bi-pin Holders

In the past tubular fluorescent lamps often had bayonet caps, but in recent years bi-pin caps have become popular, mainly because they are simpler, smaller, and lamp replacement can be made easier.

Some manufacturers have found it worth while to design bi-pin lampholders specially suited to a particular range of fittings. Such a lampholder is shown in Fig. 6.2. This is a plastic encased pedestal holder with phosphor bronze contacts and brass terminals, which has the following features; spring-loading to simplify relamping, a protruding rim which grips the lamp, thus reducing the load placed on the contact pins by the weight of the lamp, and an earth spring contact which connects the lamp cap to earth before the mains connection to the pins is made. Another type of holder is shown in Fig. 6.3. This is a grip-pin holder and is intended to give the thinnest possible holder while providing a firm connection. With this type of holder some other means of supporting the lamp must be provided since it is the lamp that supports the holder.

The temperature rise at the caps of tubular fluorescent lamps is not sufficient to create the problems encountered with tungsten filament lamps.

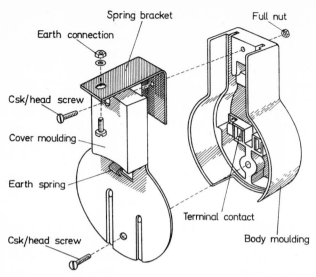

Fig. 6.2. Pedestal type bi-pin lampholder. (*By courtesy of Atlas Lighting Ltd.*)

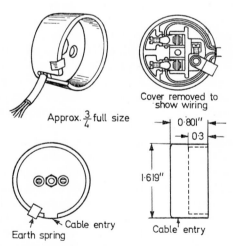

Fig. 6.3. Grip-pin bi-pin lampholder. (*By courtesy of Atlas Lighting Ltd.*)

Wiring of Fluorescent Fittings

Since the wiring of fluorescent fittings does not usually have to withstand high temperatures, standard grade PVC flexible cable is generally used. The wiring is kept away from the heat dissipating surfaces of chokes, and transformers as far as possible, but when this cannot be done the high temperature grade of PVC is used.

BS 3820: 1964 specifies that the conductors used for the internal wiring of the fitting shall be of suitable type and size, and that no conductor shall be less than 14/0076 or equivalent.

In practice a common size for the wiring of fluorescent fittings is 23/0076.

REFLECTORS

A list of materials suitable for the manufacture of reflectors is given in Table 6.1.

Each material has its own advantages and disadvantages. Sheet steel is commonly used for diffuse reflecting fittings, since it has a high mechanical strength, and may be readily pressed, spun, or fabricated into the desired shape. It is suitable for mass production as well as "made to measure" methods. Compared with aluminium or plastics it is heavy, but in addition to being strong it is relatively cheap.

A predominantly diffusing finish is obtained by either stove enamelling or vitreous enamelling. The material must be thicker for the latter treatment since a specially robust construction is necessary to avoid buckling and distortion due to the high temperatures used in processing (some 800°C). Acrylic resin enamel is also finding increasing use since it has better corrosion resistant properties than stove enamel, without the brittleness of vitreous enamel, which is liable to chip and crack. Sharp edges and corners should be avoided in the design of painted reflectors as at these points the paint film is thinner and easier to damage.

Aluminium has the advantages of light weight, ease of spinning and fairly good corrosion resistance, although ordinary aluminium will rapidly corrode in an alkaline atmosphere. The anodizing process is the formation of a hard film of oxide on the aluminium surface, which gives protection against corrosion. Where corrosion due to an alkaline atmosphere is likely, a silicone aluminium alloy is often used. A disadvantage of aluminium is the

TABLE 6.1. REFLECTOR MATERIALS

(a) *Diffuse reflectors*

Material	Finish	Temperature limit	Total reflection factor
Sheet steel	Stove enamel Acrylic resin enamel Vitreous enamel	90 °C 90 °C 200° C	Up to 80%
Aluminium	Stove enamel Sand blasted Etched	90 °C	
Polyvinylchloride (PVC) Opal Perspex (acrylic plastic)		70 °C 80 °C	

(b) *Specular reflectors*

Material	Notes	Specular reflection factor
Aluminium	Anodized and polished	70%
Super purity aluminium	Electrolitically polished and anodized	80%
Silvered glass	Silver or aluminium reflecting coating backed with copper or lead	85–90%
Plated metals	Chromium, rhodium, etc.	60–70%
Stainless steel		60%

electro-chemical action which takes place when it is in contact with some other metals or alloys such as brass, copper, phosphor bronze, or nickel. Care must be taken therefore, to use suitable materials such as stainless steel or cadmium plated steel for accessories. The use of aluminium as a specular reflector has greatly increased with the development of new techniques for chemical and electrolitic polishing. Super-purity aluminium has a very high reflection factor but is seldom used because of its softness. Polyvinylchloride finds use where the atmosphere is highly corrosive, but cannot be used at temperatures of 70°C or above and lacks the rigidity of the metal reflectors. Opal Perspex (a form of acrylic plastic) may be used where transmission as well as reflection is required. But it has a temperature limitation of 80°C and is unsuitable for use in public places, such as cinemas, which are subject to special regulations since it will "support combustion".

Silvered glass has excellent reflecting properties and may be worked, before silvering, by blowing, bending, or pressing. It is, however, vulnerable to thermal or mechanical shock and has the added disadvantage of being much heavier than aluminium, which has largely displaced it for specular reflectors.

The plated metals do not find extensive use and stainless steel is limited to applications where the high cost is justified by its corrosion resistant properties.

Prismatic glass may be used as a reflector by utilizing the property of total internal reflection. The Holophane Company have designed many fittings utilizing this principle alone. Since the problems associated with manufacturing banks of reflecting prisms are almost identical with those of manufacturing refracting prisms the section on refractors deals with this topic.

REFLECTOR HOUSINGS

Sheet steel and aluminium are the chief materials used for the reflector and control gear housings. Die-cast aluminium silicon alloy is now used extensively for street lighting fittings in place of cast-iron. When sheet steel or aluminium is used for a housing, such as the spine or chassis of a fluorescent fitting, it should be remembered that the strength and rigidity depends as much on the shape of the channel as on the thickness of the material used. Lengthwise forming and cross-brackets greatly strengthen sheet metal housings.

The common method of fabrication employs spot-welding for cheapness, although gas welds are sometimes used to improve the appearance of the joint.

In general the welding of aluminium is more difficult than the welding of steel, but spot welding is usually an economic method.

An alternative to a welded joint is seaming. In this process the two pieces of sheet metal are hooked together and then compressed. An example of this type of joint is seen in the manufacture of the tins for canned food. Another alternative is riveting, which is occasionally employed. Plastics are sometimes used for parts of the housing. Such materials may be pressed or formed into the desired shape and the shape usually imparts the necessary rigidity.

REFRACTORS

Refractors are made from glass or acrylic. Glass is used almost exclusively for lens systems, Fresnel lenses, spreaders for floodlights, and prismatic ware such as bulkhead fitting covers because of the high temperatures usually encountered. Prismatic bowls for street lighting fittings are often made from acrylic plastic although glass is still used by some companies, usually those who have been making lanterns for a long time. The newer entrants to this field usually prefer acrylic plastic, partly because of its light weight but also because it gives the designer more freedom to experiment with new shapes. If carefully designed, acrylic plastic refractors may be used with tungsten filament lamps. The problem is the thermal one of keeping the temperature of the material below about 80°C. This may be achieved either by suitable separation of the material and the lamp, for example by increasing the size of the refractor bowl, or by providing some simple form of cooling. Acrylic plastic has a low thermal capacity and so is appreciably cooled by the slightest movement of the air. For this reason it is possible to make a street lighting refractor of this material for use out in the open, which would be unsatisfactory in a draught-free enclosure.[2] Where high impact strength is required, as in vandal-proof street lanterns, polycarbonate or cellulose acetate butyrate can be used. These materials result in a more expensive lantern, and are more quickly affected by ultraviolet radiation. Polycarbonate is particularly susceptible to the yellowing caused by ultraviolet radiation.[3]

Glass refractors are usually pressed and care must be taken to ensure that all the internal flutes have a direction which allows the internal former to be withdrawn. Flutes which do not meet this condition must be formed on the outside so that the former may be split to allow removal of the refractor after pressing.

Since horizontal external prisms are likely to be difficult to clean, glass refracting systems sometimes consist of two parts: a large refracting bowl with a smooth external surface and vertical internal flutes, and a small inverted bowl refractor carrying the

7*

horizontal flutes. This is mounted inside the large bowl and fitted round the neck of a vertically burning lamp.

Acrylic plastic refractors may be pressed, machined, extruded, or injection moulded. One of the earliest methods of using this material was to cement a bank of machined prisms onto the inside wall of a clear acrylic plastic enclosure (Fig. 5.10, p. 149). By this means a smooth surface can be obtained on both the internal and external surfaces of the enclosure. Score marks caused by the cutting tool must be removed by polishing, and this adds to the cost of machined prism banks. Instead of machining the prism bank, the extrusion process has been tried, since this is a fairly cheap method of mass production, but the resultant prisms usually lack the precision required for accurate light control. Improvements in techniques are still taking place and greater use of this method is to be expected in the future; it already finds use for indoor lighting fittings.

Injection moulding allows detail of considerable complexity to be incorporated to a standard of accuracy similar to that associated with machining, without the problems of access sometimes encountered with machining. The tools for injection moulding are, however, very expensive, running into thousands of pounds, and cannot be modified without adding considerably to the cost. For this reason two conditions are essential before injection moulding becomes an economic proposition: (1) the quantity to be manufactured must justify the cost of the tools, (2) the design problems must be solved before the tools are made, since only minor modifications can be accommodated economically afterwards.

The method used by one designer[4] was to construct ten times full-size sectional models of the prisms and examine their behaviour with a special goniometer. This incorporated a highly directional light source to beam light rays into the prisms, and a carefully screened photocell to detect their change in direction. Probably a better method is to have the prism bank machined and tested as a whole. The cost of such a bank is negligible compared with the tool costs.

The lantern referred to above is shown in Figs. 6.4 and 5.6 Plate section). The lamp enclosure was injection moulded in two halves, which were then cemented together. The aperture for insertion of the lamp is at one end and is hermetically sealed with a sealing cap held in place by two quick-release clips. Small ventilation filters are provided in the sealing cap to allow the unit to breathe during heating and cooling. The ingress of dirt is in this way reduced to a minimum.

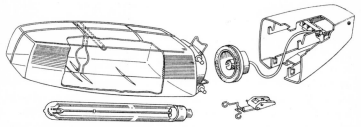

FIG. 6.4. Exploded view of a sodium street lighting lantern. (*By courtesy of Atlas Lighting Ltd.*)

DIFFUSERS

Diffusers for tungsten filament lamp fittings are commonly made from "opal" glass. The opal material is a glass containing particles of calcium fluoride which scatter the light. Pot opal, which consists entirely of this material, has the disadvantages of a low transmission factor (20–40%), and a tendency to be brittle. In practice two- or three-ply opal glass is more common. These glasses consist of clear glass coated on one or both sides with pot opal. This arrangement improves both the mechanical and the transmission properties, while still maintaining good diffusion. In recent years a satin finish has become popular for opal glassware, because it reduces specular surface reflections. The satin finish is produced by light acid etching. Diffusers made from glass are usually blown but certain forms may be pressed.

Acrylic plastic and polystyrene are manufactured in opal translucent form, and are available in a number of grades. The possibility of using these materials for diffusers with tungsten filament lamps depends on the solution of the thermal problems involved (see the section on refractors). The same applies to their use with discharge lamps such as the HPMV lamp.

The materials are well suited to the requirements of diffusers for use with fluorescent lamps where there is far less heat to be dissipated for a given area of diffuser.

Methods of working include: blow moulding, vacuum forming, and extrusion, all of which are suitable for the manufacture of diffusers.

The choice of method depends upon the shape of the diffuser and the number required. Blow moulding and vacuum forming are suitable for bowl and dish diffusers, whereas extrusion is suitable where channel section diffusers are required in large numbers.

Other materials that find limited use are glass fibre, etched and patterned glass, fabrics, and vinyl opal polymer foil. The latter material is often used for the moulded dishes and corrugated sheets associated with luminous ceiling systems. It has the advantage of being available in a grade that does not support combustion.

When plastic materials are used these should be treated to stop the collection of electro-static charges, which cause the rapid formation of a dust film. In addition, light stabilized grades of plastic should be used wherever possible to avoid yellowing of the material.

SCREENS

It is often necessary to enclose a lamp for mechanical rather than optical purposes, perhaps to protect it from the weather or to ensure that if the lamp breaks it will not shower the surroundings with broken glass or cause an explosion. For example, mercury vapour lamps used in open reflectors for area floodlighting at one time had the protection of a glass sleeve to prevent the lamp from being directly exposed to rain splashes. Food and sweet factories require protection from broken glass, while areas where inflammable materials or gases are handled require protection from fire and explosion.

In many cases the refractor or diffuser bowl will also act as a screen, but when these are not required, clear glass or acrylic bowls, covers, or sleeves are used. Which of these is used is dictated by the general design of the fitting. A fitting with a circular spun or pressed reflector will often have the mouth closed by a circular dish of clear glass which may be wired for additional strength. Fluorescent reflector fittings sometimes have acrylic plastic panels fitted over the mouth of the reflector. Bare fluorescent lamps or reflector fittings without end caps frequently employ a glass or Perspex sleeve.

Care must be taken to ensure that such screening does not cause the lamp to run hot, since this will reduce the light output of a fluorescent lamp.

LOUVERS

These may be manufactured from diffuse or specular materials such as stove-enamelled sheet steel, anodized aluminium with diffuse or specular finish, white translucent acrylic plastic, pearl finish polystyrene, or metal coated plastic.

Sheet metal louvers are generally of a slotted construction similar to that used at one time for the construction of cardboard egg containers, the peripheral members being riveted or welded to the ends of the louver fins.

Plastic louvers are usually moulded in section which are cemented together to form larger panels.

REFRACTOR AND DIFFUSER HOUSINGS

The construction of refractor and diffuser housings is similar to that of reflector housings.

Tungsten filament units such as heavy duty bulkhead fittings have a cast-iron body supporting the refractor and the lampholder, and are finished with stove enamel or galvanized. For outside use a die cast aluminium alloy body is sometimes adopted. For highly corrosive conditions porcelain is used for the body, the prismatic glass is seated in a heavy silicone rubber gasket and all external screws made of stainless steel. Porcelain is expensive and susceptible to mechanical shock, and so it is only used where its corrosion-resistant properties are essential.

Light duty bulkhead fittings have pressed steel or aluminium bodies. Great care has to be taken to make sure such fittings are not used in unsuitable situations. In one case where bulkhead fittings with pressed aluminium bodies had been used in the saline atmosphere of a bacon factory, the fittings failed in less than 2 months.

The corrosive action at the points where the fixing screws passed through the back of each bulkhead had opened the holes to such an extent that all the fixings had been destroyed and the fittings were hanging, supported only by their supply cables.

Glass fibre is a material which might be considered for certain situations, such as a cold store, but its heat insulating properties must be taken into account if heat dissipation problems are to be avoided.

For street-lighting fittings cast-iron, silicon aluminium alloy, and magnesium aluminium alloy are used. Plastics are also used where appropriate. One particular design of street-lighting lantern has an opaque canopy made from coloured PVC supported by an aluminium spine (Fig. 5.15, Plate section).

Fluorescent fittings generally have a sheet-steel spine supporting either a reflector or a diffuser, although aluminium is occasionally used.

Fittings for incandescent or mercury vapour discharge lamps commonly employ sheet metal spinnings to enclose the lampholder connections and support the diffuser (see section on reflector housings).

CONTROL GEAR

Just as the design of the lamp used in the lighting fitting is generally outside the province of the fittings designer, so to a large extent is the design of the control gear for the lamp. However, since the control gear is often incorporated in the fitting and sold as part of the fitting, it is necessary for the designer to have some knowledge in this field.

It is quite likely that the fittings designer may be involved in setting the desirable size of the control-gear components or in the purchasing of suitable components from other manufacturers. For this reason an outline of the main requirements for and functions of the more common components is given. In the case of the two most common items, i.e. chokes and capacitors, an indication of design procedure is given to illustrate the factors involved.

One of the most attractive features of the tungsten filament lamp is the fact that the only form of control gear required is a suitable switch and possibly a fuse in the case of tungsten iodine lamps to avoid arcing after failure of the filament. (Tungsten filament lamps and the latest tungsten iodine lamps incorporate a fuse in the lamp.) With arcs and discharge lamps of all kinds additional control gear is necessary. This is because the effective lamp resistance falls as the lamp current increases, and the ballast is required to limit the lamp current.

Stability may be imparted by placing an impedance in series with the light source.

The requirements for such an impedance or ballast are:

1. It should ensure that the correct voltage is applied to the lamp.
2. It should not distort the current waveform unduly since this distortion may reduce the lamp life and accentuate lamp flicker.
3. It should consume the smallest possible amount of power.
4. It should be noise free.
5. It should provide favourable starting conditions for the lamp.

Operation from an a.c. Supply

Conditions 1, 2, and 4 are fulfilled by a resistive ballast, and by careful design and utilization of the electric field set up between the lamp filaments and adjacent earthed metalwork, the starting conditions can be made reasonably satisfactory.

Resistive ballasts find use in fluorescent lamp circuits for domestic applications, where the fact that the ballast consumes as much power as the discharge lamp is tolerated since this type of ballast reduces the cost of the fitting. For this application tungsten filament lamps are often employed as a convenient means of limiting the current, providing additional interest to the appearance of the fitting, and a small amount of additional light. This additional light is particularly valuable at the instant of switching on the supply to the fitting since it bridges the small but annoying delay in the striking of the discharge lamp.

Resistive ballasts are also used for small special purpose discharge sources such as the ultraviolet lamps used for medical purposes.

The use of a capacitor to form a ballast satisfies conditions 1, 3, and 4. The waveform distortion is extreme and in general rules out the use of a purely capacitive ballast. However, capacitors are often used in conjunction with inductive ballasts and this use is dealt with later.

The ballast which most nearly satisfies all the requirements listed above is the inductive ballast or choke, which in its basic form is simply a coil of insulated wire wound on a laminated iron core, containing an air-gap.

CHOKE DESIGN

The supply voltage in this country has a tolerance of $\pm 6\%$ on the nominal value. To avoid excessive variation of lamp wattage due to variation of supply voltage, it is necessary for the volt-drop across the ballast to be made greater than that across the lamp.

The large volt-drop required across the choke is made possible by the phase displacement between the lamp and choke voltages.

The impedance of the choke is determined by the required lamp current and voltage. The minimum volume of the choke is decided by the volt-amperes which it must absorb and the permissible temperature rise and power loss.

In common with other iron-cored devices, the efficiency is a maximum when the core loss is equal to the copper loss. This requirement must be weighed against the fact that the material cost is a minimum when the cost of the core is equal to the cost of the coil.

An important feature of choke design is the size of the air-gap in the iron core. Most of the ampere-turns are absorbed by this air-gap. The main function of the iron core is to define the magnetic path and reduce the number of ampere-turns to practical proportions. In practice the size of the air-gap is difficult to calculate accurately, owing to the effects of magnetic fringing. For this reason it is common to adopt a construction which allows the air-gap to be finally set on a test bench during manufacture. It is important to ensure that the iron is not worked under saturation conditions since this would produce variable choke inductance. The presence of the air-gap keeps the magnetic flux in the core below the value at which saturation occurs.

The ultimate shape of the choke is influenced by the necessity to house the choke in a particular cross-sectional area, e.g. the spine of a fluorescent fitting. The spine of a fluorescent fitting is usually made as slim as possible for reasons of appearance and cost. This accounts for the popularity of the long, slim choke, even though it is well known that it is more efficient to have one of cubic shape.

Choke Calculations

Practical design is often simply the modification of an existing design to meet new requirements. An outline of one design procedure is given below.

A diagramatic view of a "core" type choke is shown in Fig. 6.5.

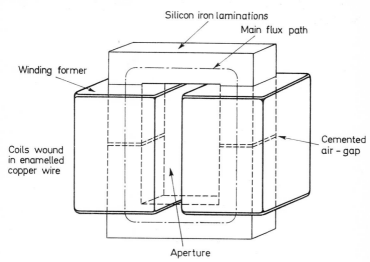

FIG. 6.5. Core type choke.

Method

1. Determine the approximate voltage and current of the choke during operation.

   Choke current = known lamp current.

Although the voltage wave form is not sinusoidal an approximate value for choke voltage (V_C) is obtained by making the assumption of a sinusoidal wave form.

In Fig. 6.6(a) and (b) V_S and V_T are known and V_R (choke loss component) is estimated from previous experience (about 10–15% of V_L):

$$V_L = \sqrt{[V_S^2 - (V_T + V_R)^2]}$$

and

$$V_C = \sqrt{(V_L^2 + V_R^2)}.$$

The exact choke voltage setting is determined experimentally.

7 a*

2. Calculate the number of turns on the choke.

If V_L is the r.m.s. value of induced voltage required:

$$\text{Turns} = \frac{V_L}{4\cdot44 \times \text{flux density} \times \text{core area} \times \text{frequency}}.$$

For the silicon irons used a suitable flux density is $1\cdot2$–$1\cdot3$ webers/m².

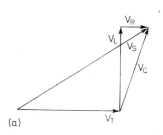

(a)

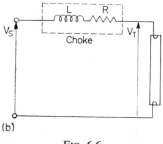

(b)

Fig. 6.6.

An empirical formula for core area is

$$\text{Area (cm}^2) = \frac{\sqrt{\text{Power}}}{5\cdot58}.$$

In practical design this value of core area would normally be modified to make use of an existing lamination stamping or to obtain a choke with a specified cross-section. The effect of core area on losses and cost must also be taken into account in fixing its value.

3. Choose wire size and determine coil size.

The wire size is governed by (a) copper loss of winding, (b) acceptable temperature rise of coil.

Item (b) depends upon coil shape and size, choke construction, and filling and choke surface area.

A current density of 310–460 A/cm^2 is usually found satisfactory.

Obtain the turns per layer and number of layers from wire tables. The coil size can then be estimated making allowance for the coil former, insulation and interleaving paper.

4. Compare the estimated coil size with the proposed lamination stampings and choke container to see if these are compatible. If not make adjustments in the coil, core area, or laminations and recalculate the values.

5. Calculate an approximate value for the core air-gap to give the desired flux density.

Ampere turns for gap = total ampere turns − iron ampere turns.

$$\text{Length of gap} = \frac{\text{Ampere turns for gap}}{\text{Ampere turns/cm for air}}.$$

A common technique is to make a double air-gap (Fig. 6.5) which is adjusted on the test bench before the cement hardens to give the correct choke impedance.

Materials

Core

The choice of sheet steel for the core laminations is influenced by the following factors:

(a) the higher the silicon content the lower the iron losses, but the greater the cost of the core construction.

(b) the thinner the laminations the lower the iron losses, but the amount of material that can be housed in a given space is reduced by the thickness of the inter-lamination insulation, and the cost rises.

In practice it is found that 1 or 2% silicon steel laminations of the order of 0·02 in. thick is the most suitable compromise.

Winding

The winding is generally of enamelled copper wire mounted on a fibre or plastic bobbin or even just a cardboard former. Each layer of the winding is separated by a strip of paper from the next layer. The size of wire is dictated by the power loss acceptable in the winding. An efficient choke for an 80 W lamp for use with a 230 V supply would have a winding resistance of about $9\,\Omega$ and the total choke losses would be about 12–15 W, although a slim choke could well have a resistance of $16\,\Omega$ and a loss of the order of 20 W.

Tappings

Bringing out tappings from a choke increases both the cost of construction and the possibility of faults developing where the tappings pass through the winding. For this reason it is preferable to use untapped chokes.

Housings

The sheet-steel container into which the choke winding is placed is required for reasons of safety as well as to protect the choke winding, to screen the surrounding metal work from the stray field, and hold the choke filling.

The choke filling helps to reduce the noise and improve heat transfer. To avoid the possibility of the filling material leaking, modern practice is to use a thermo-setting polyester resin. The thermal conduction is improved by loading the material with silica. The material used should have a certain amount of elasticity when set so that it acts as a cushion between the choke and the case to avoid transferring any core vibrations to the metalwork of the fitting.

Heat extraction

Tests have shown that the most effective way to remove heat from a choke is to attach it to a heat sink. Generally this is provided by the body-work of the fitting. Ventilation, while helpful and desirable, is not as effective. For this reason the temptation to mount the choke on a resilient mounting is usually resisted and the choke is bolted directly to the metalwork of the fitting. The temperature limit for the winding insulation is generally taken at 105 °C for a designed average life of 10–20 years. This temperature relates to class A insulation with the layers interleaved with paper.

CAPACITORS

Once the decision to use an inductive ballast has been taken, the problem of the lagging power factor which it produces (about 0·5) must be faced. The supply authorities expect that a power factor of at least 0·8 should be maintained in a lighting installation. This value of power factor may be achieved by bulk correction at the supply terminals or by individual correction at each fitting. It has become common practice to provide each lighting fitting above 20 W with a power-factor correction capacitor. This form of correction ensures that the capacitor draws current only when the fitting is in operation.

Capacitor Design

The design of a good capacitor is the result of the accumulated knowledge and experience of the designer and the organization to which he belongs.

The type commonly used in lighting fitting control gear circuits is the impregnated-paper capacitor. This consists of a pair of aluminium foil electrodes separated by a number of Kraft paper tissues (a wood-based paper) generally impregnated with chlorinated diphenyl, although mineral oil, petroleum jelly, and other substances are also used as impregnants. The reason for the increase in popularity of chlorinated diphenyl is that by virtue of its higher permittivity it reduces the quantity of materials required for a given capacitor and hence the cost.

Capacitor Calculations

The basic equation for the capacitance of a parallel plate capacitor is

$$C = 8\cdot85 \times 10^{-6}\ \varepsilon_r A/d \text{ micro-farads,}$$

where ε_r = relative permittivity, or dielectric constant of the dielectric material, A = area of one plate in square metres, d = distance between the plates in metres.

The importance of this equation lies in the fact that it shows the relationship between the permittivity, the area of the plates, and the thickness of the dielectric. In practice the number of plates and the method of construction bring modifications to the simple formula, but the relationship between the three quantities mentioned is the basis of the design.

The thickness of the dielectric is governed by the voltage at which the capacitor is required to work. The allowable stress in an impregnated paper dielectric is 15–25 V/μ, and papers are available from 6–12 μ thick.

The quality of capacitor tissue has reached a very high standard, but, even so, there will be weak spots of the nature of conducting particles and other imperfections (such as unreduced shive) which effectively reduce the thickness of the dielectric at particular points. For the large areas of dielectric needed for capacitors it becomes necessary to use at least two layers of tissue between foils so that the possibility of coincidence of such weak spots becomes unlikely.

The use of three layers even for the same overall thickness of dielectric makes the possibility of coincidence of weak spots exceedingly remote. However, for a typical dielectric thickness of say, 24 μ, it is more expensive to use 3 layers of 8 μ compared with two layers of 12 μ.

The effective relative permittivity is the result of the combination of that of the paper and that of the impregnant. The combined permittivity is influenced by the method of manufacture, and lies between 5 and 6 when chlorinated diphenyl is used as the impregnant. Mineral impregnants give about 70% of this value.

From previous experience, the number of square centimetres of plate area per micro-farad will be known for any particular design. In practice this area is translated into terms of a number of turns to be wound on a given diameter mandrel, for a specified foil width, and for the particular lay-up of foils and paper.

Construction

The method of laying up the paper and foil and inserting the connecting lugs is shown in Fig. 6.7. The second layer of dielectric is essential since without it rolling would short circuit the plates.

A consequence of this construction is that two capacitors in parallel are formed by the roll. The paper and foil interleaved in this manner are wound on to a mandrel, which is split to allow easy removal of the finished roll.

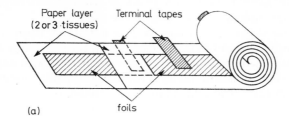

(a)

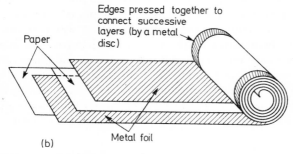

(b)

FIG. 6.7. Impregnated paper capacitor. (a) Terminal tape type. (b) Off-set foil type.

A popular form of construction is one in which the finished cylindrical roll is flattened by pressing between parallel platens after removal from the mandrel. This flattening eliminates the waste space occupied by the mandrel and has the added advantage that it reduces the distance between electrode foils, resulting in an increase in capacitance per unit volume.

If a container of the same cross-section as the flattened roll is used the minimum overall volume for the capacitor is obtained. Also, the quantity of free impregnant is a minimum thus reducing the risk of leakage of impregnant with temperature variation.

The metal container may be spun or drawn and after insertion of the capacitor roll is sealed and fitted with terminals or insulated flexible leads

For safety in handling, a discharge resistor is fitted between the terminals so that the terminal voltage will fall to less than 50 V within one minute of switching off the supply.

In some capacitors an internal fuse is fitted to open-circuit the capacitor in event of failure. One consequence of fitting a fuse is that it would be possible for a large number of capacitors to fail in an installation without this becoming apparent until the rise in current taken from the mains was detected.

Life

In the design of a capacitor for a lighting circuit the stresses to which the materials are to be subjected are chosen to give minimum cost of capacitor for an average life of 10 years.

It is generally accepted that the life of paper capacitors varies inversely with temperature and overheating will therefore cause premature breakdown of the capacitor dielectric. To avoid this breakdown care must be taken not to exceed the temperature for which it was designed (about 70 °C for the type described above). The position of the capacitor in the control gear housing is therefore important and it should be kept away from chokes or transformers which are dissipating power in the form of heat.

STARTING DEVICES

The control gear must limit the current passed by a discharge lamp, but in addition it must assist starting where necessary. The high pressure mercury vapour lamp has a built in auxiliary electrode which initiates the discharge, and further starting gear is unnecessary. On the other hand, the low-pressure mercury vapour discharge of the tubular fluorescent lamp requires preheating of the cathodes and either a voltage surge or utilization of the electric field which exists between the lamp cathodes and the earthed metalwork of the lighting fitting to start the discharge. Preheating and a voltage surge are provided by incorporating a starter switch in the lamp circuit (Figs. 6.8 and 6.10).

When the supply is switched on the starter provides a path through the lamp cathodes to produce preheating. The switch then opens automatically, interrupting the heating current. Since this heating current also passes through the choke, the choke field collapses. The collapse of the choke field releases stored energy which produces a high voltage between the lamp cathodes and causes the lamp to strike. The method utilizing the electric field usually employs constant cathode heating, which is provided by a cathode heating transformer.

The sodium lamp also requires a high starting voltage and this is either produced by a starter switch–choke combination or by a "leaky flux" transformer, depending on the design of the lamp. Linear sodium lamps use a choke and starter switch, whereas U-tube sodium lamps use the transformer.

The starting devices which will be considered are:

1. Starter switches.
2. Cathode heating transformers.
3. Semi-resonant starting circuits.
4. Leakage flux transformers.

Starter Switches

There are two main types of starter switch, and in order of popularity they are in the glow starter switch and the thermal starter switch.

Glow Starter Switch

The glow switch consists of a pair of bi-metal contacts sealed in a small glass bulb filled with argon gas. The type of circuit in which it is used is shown in Fig. 6.8. When the supply is switched on the whole mains voltage appears between the open contacts, generating an arc discharge. The heat from the discharge closes the bi-metal contacts causing the pre-heat current to flow. The closure of the contacts extinguishes the arc, the bi-metal contacts cool and open, causing the lamp to strike. A small radio interference suppressor capacitor is fitted between the contact connections outside the glass bulb. The glass bulb is usually mounted on a paxolin or plastic base and inserted into a small cylindrical metal canister (Fig. 6.9). The base has metal studs or pins pro-

truding from it which are connected to the bi-metal contacts.
A suitable insulated socket must be mounted in the control gear
housing to receive the metal studs of the starter switch so that it
may be connected into the control gear circuit. Starter switches
of this type are expendable items and normally last about twice
as long as a fluorescent tubular lamp.

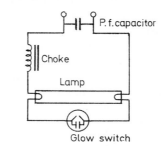

FIG. 6.8. Glow starter switch circuit.

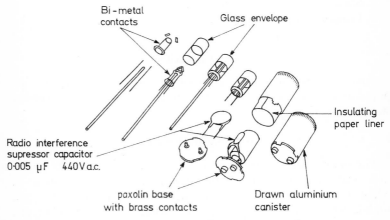

FIG. 6.9. Exploded view of a glow starter switch.

Thermal Starter Switch

Externally a thermal starter switch has a similar appearance
to a glow switch, except that it sometimes employs a larger size
of canister. It also has a pair of bi-metal contacts, but these are
initially closed and not open as in the glow starter. The contacts

are sealed in a glass bulb together with a small heater coil. The bulb is filled with a suitable gas to improve the thermal link between the heater coil and the contacts. The circuit for this form of switch is shown in Fig. 6.10.

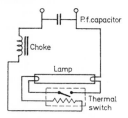

FIG. 6.10. Thermal starter switch circuit.

When the supply is switched on a current flows through the lamp cathodes, the choke, and also the heater coil in the starter switch. The heater coil raises the temperature of the bi-metal contacts and they separate, interrupting the current through the choke, and the consequent voltage pulse causes the lamp to strike. Once the lamp strikes the lamp current flows through the starter heater and the bi-metal contacts remain open.

This form of switch is more complicated than the glow switch but is useful where a longer pre-heating time is required. The thermal starter has found use with the linear sodium lamp as well as fluorescent tubular lamps.

Like the glow starter the thermal starter switch has a limited life. Normally these switches should last at least as long as the fluorescent lamp.

Cathode Heating Transformers

A circuit employing a voltage fed cathode heating transformer is shown in Fig. 6.11.

An auto-transformer is used for simplicity and economy. The impedance of the transformer winding is much higher than that of the choke and so initially most of the supply voltage is applied across the ends of the lamp. The secondary tappings on the transformer winding produce an initial voltage of about 12 V across each cathode and hence a rapid rise to emission temperature.

In addition the electric field set up between the cathodes and the adjacent earthed metalwork helps to ionize the gas in the arc path and the lamp strikes. Once the lamp has struck the lamp current passes through the choke and causes a reduction in voltage across the auto-transformer. This reduces the cathode heating.

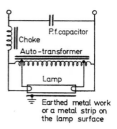

FIG. 6.11. Circuit using a voltage-fed cathode-heating transformer.

The transformer is designed to have a high reactance and so there is no air-gap, but otherwise the materials used are similar to those described in the section on choke design. A small ceramic radio-interference suppressor capacitor is normally fitted inside the transformer housing so that when the circuit is connected, it is across the ends of the lamp. A twin lamp circuit employing a current transformer for cathode heating is shown in Fig. 6.12.

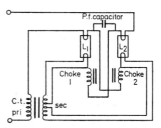

FIG. 6.12. Circuit using a current-fed cathode heating transformer.

The current-fed cathode heating transformer must have a primary winding capable of carrying the supply current to the lamp and separate secondary windings to carry the cathode heating currents.

Choke 1 is connected to the neutral via the cathode of lamp (L_2) and its circuit is completed through the lamp (L_1), and the current transformer primary. Choke 2 is connected to the line via the cathode of lamp (L_1) and the primary of the current transformer, and its circuit is completed through the lamp (L_2).

When the supply is switched on the choke circuits are not in operation (the lamps being out) and so the power factor correction capacitor governs the current flowing through the primary of the current transformer and two of the lamp cathodes. The current in the primary produces a corresponding current in each of the secondaries and so provides heating current for the other two cathodes. When the lamps strike the choke circuits are completed and the chokes are in effect placed in parallel with the p.f. correction capacitor. The lagging component of the current passing through the chokes compensates the leading current taken by the capacitor and the current from the mains is reduced. This in turn reduces the level of cathode heating at both ends of each lamp.

Semi-resonant Starting Circuit

Some of the circuits for controlling fluorescent lamps have already been described. One which has been revived with the introduction of the 5 ft. 65 W fluorescent tube is the semi-resonant start circuit (Fig. 6.13). The starting conditions are indicated in the vector diagram given in Fig. 6.14.

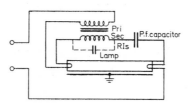

FIG. 6.13. Semi-resonant starting circuit.

With the lamp out the current in the primary and the secondary is the same. They are wound in opposition so that their voltages almost cancel. The capacitor voltage is therefore approximately equal to the mains voltage (i.e. $V_c \approx V_m$). However, a local circuit is formed by the secondary winding and the capacitor. In this local circuit the induced secondary voltage (V_s) is added to the capacitor voltage (V_c), since it is in antiphase with the primary voltage. The tube voltage therefore exceeds the mains voltage, being about 280 V on 240 V mains.

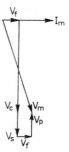

FIG. 6.14. Starting conditions for semi-resonant circuit. I_m = mains current. V_f = filament voltage. V_m = mains voltage. V_p = primary voltage. V_s = secondary voltage.

When the lamp is running the primary current is the vector sum of the capacitor current and the lamp current. The secondary current is simply the capacitor current. Because of the phase and magnitude differences in the two currents the capacitor and secondary voltages are no longer in phase. Under this condition the primary acts as a choke for the lamp.

As in other circuits an earthed starting strip or surface is used. An HRC fuse is usually fitted to protect against capacitor failure, and a small radio interference suppressor capacitor is placed across the secondary winding.

The Leakage Flux Transformer

Some lamps such as the U-tube sodium type are started by means of a step-up transformer. Current limitation is still necessary and so the leakage flux transformer combines the functions of a voltage transformer and a choke.

In a transformer some of the flux produced by the primary winding does not link the secondary winding. This "leakage" flux finds a return path in the space between the primary and secondary windings. Similarly, when current flows in the secondary, part of the resultant MMF also produces leakage flux. The leakage fluxes generate e.m.f.s in the primary and secondary windings, which cause volt drops and reduce the output voltage.

In ordinary transformers this voltage loss is undesirable, and the secondary and primary are wound close together to reduce the leakage flux.

In the leakage flux transformer, the primary and secondary are separated to increase the leakage. The reluctance of the main leakage path can be reduced by inserting additional laminations as magnetic shunts (Fig. 6.15).

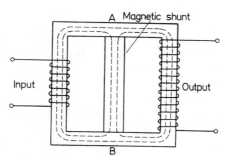

FIG. 6.15. Leakage transformer.

These shunts simply reduce the reluctance between points A and B and so the flux through the secondary winding is unaltered when on open circuit. The volt-drop caused by the no-load current is negligible and the full secondary voltage is obtained at the output terminals. Once the lamp strikes the load current flowing in each winding causes a large volt-drop. Thus the leakage flux transformer produces a large voltage regulation, and it is this feature which makes it suitable for the control of discharge lamps.

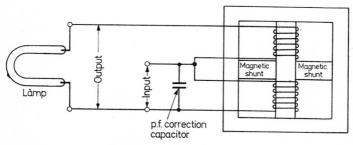

FIG. 6.16. Auto-transformer.

Compared with choke and starter switch control it has the disadvantages of greater cost, bulk, and lower power factor. However, it is used where lamp design precludes the use of a starter switch and choke. To reduce the cost an auto-transformer version is employed in many circuits, but the principle of operation is similar to that described above (Fig. 6.16).

HIGH-FREQUENCY OPERATION

The inductive reactance of a choke is given by the equation $X_L = 2\pi f L$, where L is the inductance in Henrys and f the frequency of the supply in cps. The higher the value of f the smaller the value required for L to give a specified value of inductive reactance. Reducing L enables the amount of choke material to be reduced, and the result is a much smaller and lighter choke. The efficiency of a fluorescent lamp also increases with increase in supply frequency. The gains achieved in this way are partly offset by the necessity to use higher grade magnetic materials.

A number of high-frequency installations have been put into operation, mainly in the United States. The disadvantage of high-frequency operation is the need for a frequency converter, and at the time of writing it is not generally considered economic. However, considerable use is made of inverters, which change direct current supplies to high-frequency alternating current (up to 10 kc/s) for transport purposes (see section on direct current operation of fluorescent lamps). High-frequency operation produces conditions more favourable to capacitor ballasts and these are sometimes used.

DIMMING

The light output from fluorescent lamps can be controlled by means of dimmers provided that the cathodes at each end of the lamp can be kept at emission temperature. A simple dimming circuit is shown in Fig. 6.17.

The lamp is choke controlled as in an "instant start" or "quick start" type of circuit, but the cathode heating transformer is fed direct from the mains so that the voltages on the secondaries are independent of the lamp voltage. The lamp voltage may then be reduced by means of a series resistance. Dimming circuits employing thyratrons have been used in large installations to reduce the dimmer power loss, and recently silicon controlled rectifiers (thyristors) have replaced thyratrons because they are smaller and more robust. Another method is to employ saturable reactors to control the main circuit current.

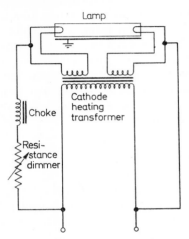

FIG. 6.17. Dimming circuit.

DIRECT CURRENT OPERATION

Fluorescent discharge lamps may be operated from a direct current supply, but the necessity to use a resistive ballast introduces very high power losses in the ballast. In addition the migration of positively charged mercury ions towards the cathode (cataphoresis) results in low light output from the anode end of the lamp. For this reason, when the lamps are operated directly from a d.c. supply, it is necessary to incorporate a reversing switch in the circuit to change the direction of the current through the lamp every few hours. When a resistance ballast is used the choke is still required in order to produce the inductive voltage surge when the starter switch contacts open.

For many purposes it is better to use an inverter and change the direct current into a high frequency alternating current (up to 10 kc/s). The design of suitable inverters has been simplified by the advent of the power transistor and this method of operation is used extensively in trains, aircraft and motor vehicles.[5]

HEAT DISSIPATION

Throughout the foregoing sections, reference has been made to the permissible operating temperatures for the various components. These temperatures are determined mainly by safety considerations.

Overheating damages the electrical insulation, and hot metalwork or glass may cause burns to anyone touching the fitting. In some atmospheres an overheated fitting may ignite inflammable gases or dust. Plastic enclosures can be distorted by overheating and this would spoil the appearance and performance of a fitting.

All the electrical energy absorbed by the lamp, and sometimes the control gear as well, must be dissipated at the fitting. The possible methods of heat dissipation and hence reduction in the operating temperature of the fitting are:

1. Radiation.
2. Convection.
3. Conduction.

Most of the heat is removed from the fitting by radiation and convection, although conduction often provides the solution to the problem of removing heat from particular components within the fitting.

The amount of radiation per unit area is governed by the emissivity of the metalwork of the fitting. Painting increases the emissivity, though the colour of the paint makes little difference in this respect. The radiation may be increased by making the enclosure larger. This also increases the surface area from which heat can be removed by convection.

The extent to which a glass or plastic enclosure is heated by the source radiation depends upon the spectral distribution of the source and the transmission factor of the enclosure to that particular range of radiation. It is found that some discharge lamps cause greater heating than tungsten lamps because they produce a larger proportion of long wavelength infrared radiation.

Whenever possible ventilation should be provided so that convection currents of air may pass through the fitting. Ventilation of fluorescent fitting often results in a better light-output ratio, since it helps to maintain the lamps close to their optimum operating temperature (about 40 °C).

In outdoor fittings over-cooling will reduce the light-output ratio.

COMBINED LIGHTING AND VENTILATING SYSTEMS

Where high levels of illumination are used, a substantial amount of heat is produced by the lighting fittings. This can be usefully employed in warming the working space when the outside temperature is low, but has to be removed when the outside temperature is high. The necessary temperature control can be effected by ducting air through the lighting fittings. When illumination levels are high these are nearly always fluorescent, so that combining the lighting and ventilating systems also allows the temperature of the tubes and control gear to be controlled. An added advantage of the combined system is that separate intakes or outlets for the ventilating system do not have to be made in the ceiling.

The air can either be drawn in through the fitting[6] (Fig. 6.18a) or through ducts separate to the fitting (Fig. 6.18b). The dis-

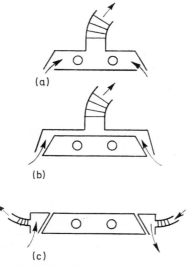

FIG. 6.18. Air-handling fittings.

advantage of the first system is that the deposition of dirt is likely to be very much greater. Figure 6.18(c) shows a system that enables air to be extracted and conditioned air to be given out at the same time.

Fittings have been made with ducts (Fig. 6.19) through which cooled water is circulated. Systems using these are very expensive.

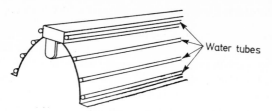

FIG. 6.19. Water-cooled fitting.

FLAME-PROOF FITTINGS

The design of this type of fitting is highly specialized and there are certain stringent requirements to be met. BS 229: 1957 divides the flammable gases and vapour into four groups, namely:

Group I. Methane.

Group II. Petroleum vapours and some industrial gases and vapours.

Group IIIb. Town gas and coke-oven gas.

Group IV. Hydrogen and acetylene.

The Ministry of Power have a testing station of Buxton where fittings are type-tested and given a flame-proof certificate and number if they prove acceptable.

The British Standard for flame-proof electric light fittings is BS:889, and this should be consulted for detailed requirements. Some of these may be listed as follows:

1. An internal explosion must not ignite an external inflammable atmosphere.
2. An internal explosion must not break the fitting or the glass.
3. The fitting must not become hot enough to ignite the external inflammable atmosphere. The limiting temperature is 50 °C for ambient temperatures between 15 °C and 35 °C.
4. The terminal box and lamp housing must be separately flame-proof, and a flame-proof seal must be provided where the leads pass from one to the other.

Fittings designed to meet the requirements listed in BS 889 are usually very heavy, with thick metal flanges and cooling fins. The glass used has to be specially toughened and tested. For these reasons flame-proof fittings are expensive.

Only the simplest of reflectors or refractors are used in flame-proof fittings, since the more complex forms of control would greatly increase the cost of the fitting.

TESTS

In order to ensure that the lighting fitting is electrically and mechanically safe, and will withstand the conditions for which it is designed, it should pass the various tests laid down in BS. 3820 : 1964 for general purpose lighting fittings. Other British Standard Specifications cover the more specialized classes of fittings: BS 1788/1964 for street lanterns, BS 3541 for hospital lighting fittings, and so on as listed in BS 3820.

In BS 3820 there are thirty-nine clauses detailing tests and checks which the fitting must pass. Not every type of fitting has to pass all the tests; the tests which are appropriate to the type of fitting being tested are given in a table. It is unnecessary to describe all of them here, but some of the more interesting ones have been selected to indicate the range and comprehensiveness of the specification.

Constructional and Dimensional

The tests in this section are designed to ensure that the fitting is mechanically sound. Fixing arrangements must be strong enough to support the weight of the fitting and any additional load that may be imposed on the fitting during installation. Assembly, installation, and maintenance must be able to be carried out without unduly stressing the fixing holes. Surfaces must be suitably protected to withstand corrosion, and the materials of which the fitting is made must not deteriorate during normal life.

Requirements of Enclosures

In this section tests for drip-proof, rain-proof, jet-proof, water-tight, submersible, dust-proof, and dust-tight fittings are described.

The rain-proof test, which is applicable to street lanterns as well as to other outdoor fittings, is carried out with the apparatus shown in Fig. 6.20 (facing p. 216). The semicircular tube, which sprays jets of water, is oscillated about an angle of 60° from the downward vertical. At the end of a specified time water must not have accumulated in the fitting if it is a street lantern. And for other fittings any accumulation of water must not interfere with its operation.

Jet-proof fittings are subjected to a jet of water of specified pressure, and water must not enter the fitting when the drain holes are closed.

Watertight fittings are tested by submersion after being run until their temperature exceeds that of the water by 5–10 °C, and the lamps switched off.

Figure 6.21 (facing p. 217) shows the apparatus used for the dust-proof test. Talcum powder is circulated outside the fitting, which has air drawn through it.

Electrical Requirements

The electrical requirements are concerned mainly with safety.[7] All metal parts which may become accidentally alive must be connected to earth. Live parts, except the lamp-holders, must be provided with covers and these must withstand reasonable mechanical forces. Electrical insulation between live parts and all external parts must be adequate to prevent electric shock and electrical breakdown. The insulation resistance is tested by applying 500 V between the conductors and the external metal parts. The resistance must not be less than 2 MΩ. When a specified alternating voltage is applied breakdown or flashover must not take place. The specified voltage varies from 250 V to 3500 V according to the class of fitting.

Thermal Requirements

These are to ensure that no part of the fitting becomes excessively hot.

The fitting is suspended in a special chamber. The ceiling and at least three of the walls of this are double. The walls are made of metal perforated with holes 2 mm in diameter. Fittings are suspended in the normal working position, ceiling and wall mounted fittings being fixed to a matt black wooden board.

The temperature measurements are made with fine wire thermocouples held in position by either mechanical clamping under

FIG. 6.20. Rain-proof test apparatus. (*By courtesy of Atlas Lighting Ltd.*)

FIG. 6.21. Dust-proof apparatus. The air filter to the pump, the manometer, and rate of air flow gauge (left to right) can be seen on the right. These are connected to the fitting. (*By courtesy of Atlas Lighting Ltd.*)

existing screws, soldering, adhesive, or special mechanical holders. The temperature of supporting surfaces (such as the black painted ceiling or wall) is measured by attaching a black copper disc to the thermocouple and sinking it to the level of the surface.

The e.m.f. developed by the thermocouple is measured by a potentiometer. The cold junction is kept in a Dewar vessel containing a suitable liquid to prevent rapid changes in temperature. The temperature rise is found by subtracting the ambient temperature in the enclosure from the sum of the cold junction temperature and the measured rise of the thermocouple.

During the tests the temperature of the chamber must be kept at 25 ± 5 °C. The lighting fittings must be equipped with cables, reflectors, and the like. Lamps must be selected according to the relevant British Standards; filament lamps and discharge lamps (other than fluorescent) being run at rated wattage, and fluorescent lamps being run at rated voltage.

Temperatures of the incoming supply cable, lamp cap, and other components and touchable parts must not exceed the specified limits.

Photometric

The methods for carrying these out are given in Chapter 7.

REFERENCES

1. KEEN, J. and STEPHENSON, H. F., *Trans. I.E.S. (London)* **27**, 45 (1962).
2. STEVENS, R. W., *Trans. I.E.S. (London)* **25**, 151 (1960).
3. VAN DUSEN, V. A., Optical plastics applications in street lighting luminaires, Preprint No. 32, *Illum. Engng. (N.Y.)* 1965.
4. STEVENS, R. W., *Trans. I.E.S. (London)* **25**, 152 (1960).
5. DAVIES, I. F. and DUNTHORNE, D., *J.I.E.E.* **6**, 227 (1960).
6. ROBERTS, G. G., *J. Inst. Heat. Vent. Engrs.* **31**, 349 (1964).
7. *Regulations for Electrical Equipment of Buildings*, I.E.E., 14th ed., 1966.

CHAPTER 7

PHOTOMETRIC MEASUREMENTS

ACCURACY

In taking photometric measurements on fittings we want to achieve results that are as accurate as possible. But in reaching an idea of the accuracy we need, we have to bear in mind the use to which the data will be put. It is obviously wasteful both of time and money to try to make measurements having a degree of accuracy that bears no relation to what is required in the field.

For instance, most of the readings taken on indoor fittings are used to calculate utilization factors, and from these illumination values in lighting installations. Even if the polar curves are very accurate it has to be recognized that the utilization factors may have a degree of inaccuracy amounting to 10% owing to assumptions made in their derivation. Then, in the lighting installation itself, the lighting engineer will probably not be able to measure reflection factors accurately, and in any case it is doubtful if he will be able to allow for windows and furniture accurately. Other sources of error can be caused by variations in lamp output and voltage fluctuation, tolerances in the lighting fittings themselves, and fluctuations in temperature with fluorescent fittings.

All this is not to advocate inaccurate photometry, but, rather, a sensible degree of accuracy. Obviously to try to obtain an accuracy of $\pm 0.1\%$ in the measurement of light output ratio would be a waste of time and money. It could be argued, however, that it may be useful to obtain an accuracy of $\pm 1\%$ not so much for calculation purposes but for comparison purposes.

It is the object of this chapter to describe the experimental procedures and apparatus necessary to achieve this degree of accuracy. Obviously meticulous attention to experimental procedures and first-class apparatus are needed.

THE PHOTOCELL

Except, perhaps, for luminance measurements, measurements by visual comparisons have been completely superseded in routine laboratory work by those taken by photocell. This demise of visual photometry has taken place because the photocell allows the measurements to be taken faster and reduces the tedium associated with photometric work. Also, provided certain precautions are taken, the photoelectric cell is more accurate and consistent. The two types of photocell used in photometry of fittings are the photovoltaic and the photoemissive cell. The former is by far the most usual because of the simplicity of its associated circuits, and will be described first.

THE PHOTOVOLTAIC CELL

The construction of the photovoltaic cell,[1] also known as the barrier-layer or rectifier cell, is shown in Fig. 7.1.

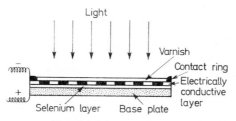

FIG. 7.1. Photovoltaic cell.

The base plate, usually steel or aluminium, carries a layer of metallic selenium, which is light sensitive. The electrically conductive layer, applied over the selenium layer, is sufficiently thin to allow light to reach the selenium. But at the same time it is electrically continuous because it acts as the negative pole. In modern cells it consists of cadmium oxide, though gold and platinum have been used in the past. It is applied by sputtering.

The base plate forms the positive contact, and a strip of Wood's metal sprayed onto the edge of the top surface forms the negative contact. The front surface of the cell is protected by a transparent varnish.

8*

The action of the light is to release electrons from the upper surface of the selenium. These maintain a flow of current through an external circuit connected between the positive and negative contacts.

Normally the cell is used in a mount providing spring contacts to the base plate and a negative contact strip. To minimize the obstruction of obliquely incident light the projection of the mount in front of the cell should be as small as possible. In a more robust construction, the potted photocell, wires are soldered to the contacts on the photocell and the whole is cast in Araldite resin. Besides eliminating possible trouble due to faulty spring contacts, this construction is more proof against deleterious atmospheric conditions.

Spectral Response

The spectral response of the photovoltaic cell has its peak sensitivity at approximately the same wavelength as that of the eye. On either side of this it is more sensitive than the eye, but it is possible to obtain fairly good correction by means of a gelatine filter marketed especially for the purpose.

TABLE 7.1. COMPARISON OF SPECTRAL SENSITIVITY OF MEGATRON TYPES M AND MF CELLS WITH CIE CURVE

Wavelength (μ)	Type M cell	MF cell-filter combination	CIE curve
0·40	1·42	0·13	0·04
0·42	2·68	1·06	0·4
0·44	4·45	2·95	2·3
0·46	6·9	6·15	6·0
0·48	13·9	13·6	14
0·50	38·6	39	32·2
0·52	74	76	71·4
0·54	94	97	95·7
0·56	100	100	100
0·58	91	87	87·6
0·60	70·5	64	63
0·62	46·2	40	38
0·64	23	18·9	17·6
0·66	11	8·8	6·1
0·68	5·8	4·5	1·7
0·70	3·7	2·9	0·41

(By courtesy of Megatron Ltd.)

Megatron produce two types of cells, the M and MF, with excellent correction. Table 7.1 compares the irperformance with the CIE curve. They also produce a cell that matches the CIE Standard Observer for Scotopic Vision very closely.

These cells give such excellent correction that it is far better to use them than use uncorrected cells and apply correction factors. However, a list of correction factors is given below for Megatron type B cells in order to give an idea of the order of correction involved. They should be used cautiously since they vary from make to make of cell, and the names by which manufacturers refer to colours of fluorescent tubes do not always agree.

Light source	Factor
Tungsten	1·00
Mercury 80 W and 125 W	1·25
Mercury 250 W and 400 W	1·33
Sodium	1·37
Fluorescent daylight	1·06
Fluorescent warm white	1·15

Sensitivity

It is essential in photometry that the current output of the photocell should be proportional to the illumination (unless the photocell galvanometer combination is specially calibrated). As can be seen from Fig. 7.2, this requirement is most nearly achieved when the circuit resistance is low. Actually, the graphs tend to mask small departures from linearity and for the most accurate work the illumination should not be allowed to rise above 25 lumens/ft^2, as well as which the circuit resistance should effectively be zero.

Cell size also affects linearity. The closest approach to linearity is obtained by using the smallest cell compatible with obtaining sufficient current to be properly measured.[2] For with such a cell, the resistance of the electrically conducting film is at a minimum. Also, since the current is small, the voltage drop due to the circuit resistance will be kept down. Hence large cells are not so much useful for obtaining a large output at high levels of illumination, as for obtaining sufficient current to measure at low levels.

Figure 7.2 substantiates these facts. When the circuit resistance is 100 Ω, the output is very nearly proportional to the cell size. But when the circuit resistance is 3000 Ω the output is only doubled at 25 lumens/ft² and is hardly increased at all at 200 lumens/ft²,

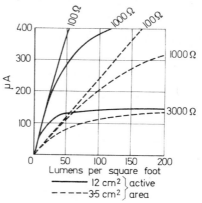

Fig. 7.2. Effect of circuit resistance on sensitivity of photovoltaic cell.
(*By courtesy of Megatron Ltd.*)

Effect of Temperature

The output of the barrier layer cell varies with temperature, but the variation is least when the circuit resistance is zero. This fact provides another reason for using a low circuit resistance.

Fluctuating Light Sources

The output of all light sources varies on the a.c. mains with the periodicity of the cycle. Fortunately, the photocell obeys Talbot's law and the current will correspond to the average value of illumination providing that the characteristics of the galvanometer are such that the indication is steady. There is a departure from this at high values of circuit resistance and also if the frequency of interruption is low.

Oblique Light Incidence

At angles of incidence above 60° or so, the lacquer tends to reflect a significant amount of light, which, therefore, does not reach the selenium layer. Thus the reading is less than it should be according to the cosine law of illumination. At 60° the error is about 10% increasing to 40% at 85°. For a hemispherical sky[3] the error is stated to be from 8% to 10% for a cell calibrated with normally incident light.

Some compensation for this cosine error, as it is usually called, can be made by using a matt lacquer. A more refined method is to omit the lacquer and cover the cell with a hemispherical dome of transparent plastic (Fig. 7.42, facing p. 265). Unfortunately, if the light is parallel to the cell surface the dome will reflect some of the light on to the photocell. But otherwise the error is small and is only 10% at 85°. In applications where the light is incident at all angles the error would be negligible.

Opal perspex with a matt surface provides another alternative, when it is placed over the cell. At high angles of incidence, however, it reflects the light specularly so that the reading is too low. This can be compensated for by allowing the light to reach the cell through the edges of the perspex. The readings at very high angles will then be too high, but can be corrected by using a screening ring as in the construction[3] shown in Fig. 7.3. This gives a good correction over the whole range of angles.

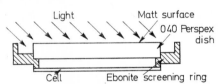

FIG. 7.3. Correction device for oblique light incidence.

When only one light source is being measured, as is usually the case in a photometric laboratory, the most accurate method of compensating for the reflection loss is to tilt the cell so that the light is incident normally. The readings are then multiplied by the cosine of the angle of the tilt. However, this method is valid only if the source can be regarded as a point.

Uniformity Over Cell Surface

Owing to the resistance of the electrically conductive layer, the sensitivity of the cell varies over its surface, the centre being the least sensitive area. Care should therefore be taken to ensure that the whole of the cell is illuminated otherwise incorrect readings may result.

Fatigue

Cells vary in the amount of fatigue they show. Generally speaking, a cell that is short circuited and exposed to a high level of illumination will drop a little in output after reaching its maximum, but after being on open circuit the output will increase a little.[4] Both these effects are reversible and the cell will recover its original properties after a while.

Another undesirable property is that an unilluminated photocell that is subsequently exposed to light may take a minute or so to reach its final value. This effect is especially pronounced when the level of illumination is low.

The Equivalent Circuit

This[5] is shown in Fig. 7.4. g is a perfect photoelectric generator which produces a current i_g proportional to the illumination, C is the effective capacitance of the cell, R_s its series resistance, and r the equivalent of the barrier-layer resistance. R is the resistance of the external circuit.

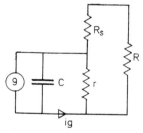

FIG. 7.4. Equivalent circuit of photovoltaic cell.

The undersiable properties of non-linearity, temperature dependance, and fatigue can be partly attributed to the variation of r with illumination and temperature. These effects can therefore be reduced by making the effect of R and R_s as small as possible so that r is short-circuited. Methods of doing this will be discussed under the following section on circuits.

Circuits

In considering the suitability of different types of circuit for use with the photovoltaic cell, there are two restrictions which must be taken into account. Firstly, if the linearity of the photocell is to be preserved, the effective resistance of the circuit must be as small as possible. Secondly, any shunts that are used should not have such a low resistance that the galvanometer is unduly damped.

A circuit[6] with a variable shunt is shown in Fig. 7.5(a). The values of resistance marked are suitable for use with a galvanometer G of internal resistance $50\,\Omega$ and critical damping resistance

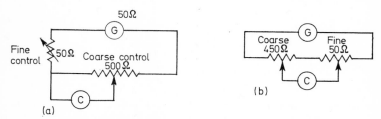

FIG. 7.5. Simple circuits for use with photovoltaic cells.

$500\,\Omega$. It will be noted that variation of the fine control does alter the damping resistance, but only to such a small extent that it has no discernible effect. The maximum resistance that the cell looks into occurs when the coarse control approaches its mid-point position. In the circuit shown this amounts to about $150\,\Omega$ which is sufficiently low for most purposes.

Figure 7.5(b) shows an alternative circuit in which the galvanometer looks into a constant resistance.

For more accurate work a circuit presenting zero resistance to the photocell should be used. The drawback of this type of circuit is that a balancing operation has to be carried out every time a reading is taken, which is a time-consuming and tedious process if numerous readings have to be taken. The basic circuit is shown in Fig. 7.6 and is due to Campbell and Freeth.[7]

P is a potentiometer which is used to balance the current flowing through the galvanometer G from the cell C. The arrows indicate the direction of the Maxwell circulating currents, and it can be seen that if the polarity of C is such that it drives the current from X to Y, P must be arranged to drive it in the reverse direction.

To operate the circuit, P is adjusted until G shows a null deflection, the two currents then being equal. When this balance is achieved the potential at X is the same as that at Y, and C is effectively short-circuited. The short-circuit current can either be read

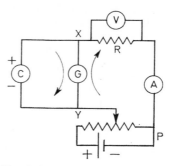

Fig. 7.6. Campbell–Freeth circuit.

directly by an ammeter A or a voltmeter V across the resistance R. For greater precision V can be replaced by a potentiometer, which by suitable switching can use the galvanometer G to economize on instruments. In another variant V and A are both omitted and P is a calibrated potentiometer that measures the voltage across R as well as supplying the balancing current. Since, however, it is supplying current R must be made large enough so that its calibrations are not upset. In the circuit[8] shown in Fig. 7.7 an economy

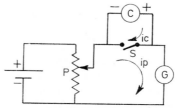

Fig. 7.7. A variation of the Campbell–Freeth circuit.

of instruments is effected by using a short-circuit key S across the cell C. P is an uncalibrated potentiometer which is adjusted until depression of S does not affect the reading of G. When this balance point is obtained the current (i_p) flowing through S and due to

P must be equal and opposite to that (i_C) due to C, and, therefore, G registers the short-circuit current of C.

In all these variations of the Campbell–Freeth circuit the resistance, and, therefore, the sensitivity, of the galvanometer can be as high as desired without upsetting the linearity of the photocell, since this is working under short-circuit conditions when balance is obtained.

A circuit designed by Wyatt[5] is more accurate than the Campbell–Freeth since it eliminates the effect of the resistance R_s and r (Fig. 7.4) of the cell, and the short-circuit current of g is measured.

The circuit (Fig. 7.8) is of the bridge type. $ABCD$ represents the bridge. The cell is in the arm AB (the symbols meaning the

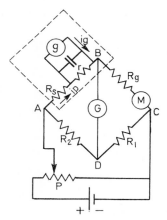

FIG. 7.8. The Wyatt circuit.

same as in Fig. 7.4) and is shown enclosed by the dotted line. G is a galvanometer. M is a meter for measuring the current flowing in BC. P is a potentiometer for adjusting the current flowing in the arms of the bridge. The polarity of the battery is arranged so that it opposes the current flow of the current from g, in r.

The resistors R_g, R_1, and R_2 are chosen so that $R_g/R_s = R_1/R_2$. For convenience, R_1 and R_g can be made equal, in which case R_2 must be made equal to R_s.

When illumination is falling on the photocell, a balance can only be obtained when the voltage drop across r is zero, that is, when g is short-circuited. This is the condition that we want for the best linearity. It will only occur when the current i_g flowing through r and generated by g is equal and opposite to that current i_p generated by P; that is, when $i_g = i_p$. G will then show a null deflection since the bridge will be balanced. The current in AB (i_p) will be equal to that in BC, and can be measured by M.

The value of R_2 has to be found in a preliminary experiment by determining which value of it gives the best linearity. Wyatt found that to get best results its value has to be altered according to the range of illumination values being measured.

A circuit in which the photocell current is only partially balanced out is shown in Fig. 7.9. The Mallory cell drives the

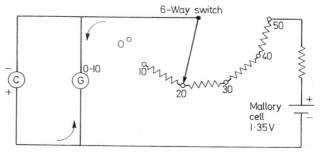

Fig. 7.9. The Harrison circuit.

current in opposition to the photocell current. The 6-way switch is rotated until the galvanometer gives a deflection on the scale (that is the deflection must not be negative or greater than full scale). The indication shown by the galvanometer is then equal to the out of balance current and is added to the indication of the switch. When the switch is at zero the galvanometer is direct reading. This circuit has the advantages of effectively increasing the scale length from 10 cm to 60 cm, and of eliminating the tedium of the balancing operation. The voltage of the Mallory cell should be checked periodically. Also, if the photocell is changed, the new one must have a resistance that is suitable for the circuit. This circuit is used on instruments marketed by W. Harrison.

In order to operate an automatic recording instrument such as a milliammeter driving a pen over a moving roll, it is necessary to amplify the output from the photocell. But unfortunately this presents difficulties because of the cell's comparatively low resistance and the inherent instability associated with d.c. amplifiers that rely solely on electronic means. Conversion of the current into a.c., so that an a.c. amplifier can be used, may not be feasible if the light falling on the photocell is intermittent. There are, however, various d.c. amplifiers on the market that can be used with photocells and these usually rely on some other means than electronic for their mode of operation.

Digital voltmeters, especially those which provide an automatic print-out, are becoming popular, but even with these it may be necessary to use an amplifier to get sufficient voltage.[9]

PHOTOEMISSIVE CELL

The photoemissive cell is capable of better linearity and greater stability than the photovoltaic cell and its use should be considered where greater precision is required. However, it suffers from the drawback that its associated circuit is more complicated and involves the use of some sort of valve amplifier.

The production of electric current by the photoemissive cell depends on the action of light in releasing electrons from the cathode. To draw the electrons towards the anode, its potential is made some 30–50 V higher than that of the cathode by connecting an appropriate source of potential across the cell.

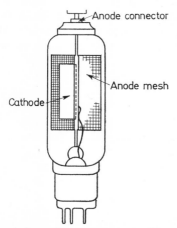

FIG. 7.10. Photoemissive cell: vacuum type. (*By courtesy of Rank Electronic Tubes.*)

Theoretically, the rate of emission of electrons should be proportional to the illumination, providing that this is of constant spectral composition. But to ensure that the response of the cell as a whole is linear, the cathode must be electrically continuous and the electric field uniform. This latter requirement rules out the use of cathodes that are directly deposited on to the glass envelope, since some of the cathode material is inevitably deposited beyond the boundary of the area intended to receive it.[2] As these outlying parts will not be in good electrical contact with the cathode proper they may attain a potential such that emission from them is reduced when they are called upon to produce relatively high currents.

In order to achieve a uniform field and an electrically continuous cathode, the anode is best made of a cylindrical wire mesh with the cathode placed in its axis. This construction is adopted in the Rank Electronic Tubes type VB shown in Fig. 7.10, which has a Bi–O–Ag–Cs cathode.

Spectral Response

The spectral response of this cell does not match that of the eye. However, by using a suitable solution of cupric chloride and potassium dichromate to correct respectively the blue and red ends of the response, and cobalt ammonium sulphate to correct the region around 500 mμ, a very good match can be obtained.[10] The solution is contained in a cell held in front of the photoemissive cell. A typical residual error curve is shown in Fig. 7.11. For the photometry of specific lamps such as mercury and sodium

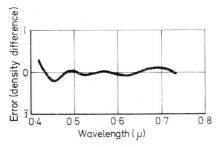

Fig. 7.11. Final residual error curve after correction by cupric chloride, potassium dichromate, and cobalt ammonium sulphate. (*By courtesy of the Director of the NPL.*)

vapour, fluorescent lamps, and tungsten lamps at various colour temperatures, better correction can be obtained if most attention is paid to the middle of the spectrum since the ends are relatively unimportant. The use of this compromise technique gives a very good degree of correction.

Circuit

The circuit is of the current balancing type, and is shown in Fig. 7.12(a). A galvanometer alone is not sensitive enough to

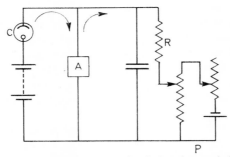

FIG. 7.12 (a). Current balancing circuit for photoemissive cell.

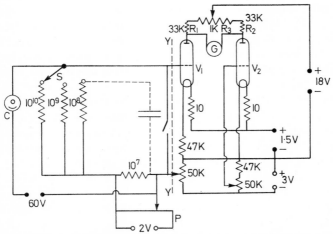

FIG. 7.12(b). D.C. amplifier for use with photoemissive cell. (*By courtesy of the Director of the NPL.*)

detect the balance point and a valve amplifier has to be used. In Fig. 7.12(a) the photocell C with its accompanying batteries generate a current in the clockwise direction, whereas the potentiometer P generates a current in the opposite direction to produce a balance, indicated by a galvanometer fed from the valve amplifier A. Since P is supplying current, its resistance should be small compared with that of R so that its calibration is not upset. This high resistance also increases the sensitivity of the system.

The fluctuating intensity of discharge lamps may generate a ripple in the current from the photocell. This could possibly cause an error in the null indication of A. It can be eliminated by connecting a capacitor as shown.

Before measurements can be taken, the dark current has to be balanced out by setting P at zero and adjusting A until the galvanometer shows no deflection. When the cell is illuminated, the measurement is taken by adjusting P until the galvanometer once more shows a null deflection. Under this condition the reading is proportional to the additional current generated by illuminating the photocell.

Many amplifier circuits[10] have been devised, and a typical one developed by the NPL is shown in Fig. 7.12(b). The switch S provides ranges of sensitivity. The amplifier itself is on the right-hand side of the line YY. It is basically a Wheatstone bridge circuit, the galvanometer G indicating the balance position. V_1 and V_2 (ET3, ME 1401, or ME 103) are electrometer triodes (triodes having a very high input resistance to avoid diverting current from the grid leak resistor), which provide two arms of the bridge. Resistors R_1 and R_2 together with the other variable one R_3, provide the other two arms.

The out of balance current in the left-hand circuit changes the grid bias of V_1 thus altering its effective resistance. This is of course registered by G. The dark current is balanced out by adjusting R_3 with P set to zero. Thenceforth when the light falls on the photocell the balance is restored by adjusting P, as described above.

Great care must be taken in the choice of components. The two valves should be matched as closely as possible, final equality being obtained by adjusting the grid bias. The resistors must be of the "gold–pink" tolerance–stability quality, but the grid coupling ones of values 10^{10}, 10^9, and 10^8 Ω must be of the highest quality obtainable, with low temperature coefficients.

The circuit must be screened to avoid stray disturbances being picked up. Also no light should be allowed to reach the triodes since these are sensitive to light. Silica gel should be placed in the screened boxes to avoid leakage paths caused by condensation. If the various boxes are separate, they should be connected by screened leads and earthed if they are metal.

Photocell Housing

Since the cathode does not have uniform sensitivity over its surface, and in any case would not respond to the cosine law of illumination owing to its configuration, it is necessary to house the photocell in a box with a diffusing screen. The spectral transmission characteristics of the diffusing screen must be taken into account in calculating the colour correction filter for the photocell.

TESTING LINEARITY OF PHOTOCELLS

The linearity of photocells can be tested on a photometric bench, but this method is not very convenient. The following method enables the photocell and its associated circuit to be tested on the apparatus on which it is being used.[11] A number of lamps are mounted in an internally whitened box having an aperture, which is preferably covered with a diffuser. The procedure is to check that a reading obtained with any combination of lamps is equal to the sum of the readings obtained with the individual lamps. This method enables the linearity to be checked for a range of illumination levels varying from that obtained with one lamp to that obtained with all the lamps.

DISTRIBUTION PHOTOMETRY

The object of distribution photometry is to find how the luminous intensity varies round a lighting fitting in order to plot polar curves, isocandela diagrams, and calculate the performance of the fitting. Generally speaking the type of apparatus needed for testing indoor fittings and street lanterns is the same, whereas floodlights may need special apparatus with a long light path.

Before describing the various types of distribution photometer we will discuss the problems which arise in distribution photometry.

1. Exclusion of Extraneous Light

It is very important that only the light that is to be measured is allowed to reach the photocell.

The exclusion of extraneous light is mainly achieved by using black baffles in front of the photocell so that its angle of view is restricted, as far as possible, to the cone of light from the lighting fitting. It is essential that every part of the photocell C (Fig. 7.13) is able to receive light from the whole of the fitting. It follows, there-

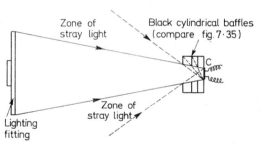

FIG. 7.13. The use of baffles for restricting the zone of stray light.

fore, that the edges of the photocell will have a field of view beyond that required (indicated by zone of stray light in the diagram). This can obviously be reduced by extending the baffled area as far from the photocell as possible. The use of black flock paper, velvet or black paint has then to be used to make the unwanted field of view as dark as possible.

Account has also to be taken of the fact that the photocell can "see" beyond the fitting, so that parts of the apparatus or walls that may reflect light must be properly darkened. The most practical way of finding what parts need attention is to view the fitting from the photocell position, any sources of stray light being noted. The bevelled edges of mirrors are apt to reflect light and should be blackened. Finally, as a check on the adequacy of the precautions, lights can be shone on to various parts of the apparatus, and surrounding building structure. Unwanted reflections will then be recorded by the galvanometer.

2. Length of Optical Path

It is essential that the optical path is made sufficiently long for the inverse-square law to apply to a reasonable degree of accuracy. There is much debate over what is a reasonable degree of accuracy and what path length is needed to give it.

One point is certain. The total, and up and down light output ratios, can be determined accurately at any distance no matter how short. This can best be understood by regarding the readings taken on the fitting (also bare lamp) as illumination values taken over specific areas of the surface of a sphere enclosing it. If these illumination values are multiplied by their respective areas the total flux will be found, since illumination times area equals flux (or lumens per square foot times area in square feet equal lumens).

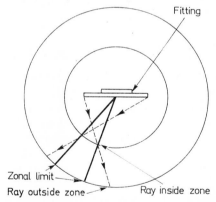

Fitting

Zonal limit

Ray outside zone

Ray inside zone

FIG. 7.14. Vertical section through concentric spheres enclosing lighting fitting.

The same is true of the up and down flux, provided the fitting is not deep compared with the test distance. However, it can be seen from Fig. 7.14 that the zonal flux will vary because rays of light will fall into different zones as the sphere size in increased.

Dunlop and Finch[12] have carried out experimental work in which they compared photometric data derived from polar curves taken at 10 and 40 ft on 8 and 4 ft fittings. In the worst case, the 8 ft fitting tested at 10 ft, the utilization factors did not differ by more than one unit in the second figure from those derived from the 40 ft data. However, there were quite considerable differences in the zonal lumens, as would be expected. In an extension of this work Riggs and Lampert,[13] who also compared polar curves taken at 10 and 40 ft on 8 ft fittings, showed that the accuracy of the transverse polar curve was good in most cases. Exceptions occurred at angles above about 75°. The axial polar curve was invariably markedly out, sometimes by as much as 30%. Their conclusion was that 10 ft photometry gives light output ratios and utilization factors that are accurate enough for practical purposes.

An argument often put forward as a justification of short-distance photometry is that since we are usually concerned with short lengths in actual installations, short distance photometry is the more meaningful. This is obviously erroneous, for all calculations depend on using true candelas. Thus, data derived by short-distance photometry could not be used to calculate accurate values of illumination by any of the usual point-to-point methods, such as the aspect factor method.

3. Position of Fitting During Test

The light output of fluorescent tubes varies with temperature, it being at a maximum between 15°C and 20°C. When the tubes are alight in the fitting they are usually working well above their optimum temperature. Hence there is a loss of light output which is sometimes considerable. Therefore, if the fitting is rotated about its own axis or mounted in other than its designed position, it is quite likely that heat will escape from it so increasing its light output.

Sodium lamps cannot be rotated about their own axis during test, otherwise the molten sodium will run round in the arc tube and is likely to run on to the electrodes. Mercury vapour lamps of the MA/V type must only be burnt vertically since convection currents bow the arc upwards on to the tube, fusing it.

For all these reasons, and because of ease of suspension of the fitting, it is better to test the fitting in the working position. Unfortunately, because of space limitations, it is often necessary to test fluorescent fittings in other positions. In such cases an allowance has to be made in one of the ways that will be described when we deal with distribution photometers.

4. Temperature Stabilization

It has already been noted that the output of fluorescent tubes varies with temperature, and it is, therefore, vital that the temperature of the test area is kept stable. Draughts should also be avoided since these can reduce the temperature of the tubes by carrying away the layers of hot air surrounding them.

LIGHT DISTRIBUTION PHOTOMETERS

Probably the most simple type of distribution photometer[14] is that shown in Fig. 7.15. The photocell housing travels around the fitting on a semicircular track, and its position is controlled

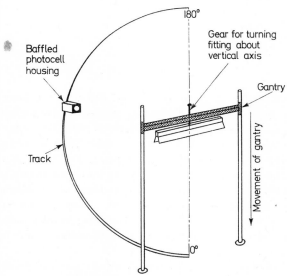

FIG. 7.15. Track distribution photometer.

by means of a flexible cable. The fitting can be rotated about a vertical axis so that a complete series of curves, at different angles of azimuth, can be taken. In order to facilitate the mounting of the fitting on the aparatus, the gear for turning the fitting is mounted on a gantry (as in the figure) or some sort of hoist so that it can be brought down to easy reaching distance.

In Fig. 7.16 the photocell housing is carried on an arm.[15] This arrangement can be space-saving compared with the simple track. For, if we want an optical path of 12 ft, say, then a head-room

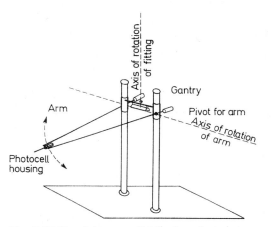

FIG. 7.16. Revolving arm distribution photometer.

of 24 ft is needed with the track system. But with the arm, intensities below the horizontal can be measured with the gantry in the top position and those above the horizontal with the gantry in the bottom position. Thus a head-room of only 12 ft is needed with the revolving arm distribution photometer, but there is the inconvenience of having to move the gantry half-way through taking a polar curve. Care has to be taken that there is no difference of temperature between the two positions, otherwise an error is likely to result when testing fluorescent fittings. In the construction of the apparatus, attention must be paid to eliminating whip and sag in the arm.

Figure 7.17 shows the revolving beam distribution photometer. The photocell and fittings housing are mounted at either end of a revolving beam. By means of the pulley arrangement shown the fitting is kept in its correct working position as the beam rotates; the central pulleys are kept stationary, but the end pulleys are free to rotate about their own axes. Sometimes gear wheels are used instead of pulleys, but over the long distances used in fittings photometry (as opposed to lamp photometry) many wheels would be needed to span the distance.

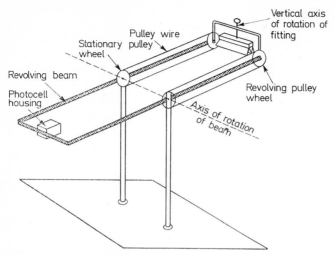

FIG. 7.17. Revolving beam distribution photometer.

This apparatus has the advantage that it is possible to have an optical path nearly equal to the height of the laboratory and make an uninterrupted sweep round the fitting. This is in contrast to the revolving arm distribution photometer, where the gantry has to be moved half-way through taking a polar curve. The fitting can be mounted on the apparatus when the fitting is at its nadir of rotation.

There are two possible snags that have to be overcome. Once again there is the question of temperature; the top of the laboratory is usually warmer than the bottom and care has to be taken that the difference is not sufficiently great to upset the readings. Secondly, air is being wafted through the fitting as the beam is moved. If this movement takes place at too great a rate it will affect the light output of fluorescent fittings.

In the types of photometer to be described next, mirrors are used to increase the length of the optical path without increasing the size of the apparatus. Unfortunately, their use introduces various possible sources of error. Firstly, the mirror is liable to sag in some positions and not in others, the sag changing the size of the image and consequently the apparent intensity. Another possible source of error is due to uneven silvering of the mirror. This causes a variation in the apparent intensity according to the orientation of the image. Also lack of trueness of the surface will cause the same sort of error. Finally, the weight of the mirror may cause sag of the arm on which it is mounted; this has to be minimized, especially if the angular measurements are taken near the axis of rotation.

Figure 7.18(a) shows a single-mirror distribution photometer. In this both the mirror and the photocell housing are fixed to the arm

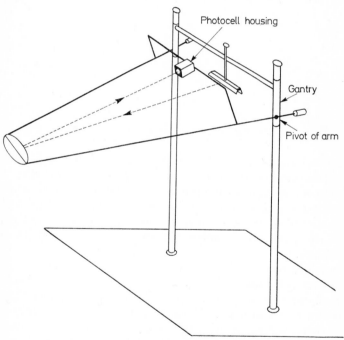

Fig. 7.18(a). Single-mirror distribution photometer.

and rotate round the fitting. As with the apparatus shown in Fig. 7.16, the movement of the gantry up and down can be used to reduce the headroom to half. If this facility is not required, then in the interests of mechanical stability it is probably better to have the pivot of the arm held to a structure that does not move with the gantry.

To save head-room, the mirror can be brought nearer the fitting and the optical path brought out sideways as in Fig. 7.18(b). If, as

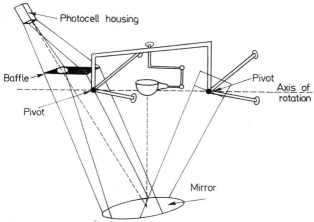

FIG. 7.18(b). Single-mirror distribution photometer—light path brought out sideways.

in Fig. 7.19, the photocell is placed in the axis of rotation and at right angles to this axis, it need not move with the arm since the angle of incidence stays constant. However, the light is incident from different directions as the arm rotates, and care has to be

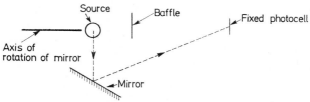

FIG. 7.19. Single-mirror arrangement with fixed photocell.

taken the photocell is equally sensitive to light changing in direction. Alternatively, two or more mirrors can be used to make the light path come out in the axis of rotation of the arm, as shown in Fig. 7.20, so that the light beam is always normal to the surface of the cell. These arrangements have the advantage that the cell can be taken as far back from the photometer as the size of the laboratory will allow, providing that the mirrors are large enough to form a complete image of the fitting.

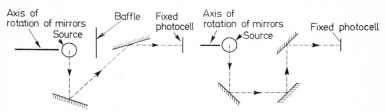

FIG. 7.20. Two- and three-mirror arrangements with fixed photocell.

In an adaptation of the beam photometer, the fitting rotates round a centrally placed rotating mirror that reflects the light into the axis of rotation. This is shown in Fig. 7.21. It effects an economy in the number of mirrors required, but suffers from the same drawbacks as the beam photometer.

In the method of inverse collimation, to be described next, the

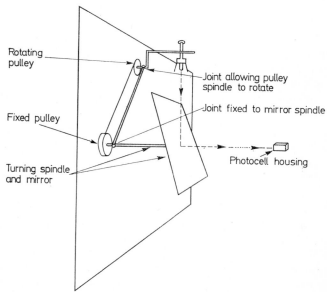

FIG. 7.21. Single-mirror arrangement with fixed photocell; rotating light source.

optical path length is shortened. Hitherto this method has been used only in the testing of projectors and floodlights, but Frederiksen of the Lysteknisk Laboratorium, Denmark, has devised an apparatus large enough for testing fluorescent fittings as well. It can be most readily understood by reference to some examples.

In Fig. 7.22(a) light from the source is focused at the aperture in the screen by the collimating lens, so only a narrow beam of light is accepted. The aperture, which is set at the focus of the collimating lens, is imaged by the second lens on to the surface of the photocell. The collection angle of the system is determined by the diameter of the aperture in relation to the focal length of the collimating lens; it is made narrower by decreasing the aperture and increasing the focal length. Errors due to aberrations in the collimating lens can be reduced by making the focal length of the lens much greater (at laest six times) than its diameter. This also reduces the error due to the light from the edges of the lens being incident obliquely on the photocell. It is essential that the collimating lens has a diameter equal to or greater than that of the source so that all the light in the direction of measurement is collected. To reduce interreflections the spacing between the lens and the source should be as great as possible. A system using a parabolic mirror, instead of a lens, can also be used [Fig. 7.22(b)].[22, 34] This allows a greater diameter of source to be measured (because it is easier to make a large diameter mirror than a lens), but it should be noted that an error is introduced by the light pick-up system due to obstruction.

Even a parabolic mirror would be too expensive for testing a 5 ft or 8 ft fluorescent fitting. Instead, Frederiksen has used perforated plates placed one behind the other to restrict the angle of collection to 4° [Fig. 7.22(c)]. Behind these a matt white surface integrates the light, which is measured by a photomultiplier. The sensitivity of a photomultiplier is necessary because the collimator allows very little light to pass.

The collimator itself is made of injection moulded black polystyrene plates 10 cm by 10 cm by 1 cm thick. The holes are 2 mm in diameter and are spaced on a 5 mm grid. Six of these plates are stacked behind each other to form an element of the collimator. Since the collimator is 6 ft in diameter, support is necessary to prevent it from sagging. The photomultiplier is baffled in such a way that it produces an equal response to a given quantity of light no matter where this enters the collimator.

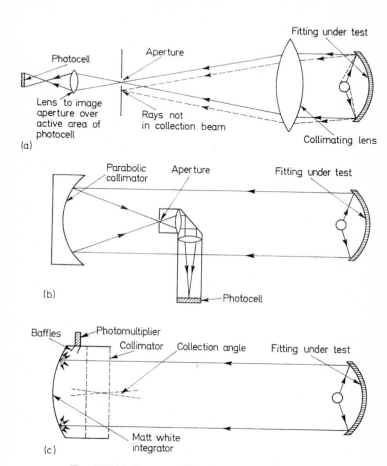

FIG. 7.22 (a). Inverse collimation by means of a lens.
FIG. 7.22 (b). Inverse collimation by means of a mirror.
FIG. 7.22 (c). Inverse collimation by means of perforated plates.

Figure 7.23 shows an apparatus suitable for use when the fitting has to be turned into positions other than its normal working position owing to lack of headroom in the laboratory.

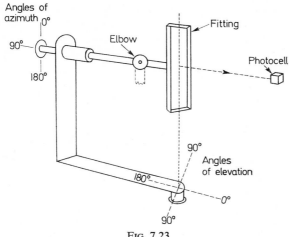

FIG. 7.23.

With this apparatus, the light output of fluorescent fittings will vary with position because of temperature variation, so a suitable means of correction has to be applied. The use of a monitoring photocell (not shown in the figure) provides the easiest method. This is mounted so that it always "sees" the fitting from the same direction and it does not interfere with the ordinary measurements. The apparatus is calibrated with the bare lamp in the normal way. The fitting is then hung on the apparatus in its working position; the elbow shown in the figure is used for this purpose. When the fitting has stabilized, a reading on the monitoring photocell is taken and the elbow is straightened so that the fitting is in the position shown in the diagram. It is then allowed to stabilize again, and another reading taken. The ratio of the two readings taken on the monitoring photocell is used as a correction factor. A similar procedure is used as whenever the angle of azimuth is changed. With some sorts of digital voltmeter, the voltage across the main cell can automatically be expressed as a percentage of that across the monitoring photocell. In this way automatic compensation can be applied. Alternatively, a potentiometer can be used in which the monitoring photocell provides the voltage normally supplied by the battery. Both these last two techniques are useful when the light source is unsteady (e.g. with MB lamps) and they could be employed on any of the other types of photometer. If only the shape of the light distribution curve is wanted, they could be used to eliminate the warming up period, providing that there is no change in light distribution during this period. With MBF/U lamps, for instance, there is a change, but not with fluorescent lamps.

BS 3820: 1964 describes an alternative method in which a lamp is used having the same light distribution as a fluorescent tube, but whose output is independent of temperature. Such a lamp can be made by using the internally phosphor-coated glass tube usually used for a fluorescent lamp. Light is provided by trafficator lamps mounted end to end axially in the tube. The optical light output ratio can be found using these tubes. This has to be corrected for any loss normally encountered due to the fluorescent tubes heating up. Temperature measurements are taken on the bottom centre of fluorescent tubes being run in the fitting. These are used to calculate the correction factor from a graph of light output against temperature. This method is very involved and could be criticized because of the spectral composition of the light from the simulated fluorescent tubes differs from that from the ordinary fluorescent tube. Also the temperature measurements add another possible source of error.

ANGULAR INDICATION AND AUTOMATION

The simplest form of angular indication comprises a calibrated disc set with its centre in the axis of rotation and a pointer fixed to the moving part. This is one of the most accurate forms of angular measurement, but it is usually not the most convenient. If pulleys are used to turn the apparatus then one of these can be used for indication purposes.

In an ingenious elaboration of this device a simple form of automation can be achieved.[16] A polar curve sheet is pinned to a board on a horizontal pulley that rotates in time with the polar curve arm. A beam of light from the galvanometer, with a cross instead of the usual single line, is arranged by a suitable mirror system to shine on to the polar curve sheet. A trace of the polar curve is automatically obtained as the polar curve arm is rotated. The curve can, of course, be simply traced with a pencil, or, if preferred, photographic paper can be used.

With all pulley and gear systems care has to be taken that slackness or backlash is reduced to negligible proportions.

For remote indication magslips are very convenient, but unfortunately the accuracy of indication is only in the order of 1° so it is usually necessary to increase the accuracy by using gears, and maybe having a coarse and fine indication system. Digital display can be obtained with shaft encoders, which are very accurate ($\pm 0 \cdot 1°$) but very expensive.

Automatic recorders in which a roll chart can be driven in time with the polar curve arm are available. In some the pen is driven by a movement similar to that of an ammeter so that an amplifier is necessary, and in others it is operated by a self-balancing potentiometer. It is important that the response is sufficiently fast to avoid the tops of peaks being flattened off and the curve being smoothed out. This caution also applies to the simple rotating polar curve sheet method mentioned above.

An extension of the self-balancing potentiometer method has been described in which a tape punch is connected to the slide wire and operates an electrically operated adding machine.[17] In a more complete system the light and electrical measurements are fed into a analogue-to-digital converter and then to punched cards thus enabling calculations to be carried out in a very brief time.

CHECKING THE ALIGNMENT OF APPARATUS

All axes of rotation should be checked for orientation; vertical axes must be truly vertical and horizontal axes must be truly horizontal.

Mirrors must be at the right inclination, and by viewing from the photocell position it can be checked that the whole of the largest fitting which the apparatus accepts is visible at all angles of elevation and azimuth.

Angular scales should be set correctly, and when the indication is remote, should be checked at the nadir, horizontal, and zenith, or other convenient positions of the arm.

If the photocell is set to read the intensity in the axis of rotation of the fitting in azimuth (i.e. nadir position if the fitting is tested in the normal working position) the reading should stay constant when a fitting (preferably linear) or fluorescent tube is rotated about the vertical axis. Variation in the reading may be caused by reflections off the superstructure, uneven silvering of the mirrors, reading not really being taken at nadir, vertical axis of rotation not passing through photocell or image of photocell, vertical axis of rotation not being truly vertical, or sag in the mirrors. The variation could also be due to the response of the photocell being dependent on the orientation of the fitting, especially if this is linear.

INTEGRATING SPHERE FOR DETERMINING LIGHT OUTPUT RATIOS

The use of the sphere in photometry depends on the principle that the illumination received on one area of a sphere from another part is independent of the relative positions of the two parts. This fact has already been proved in Chapter 2 in connection with determining the total flux emitted by a uniform diffuser. Making use of it, we can relate the illumination received on a window to the total flux emitted by a source, provided that the window is shaded from direct light by a baffle. A typical arrangement is shown in Fig. 7.24, where S is the source, W the window, and B the baffle. The inside of the sphere is assumed to be coated with paint of reflection factor ϱ and to have uniform diffusing properties.

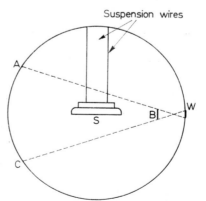

Fig. 7.24. Integrating sphere.

The intensity from the source is assumed to vary with direction. Also the source may not necessarily be in the centre of the sphere. Hence the direct illumination will vary over the surface of the sphere.

If A is the area of the sphere wall, the total flux F from the source is given by

$$F = \frac{1}{\varrho} \int L \, dA, \qquad (1.1)$$

where L is the initial luminance of an element dA of the sphere wall.

The light reflected after the first reflection will illuminate all parts of the sphere, including the window W, evenly.

Hence the illumination due to reflected light from dA received by all parts of the sphere including W will be $(1/A)L \, dA$ and the illumination due to light reflected from all parts of the sphere will be $(1/A \int L \, dA$.

From eqn. (1.1) this equals $(\varrho/A) F$.

Similarly, the illumination due to the second reflection is $(\varrho^2/A) F$. This process can be carried out indefinitely so that the final illumination E is given by

$$E = \frac{\varrho}{A} F + \frac{\varrho^2}{A} F + \frac{\varrho^3}{A} F + \cdots$$
$$= \frac{\varrho F}{A} \left(\frac{1}{1 - \varrho} \right).$$

Hence E is independent of the distribution from the source or fitting.

Theoretically, if the reflection factor of the sphere surface is known it is possible to calculate F by measuring E. But in practice the assumptions made in the theory can never be satisfied and so the sphere is only used for comparing sources; that is for substitution photometry.

There are three main departures of the practical sphere from the ideal sphere that must be considered.

1. Effect of Baffle

Flux falling on the baffle will have a smaller effect than if it fell on the sphere wall. This fact is obvious and can be verified in practice by shining a concentrating light firstly on the sphere wall and then on the baffle. Moreover, if the light is shone on a part of the sphere wall shaded from the view of the cell (*AC* in the diagram) there will be a reduction that will be nearly as great. Hence the source should be positioned in such a way that the minimum flux falls on the baffle and parts of the sphere shaded from view by the baffle. Also the baffle should be made as small as possible consistent with having all parts of the light source shaded from view. It is important that all light emitting parts of the lighting fitting are shaded from view.

To reduce the error due to shading by the baffle, some authorities advocate the use of one which is translucent, the degree of translucency required being determined by experiment. Other authorities argue that such a correction will only apply to one particular position of the source and screen and if these are materially altered a greater error than before may result.

Another suggestion for reducing the error is to paint the baffle with paint of the highest reflection factor obtainable, so reducing the amount of flux absorbed.

It can be shown by experiment that the position of the screen is not critical. Obviously it should not be too close to the window, since in this position it would reduce the view of the photocell. On the other hand, the closer it is placed to the source the more flux it will absorb. For a small source Walsh[18] recommends placing it at a third of the sphere radius from the source. Since all sizes of fittings have to be catered for, a good practical compromise is to place it half-way between the end of the fitting and the photocell.

2. Diffusion Properties of Paint

Errors must arise owing to the paint not behaving as a uniform diffuser, but these have not been investigated, and all that can be done is to make sure the finish is as matt as possible.

3. Obstruction

The fittings and the baffle interfere with the interreflection of the light. Large fittings may absorb a considerable amount of light so introducing a large error. This can be minimized by making the sphere as large as possible and by not using paint of the highest reflection factor (less the 80%), and can be allowed for by making use of the auxiliary lamp method.

In this an incandescent lamp is fixed on part of the sphere wall which is not visible from the window, that is AC in Fig. 7.24. From considerations of symmetry it is preferable if it is on the axis that passes through the window and the baffle. The auxiliary lamp is screened to prevent direct light from it reaching the source or fitting, since its function is to correct for absorption of the inter-reflected light.

To correct for absorption by the lamp to be used in the fitting, the following two readings are taken with the auxiliary lamp on:

(1) R_1 with the sphere empty.
(2) R_2 with the lamp in the sphere.

The measured output of the lamp should then be increased by R_1/R_2.

If a light output ratio is being taken then a further reading R_3 is taken with the fitting in the sphere.

The measured output of the fitting should be adjusted by the factor R_1/R_3.

The overall correction factor for the light output ratio is therefore equal to

$$\frac{R_1}{R_3} \times \frac{R_2}{R_1} = \frac{R_2}{R_3}.$$

Construction of the Sphere

The materials which have most often been used in the construction of the sphere are wood, aluminium, and mild steel. Recently fibre glass has been used as it is relatively cheap and is easy to form.[19]

Access to the sphere for painting and suspending the fitting is a problem with spheres over about 8 ft in diameter. The most common solution is to use a travelling platform which goes through a trap-door half-way up the sphere.

The erection of scaffolding may be necessary in spheres over 12 ft in diameter for the purpose of repainting, and some provision such as sockets should be made in the sphere wall to allow the scaffolding to be erected easily. An alternative approach is to have the sphere in two halves that can be drawn apart horizontally.

9*

Part of the top of the sphere can be left stationary. This can be used as a ceiling from which the fitting can be suspended and allowed to stabilize before the halves are closed together for the readings to be taken. This method overcomes the problem of the fitting heating up the sphere.

Other Shapes of Integrator

Owing to the expense of construction of a sphere other shapes of integrator are often used, particularly for lamp photometry. If the integrator is used for the purpose of comparing sources with similar light distribution, then probably the shape is not very critical. In fittings photometry, where the distributions of the lamp and fitting will usually be vastly different, then no doubt the shape is important. Keitz[20] has investigated various shapes of integrator by finding how the reading changed when a spotlight was directed on to various parts of the integrator wall. Even with the sphere, the reading fell by as much as 15 % of the maximum reading when the spotlight was directed onto the baffle or the part of the wall masked by the baffle. The maximum reading, as would be expected, was obtained when the spotlight was shone on to the part of the wall which the photocell could "see" without obstruction. With two polyhedra, one 14- the other 19-sided, the maximum error increased to 20 %, the error occuring over a greater part of the wall than in the sphere.

These figures confirm one practical detail we have mentioned already. The fitting or lamp should be tested so that as small a proportion as possible of the direct flux falls on the baffle and masked wall areas. They also indicate that it is important that before any integrator is accepted as giving results within the practical limits of accuracy required, the results should be compared with those taken on a polar curve photometer. It has been found in practice that it is possible to obtain better agreement between the two methods than the above figures might indicate. Possibly, this is due to the errors obtained with the bare lamp and fitting tending to cancel each other out, particularly in the case of fluorescent fittings, where the shape of axial distribution is usually little modified. In fact, agreement of 3 % has been reported.[21]

PRACTICAL PROCEDURES FOR TESTING LIGHTING FITTINGS

The practical procedures for testing lighting fittings are described in detail in BS 1788 and BS 3820 so there would be no point in our repeating these, but instead we shall discuss some of the basic problems involved.

1. Calibration of Polar Curves

It is usual to calibrate polar curves and any other intensity diagrams in terms of the nominal output of the lamp being used rather than the actual output of the test lamp. This procedure makes the curves very much more useful to the lighting engineer, who has to base his calculations on nominal figures. Alternatively, intensities may be expressed in candelas per 1000 lumens, or any other convenient number of lumens, from the bare lamp. This alternative avoids the necessity for rescaling the polar curve when the lumen output of the lamps is changed.

The adoption of a nominal figure is also helpful for the photometrist, who is saved from keeping standard lamps. His procedure is to choose a lamp or a number of lamps that have the correct nominal dimensions. He then ages them for the number of hours given in BS 1788 and BS 3820 and makes sure they are stable and normal in operation. His next step is to determine on the photometer the ratio of the intensity in any particular direction to the total flux from the lamp. Since this is a ratio it depends only on the shape of the light distribution of the lamp and not on its absolute lumen output. In recognition of this fact the British Standards recommend that tungsten lamps are under-run to slow their ageing. Fluorescent tubes maintain a very constant shape of distribution from one lamp to the next, and Baumgartner[15] determined that the ratio of the flux output to the intensity at right angles to the axis is 9·25. Theoretically, if the tube were a uniform diffuser this figure would be π^2.

Hence, we determine that our lamp gives, say, 10 candelas per 1000 lumens in a particular direction. So with the photometer arm in this direction we set our recording instrument to 10 units. We then put the same lamp in the fitting to be tested, run it at exactly the same voltage, and the recording instrument will be reading in candelas per 1000 lumens.

If we are using an integrator, we can use it to determine the light output ratio, and the photometer to determine the shape of the curves from the fitting. We then adjust the scale of the curves to represent the correct flux output as determined by one of the equations below.

Flux output of fitting = Light output ratio × nominal total output of bare lamps

or when each lamp gives a nominal 1000 lumens

Flux output of fitting = Light output ratio × 1000 × number of lamps.

2. Light Centre of Fitting

Ideally all measurements should be taken from the light centre of the fitting, this being the point from which the inverses quare law operates most accurately. Unfortunately, it changes its position with direction, as may be seen by considering a box-shaped diffuser fitting. Underneath the fitting the inverse square law would operate most accurately from the middle of the bottom. Whereas looking at the fitting from the horizontal, we would find it operates most accurately from the middle of the side we are looking at. Hence, ideally, we should make a compromise which gives us the least overall error, but for the sake of standardization of procedures, the relevant British Standards give the following definitions.

For street lanterns, BS 1788: 1964 uses different criteria for semi-cut-off and cut-off lanterns. The effective light centre is found by hanging the lantern on the polar curve photometer so that the axes of rotation pass through the geometrical centre of the light emitting portions. The peak intensity is then found and the lantern viewed from the photocell. The point where the line of sight to the centre of the flashed area (as seen from the peak direction) cuts the transverse plane of symmetry is taken to be the light centre. In cut-off lanterns, the light centre is taken to be vertically below the point as determined above, at a level with the bottom of the side reflectors.

For the purpose of determining the effective light centre, fittings covered by BS 3820: 1964 are divided into two classes. If the source is visible, the geometric centre of the light source is taken as the effective light centre. If the source is not visible, then the geometric centre of the light-emitting portion is regarded as the light centre.

3. Temperature Control

It has already been mentioned that the output of fluorescent tubes varies with temperature, and they give their maximum output at a temperature of about 20°C, the exact figure depending on the wattage of the tube. It follows, therefore, that the light output ratio will vary according to the temperature at which the measurements are taken. BS 3820 and BS 1788 have set the standard testing temperature at 25°C. A small variation from this value will not affect the light output unduly because both the bare lamp and the fitting outputs will be very nearly affected in the same way. The British Standards deem that the fitting should be tested between 21°C and 27°C, and, what is most important, they say that both the bare lamp or lamps and fitting must be tested at temperatures which do not differ from each other by more than 1°C.

Temperature stabilization especially over the large space taken up by a polar curve apparatus is an expensive problem to solve. Draughts must be excluded since these waft away the layers of hot air surrounding the fitting. Fan heaters have, therefore, to be used very carefully.

If the fittings are to be used at a temperature significantly different from 25°C, then the output of the fitting should be measured at this temperature. Alternatively, temperature measurements which will enable a correction to be made must be taken in the fitting. The bare lamps should still be measured at 25°C since the nominal bare lamp output is measured at this temperature. BS 1788: 1964 gives a method for correcting the light output of street lanterns to 5°C. It basically consists of finding the average air temperature inside the lantern, and using this to find a correction factor from a graph.

4. Voltage Stabilization

It is very important that the voltage is held constant throughout the duration of the test, especially with tungsten lamps where the flux roughly varies as the fourth power of voltage, so that a 1%

variation in voltage will produce a 4% variation in light output. A voltage stabilizer has, therefore, to be used, and the one selected should give an output as free from harmonics as possible.

5. Voltage Adjustment

Very often a variable auto-transformer by itself will not give fine enough voltage adjustment. The buck-boost circuit shown in Fig. 7.25 will give the required fine adjustment.

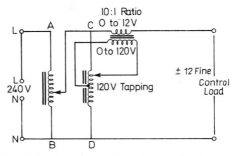

FIG. 7.25. Buck-boost fine voltage adjustment.

AB is a variable auto-transformer capable of taking the full load current. *CD* provides the fine adjustment through the fixed transformer. It need only be capable of taking one-tenth of the full load current.

Where low voltages are required, a step-down transformer fed from a variable auto-transformer can be used as an alternative to the buck-boost circuit.

6. Control Gear: Multi-lamp Fittings

The control gear generates heat so if control gear external to the fitting is used for running the lamps, it is important that the control gear in the fitting is energized when fluorescent tubes fittings are being used. However, it is preferable that the control gear in the fitting should be that operating the tubes because the heat from the tubes may affect the resistance of the windings.

It is also important that the relation of the lamp contacts to the control gear is kept constant throughout the test. When multi-lamp fittings are being tested, lamps should be used with the same control gear in the measurements on both the fitting and the bare lamp. That is, gear and lamps should not be interchanged during a test. In any case the control gear should be chosen to have as nearly equal electrical characteristics as possible and likewise the light outputs of the lamps should agree within 5%.

7. Blended Light Fittings

In these fittings two different types of lamps are used, for instance in some industrial floodlights for high bay lighting, a mercury vapour and a tungsten lamp are used in the same fitting. If we want to test the fitting with both lamps on we would have to make sure that the outputs of the lamps were in proportion to their nominal outputs and the photocell had good colour correction. These requirements are difficult to achieve. However, they can be circumvented by testing the fitting with only one lamp alight at a time, but with the other lamp in position.

The intensity in any particular direction is found for each lamp separately (the figures being based on the respective nominal output of the two lamps) and the two figures summed. From the intensity figures so obtained, the flux from the fitting can be calculated. The light output ratio is found by dividing this flux figure by the sum of the nominal outputs of the two lamps.

When an integrator is used, the light output ratios determined separately for the two lamps (designated by A and B) are combined by using the following formula:

$$\text{LOR} = \frac{xa + yb}{a + b},$$

where x = light output ratio with lamp A alight, y = light output ratio with lamp B alight, a = nominal lumen output of lamp A, b = nominal lumen output of lamp B.

8. Fluorescent Fittings with Coolers and Ventilation Holes

In Chapter 5 the purpose and mode of function of ventilation holes and coolers is explained. It is shown that these devices do not function effectively until condensation of the mercury round the cool spot is complete, this taking about 48 hr. Therefore, before testing the fitting, it should be hung up and run for this length of time before being moved to the test equipment, care being taken not to move the tubes in relation to the cooling device. So that the actual test can be completed in as short a time as possible, the bare lamp readings should be taken after the readings on the fitting.

9. Number of Polar Curves to be Taken

Unless an isocandela diagram is required, only one or two polar curves are usually required to show the distribution of the fitting. However, many more than these are needed to calculate the light output ratio, utilization factors, and so on. Figure 7.26 shows how

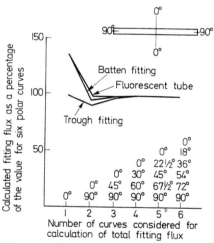

Fig. 7.26. Accuracy of calculated flux according to number of polar curves considered for fluorescent fittings.

the calculated outputs of a fluorescent tube, batten, and trough reflector vary with the number of polar curves taken. It is apparent that curves taken every 30° give a result very close to that obtained by taking them every 18°. 30° is the figure recommended for fluorescent lamps by the British Standards.

The following are the recommendations for other lamps.

BS 1788: 1964 *Street Lanterns.*	General service filament MB/U, MA/V, MBF/U lamps.	45° intervals in azimuth for bare lamps. 10° for lanterns.
	MA/U, MA/H, sodium discharge lamps, and other lamps whose rated luminous output is valid when the lamp is mounted horizontally.	18° intervals in azimuth for bare lamps. 10° for lanterns.
BS 3820: 1964	MA/V, MB/U, MBF/U, mercury discharge lamps	45° intervals in azimuth with the bare lamp mounted horizontally. 90° for fitting if lamp vertical, 30° if lamp horizontal.
	MA/U, MA/H and other lamps whose rated luminous output is valid when the lamps is mounted horizontally.	18° intervals in azimuth with the bare lamp mounted horizontally. 90° for fitting if lamp vertical, 30° if lamp horizontal.
	General service filament lamps	45° intervals in azimuth for bare lamp, and 90° for fittings.
	Sodium discharge	18° intervals in azimuth for bare lamps, and 30° for fitting.

It is also recommended that readings are taken every 10° in elevation, starting with 5°.

9 a*

THE TESTING OF FLOODLIGHTS AND PROJECTORS

Floodlights and projectors have to be tested at much greater distances than ordinary fittings since the receptor should be beyond the cross-over point (see p. 89) so that it "sees" the whole of the mirror flashed. The test distance may have to be miles in length for very parallel beams as from searchlights, but with normal flood-lights as used for football fields 100 ft is usually long enough.[22] In order to standardize testing procedures the American IES[23] has laid down that floodlights should be tested at 100 ft (but see p. 243 on inverse collimation). It also recommends that the re-ceptor should subtend 1 square degree at the light centre to even out striations, which may give very high readings locally.

A goniometer is required for measuring angles of elevation and azimuth. This usually needs to be very robust to withstand the weight of the floodlight without sagging. Two of the commonest systems of moving the fittings are shown in Fig. 7.27. In (a) the

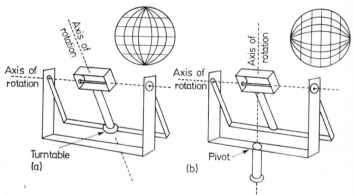

Fig. 7.27. Two forms of goniometer for testing floodlights.

part of the apparatus which moves the fitting in azimuth rotates with the fitting in elevation, so the system of coordinates is the same as is usually used on a polar curve photometer, the great circles being vertical. In the other, (b), the cradle which turns the fitting in elevation moves around in azimuth, so that the great circles pass through the axis (horizontal) of rotation of the cradle. (It should be noted that if one system of coordinates is turned through a right angle it becomes equivalent to the other.) If desired both systems can be combined in the same apparatus. Over small angles of rotation, up to 10°, the systems approximate to each other. A worm drive is useful for dividing degrees into parts, say tenths, accurately.

The receptor can be a photovoltaic cell though something more sensitive may be required at very great distances. It has already been mentioned that the American IES recommend a receptor which subtends 1 square degree at the floodlight. This can be made by using an opal diffuser, the transmitted light being collected by means of a hemispherical integrator. It is convenient to lead the photocell wires back to the goniometer to enable one person to turn the floodlight and take the readings.

It is not usually possible to calibrate the apparatus by means of the bare lamp since its intensity is not usually great enough to measure at the test distance. This difficulty could possibly be overcome by bringing the receptor nearer for the bare lamp calibration, but if a large receptor is used its angle of subtense may be too great at short distance. If this method is adopted an Ayrton–Mather shunt, presenting constant resistance to the photovoltaic cell, is useful for decreasing or increasing the sensitivity by convenient factors.

The alternative method of calibrating the apparatus is to use an accurate illumination meter, or else hold a standard lamp at a fixed distance from the receptor. The actual flux output of the test lamp should be measured so that all the readings can be multiplied by a factor to correct for any deviation from the nominal output. This is sometimes known as the direct method of photometry, and is so called in BS 3820: 1964 (though it should be noted that this specification does not deal with floodlights).

SUPPLEMENTARY PHOTOMETRIC TESTS

We will now describe the smaller photometric instruments that are needed for measurements in the lighting installation and for measurements on the fittings themselves.

REFLECTION FACTOR AND GLOSS

The reflection factor of a surface is defined as the ratio of the flux reflected by it to the flux incident on it. It depends on the angle of incidence as explained in Chapter 4 and also on the spectral composition of the incident light.

There are two types of reflection factor—specular and diffuse. The former, also known as the direct reflection factor, is defined as the ratio of the flux reflected specularly to that incident. The diffuse reflection factor is defined as the ratio of the flux reflected in all directions, except the specular direction, to the incident flux. The total reflection factor is the sum of the two.

Two of the instruments we shall describe, the PRS (Paint Research Station) and gloss heads do not give results which are strictly in accordance with the above definitions, but they have been accepted for measurements on fittings owing to their ease of use. They are available as standard instruments.

One of the most elegant methods of finding the total reflection factor for light incident in one direction only is by means of the Taylor[24] sphere shown in Fig. 7.28. The lamp housing, with its

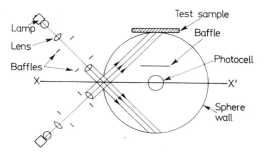

Fig. 7.28. Taylor sphere for measuring reflection factor.

optical system for rendering the light beam parallel, can be rotated through 180° about the axis XX', which passes through the centre of the sphere. The test sample is put over a hole at the top, where the beam of light falls on it when the lamp housing is in its bottom position. The photocell is in the plane of the paper. A baffle is interposed between the hole and the photocell.

The galvanometer connected to the photocell is adjusted to give zero deflection when the beam is passed out of the sphere through the hole. The sensitivity is adjusted so that full-scale deflection is given when the beam is directed on to the bottom of the sphere, the hole being covered by a plate having the same reflection factor as that of the sphere. The reflection factor of the sample is found by placing the sample in position and shining the beam on to it. The ratio of the reading so obtained to full-scale deflection gives the reflection factor.

This fact may be deduced in the following way. If F is the flux in the beam then the sample reflects ϱF lumens into the sphere (ϱ being the reflection factor of the sample). But when the lamp housing is swung into its upper position then it is as though a source of F lumens were placed in the sphere. Hence the ratio of the two readings gives the reflection factor. Actually, this is only approximately true because the sample, baffle, photocell, and entry hole for the light beam absorb some of the interreflected light. It is usually considered that a better technique is to calibrate the instrument by means of a test sample of known reflectance.

A more practical instrument for measuring total reflectance is the reflectometer head originally devised by the Paint Research Station.[25] As shown in Fig. 7.29, the head is seen to consist

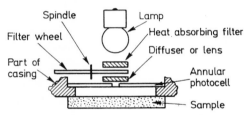

FIG. 7.29. Paint Research Station reflectometer.

basically of a light source (6 V, 6 W) that shines through a round aperture in the photocell, which faces the sample. A heat absorbing filter prevents the photocell becoming unduly hot. Just above the aperture a diffuser can be inserted if diffuse illumination on the sample is required. For direct illumination of near normal incidence, a lens is used in conjunction with a mask that has a central round aperture and is fitted between the head and the sample. Normally, diffuse illumination is used for paint finishes, and direct illumination for specular metal finishes. The head also features a wheel with tristimulus filters and a neutral density filter. Figure 7.30 (*inset Plate section*) shows a photograph of the instrument.

The instrument is calibrated by placing it on a magnesium carbonate block of known reflectance. Usually, the neutral density filter is used, but if the reflectance of the sample is low the clear aperture on the wheel is used. In this case the head is calibrated and the readings taken with the clear aperture in position. These are then multiplied by the ratio of the readings obtained on the standard block with and without the neutral density filter in position. This instrument does not give a true measure of the reflection factor, but the results are sufficiently close to the true value for practical purposes.

Specular reflectivity can be found by measuring the intensity of an image formed by the sample. Its value is equal to the intensity of the image divided by the intensity of the source. Care must be taken that the direction of known intensity of the source is the direction in which the image is viewed. These measurements can be conveniently taken on a photometric bench. Alternatively, the luminance of the image can be compared with that of the source. This is an especially useful method where measurements have to be taken on a reflector made up into a fitting. Suitable luminance meters are described in the section on luminance measurements.

The gloss head[26] (Fig. 7.31, *Plate section*) is a useful instrument for measuring the gloss of paints and specular reflectivity of metals. Figure 7.32 shows the basic components of the head. Light

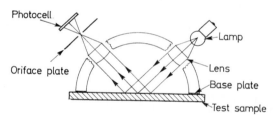

FIG. 7.32. The gloss head.

from the 6 V, 6 W lamp is rendered parallel by the lens. It is reflected by the sample held against the base plate into a similar lens, which forms an image of the filament at its focus. A plate with an aperture slightly larger than the image is fixed in the focal plane. The light which is passed through the aperture falls on to a photocell beyond. The most commonly used angles of incidence and reflection are 45°. In order to measure the gloss of paints, the instrument is calibrated by placing it on a black glass plate, this being taken as having 100% gloss.

When measuring the reflectivity of metals it is found that this instrument tends to give results which vary significantly between

FIG. 7.30. Reflectometer head (see Fig. 7.29). (*By courtesy of Evans Electroselenium Ltd.*)

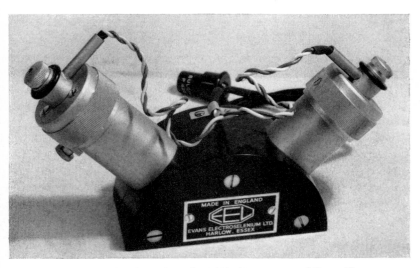

FIG. 7.31. The gloss head (see Fig. 7.32). (*By courtesy of Evans Electroselenium Ltd.*)

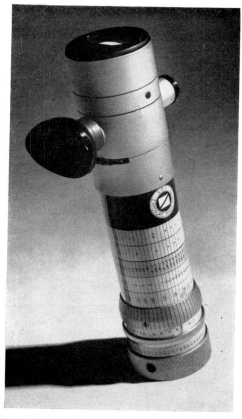

FIG. 7.39. The SEI meter. The base of the barrel is turned to obtain a balance point. The microammeter is on the top of the instrument. (*By courtesy of Ilford Ltd.*)

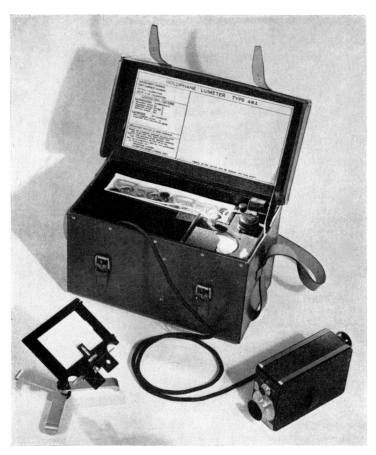

Fig. 7.41. The Holophane lumeter. (*By courtesy of Holophane Ltd.*)

FIG. 7.42. The Megatron illumination meter. Note the Perspex dome on the cell, providing cosine correction. (*By courtesy of Megatron Ltd.*)

instruments of the same type. Scott[27] found that this variability was due to differences in the filament configuration and unevenness of the glass envelope of the lamp. He modified the optical system by frosting the lamp and putting a plate with an aperture in front of it, so that this latter acted as the light source. These modifications conferred very good reproducibility between instruments and also reduced the variation between readings taken with the same instrument on the same sample. For calibration of the instrument Scott used a 45° right-angle prism with its hypotenuse lying on a black glass plate. The incident light thus passed normally through one 45° face and emerged through the other. He took the reflection factor of this to be 90%.

TRANSMISSION FACTOR

By analogy with reflection factor, the transmission factor is defined as the ratio as the transmitted flux to the incident flux. It is also dependent on the angle of incidence and the spectral composition of the incident light.

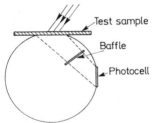

FIG. 7.33. Transmission factor; light incident at a specific angle.

With transparent plates, the easiest way of determining the transmission factor is to measure the intensity of a source with and without the plate in front of the source.[28] To minimize interreflections, the plate should not be too near the source or receptor. Alternatively, the luminance of a diffuser with and without the plate in position may be measured. Though there will be an inaccuracy due to interreflections, this could be corrected by using interreflection theory.

The integrating sphere is used for measurements on diffusing plates and, of course, may be used for transparent plates. The apparatus shown in Fig. 7.33 is an arrangement that is used for light incident at a specific angle. The cross-section of the beam should be considerably less than the size of the aperture in the sphere, since the light spreads sideways in a diffusing medium. There is a baffle between the aperture and the cell to prevent light reaching it directly from the sample. The ratio of the readings with and without the sample in position is the transmission factor, to an approximation depending on the size of the aperture and the photocell in relation to the sphere, and the reflection factor of the sample. Walsh[18] recommends multiplying the results by a correction factor obtained by directing a beam of light through another aperture into the sphere and taking the ratio of the readings with and without the test sample in position.

For diffuse incidence a lamp in an integrating sphere is used as the light source as shown in Fig. 7.34. The baffle, interposed between

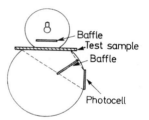

Fig. 7.34. Transmission factor; diffuse incidence.

the lamp and the aperture, prevents direct light reaching the sample. The aperture itself must be smaller than the entry hole of the receiving sphere to allow sideways diffusion in the test sample. A correction factor can be obtained as described for direct incidence.

LUMINANCE MEASUREMENTS

The average luminance of a fitting in a given direction can be found by dividing its intensity by the projected area of the fitting in that direction. If the fitting has a simple geometrical shape it is usually easy to find its projected area by calculation from the overall dimensions. Alternatively, the fitting can be photographed from as great a distance as possible, or the outline of its flashed area traced on the ground-glass screen of the camera.

Determination of the luminance of a small area presents a more difficult problem. The most simple method, which, however, is only of any use for measuring self-luminous surfaces, is to put the photocell directly over the surface to be measured. Some caution is needed in the application of this method. Even though the galvanometer may be calibrated in lumens per square foot, it will not measure the luminous emittance in lumens per square foot because of the error in the response of the cell to oblique rays. It is, therefore, necessary to calibrate the cell directly on a surface of known luminance. A convenient arrangement is to have a translucent opal surface illuminated evenly from behind. The intensity of this can be found on a photometric bench by applying the appropriate area source formula for uniform diffusers. The luminance is then, of course, equal to the area of the opal diffuser divided into the intensity, and the luminous emittance is π times this value if the opal diffuser is assumed to be a uniform diffuser. For permanence, the diffuser and the light source should be fixed into a box.

The drawback of putting the photocell directly on the surface to be measured is that the reading varies significantly with a small

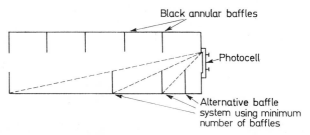

FIG. 7.35. Baffled cylinder for measuring luminance.

change in the distance. This can be overcome by holding the photocell a few inches from the light source. It is better, therefore, to mount the photocell in a black baffled box as shown in Fig. 7.35. If the surface to be measured is not of even luminance, some error may be incurred. This is due to the edges of the photocell being more sensitive than the centre and these two areas having different fields of view when the baffled box is held at a distance from the surface to be measured. The smaller the acceptance angle the smaller will be the error from this cause.

To achieve greater sensitivity it is necessary to use some sort of optical system to collect more light flux. In a simple arrangement shown in Fig. 7.36, a reflex camera is used in which a photocell is placed in the position of the plate. When the mirror is in its down position, that is at 45° to the camera axis, it reflects the light on to

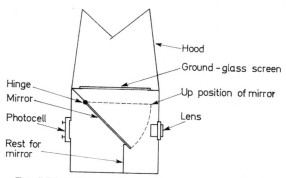

FIG. 7.36. Reflex camera used as a luminance meter.

the ground-glass screen on which the image is formed. The equivalent position of the photocell is marked on the ground-glass screen so that the camera can be aimed exactly at that part on which a measurement is required. The mirror is then lifted so that the light falls on the photocell. Since the illumination on the photocell depends on the distance of the lens from it, a correction has to be applied if the lens is moved for focusing. For many purposes this instrument is not sufficiently sensitive especially if a small angle, such as $\frac{1}{2}°$, is required.

The optical system of the Spectra-Pritchard[29] meter (Fig. 7.37) is a refinement of that used in the reflex camera. The objective

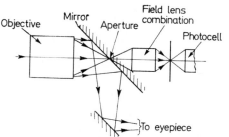

FIG. 7.37. Optical system of Spectra-Pritchard photometer.

forms an image of the test surface in the vertical plane passing through the aperture in the mirror. Light that passes through the aperture falls on the photocell after passing through the field lens. The remainder of the image is viewed through the eyepiece. In some luminance meters of this type, the opposite optical arrangement is used; the mirror serves to reflect the light onto the photocell and the direct light passes into the eyepiece. This has the disadvantage when measuring polarized light that the amount of light reflected by the mirror varies according to the plane of polarization. In the Spectra range of instruments, there is a choice of models having $\frac{1}{2}°$ or $1\frac{1}{2}°$ acceptance angle. With the most sensitive instrument, the minimum detectable luminance is 0·0001 foot-lamberts.

We will now describe some instruments that depend on visual judgements to obtain a balance point.

In using the SEI meter,[30] illustrated in Fig. 7.38, the observer views the subject through the simple telescope comprised of the

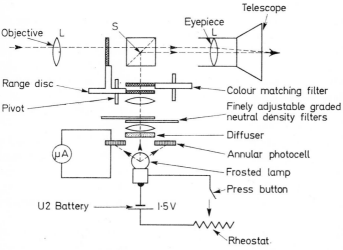

FIG. 7.38. Principle of SEI luminance meter.

objective and eyepiece lenses. This forms an inverted image. In the centre of the field there is a spot S subtending an angle of $\frac{1}{2}°$ at the object, produced by an adaptation of a Lummer–Brodhun cube.

The observer has to adjust the brightness of this spot to equal that of the image.

Light for the illumination of the spot is produced by the lamp, which has a frosted-glass envelope. This is standardized before use by adjusting the rheostat until the needle of the microammeter connected to the annular photocell is over a calibration mark. In a small portable instrument, this method of setting the output of the lamp is very much more accurate than using a voltmeter across the lamp, since the output of the lamp varies as the fourth power of the voltage. (See section on voltage stabilization.)

After the lamp has been set to the correct output, the luminance of the spot S is varied by means of the finely adjustable graded neutral density filters, until it matches that of the object. There are two filters and they are moved in opposing directions across the beam by rack and pinion. This is operated by turning the base of the instrument against the barrel, which is calibrated in footlamberts.

The range of the instrument may be altered by turning the range disc. This reduces the image brightness on the top two ranges and the spot brightness on the lowest range. Each of the three ranges of the disc alters the sensitivity by a 100 times. The total range of the instrument is from 0·01 to 10,000 footlamberts.

In order to facilitate matching of the spot, its colour can be changed from that suitable for tungsten light to that suitable for daylight, and vice versa, by means of the colour matching filter.

The SEI meter is thus very versatile for an easily portable instrument; it is only 7 in. long by $1\frac{1}{2}$ in. diameter. But it does suffer from the drawback that the measurements depend on the skill of the operator in matching the spot, though this can be improved with practice and a surprisingly good degree of consistency obtained. A photograph of the instrument is shown in Fig. 7.39, Plate section.

A similar principle is used in the Luckiesh–Taylor[31] and the Macbeth illuminometer[32] instruments, but in the latter the lamp is moved to obtain a balance.

In the Holophane lumeter[33] (Fig. 7.40, and Fig. 7.41, *Plate section*) the object flashes the objective lens, which is viewed through the eyepiece. The object is, therefore, not seen as such but as a uniformly bright disc having the luminance of the object (multiplied by the percentage loss in the optical system). This disc is seen surrounded by a ring of light reflected by the white comparison surface. The luminance of this ring is matched against the object by adjusting the range and main control knobs, which are graduated.

Light for the white screen is provided by the lamp in the whitened compartment. Two 2 V accumulators, in a separate case, supply current for the lamp, and a variable resistor enables the correct voltage to be set. The lamp is moved, by means of the calibration screw, only when the instrument needs recalibration.

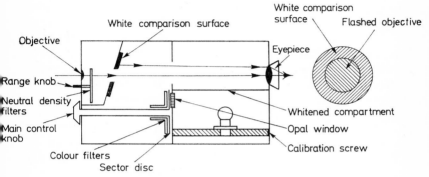

FIG. 7.40. The Holophane lumeter.

Light reaches the white surface after passing through the opal window, and the amount of this light is varied by turning the sector disc by means of the main control knob. Its colour can be altered by turning the appropriate colour filter in front of the opal window, by a control knob (not shown in the diagram). There are four filters; one for mercury light (also suitable for daylight), one for sodium light, one for bringing the colour temperature of the lamp up to 2700° K, and a 1/10 neutral density filter which increases the sensitivity of the instrument by ten times.

The range knob provides four ranges; X1, X10, X100, and X1000. It controls the light entering the instrument by bringing neutral density filters behind the lens.

Careful selection, ageing, and under-running of the lamps used in this meter confer stability of calibration over long periods.

A difficulty encountered in the use of this instrument is that of aiming it with certainty, because the image is not seen as such. This could be overcome by putting sights or a view-finder on the instrument. The field of view is 2·4°.

ILLUMINATION METERS

Meters for measuring illumination consist basically of a photo-voltaic cell connected to a microammeter or, for more sensitive meters, a spot galvanometer.

Most meters provide a number of ranges, thus enabling low levels to be measured as accurately as high levels. The provision of these ranges presents two problems. Firstly, it is found in practice that if the sensitivity between ranges exceeds 1 to 50, the shunts will damp the meter unduly. Secondly, the shape of the response curve may change with the range because of the change in the resistance that the cell looks into. In the Megatron meter (illustrated in Fig. 7.42, *Plate section*) both these difficulties are overcome by subdividing the cell concentrically. In effect the cell size as well as the circuit resistance is changed by the range switch. The concentric division of the cell preserves its circular symmetry and thus allows the cosine correction given by the dome to remain effective (see section on cosine correction of photovoltaic cells on pp. 222–3).

Luminance meters can be used for measuring illumination. The procedure is to measure the luminance of a uniformly diffusing plate of known reflection factor. In Fig. 7.41 (*Plate section*) a plate is shown for use with the Holophane lumeter; this instrument is calibrated as an illumination meter as well as a luminance meter.

MEASUREMENT OF SCALAR ILLUMINATION

A potted photocell having a table-tennis ball cemented to its surface is used as the light receptor.[35] To compensate for the reduced sensitivity of the device in the direction of the back of the

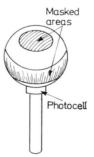

FIG. 7.43. Device for measuring scalar illumination.

photocell, areas of the ball are masked as shown in Fig. 7.43. These areas are selected in such a way that the readings obtained from the photocell are independent of the direction of the incident light.

The meter can be calibrated by using the relation

$$\text{Scalar illumination} = \frac{I}{4d^2} \quad \text{(see p. 56),}$$

where I is the intensity of the source in the direction of the photocell and d is the distance of the source from the photocell.

MEASUREMENT OF VECTOR ILLUMINATION

For this measurement two matched, cosine-corrected photocells are mounted back-to-back and connected as shown in Fig. 7.44. Exact matching is obtained by adjusting the potentiometers.

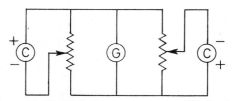

FIG. 7.44. Circuit for measuring vector illumination.

Alternatively, if uncorrected cells are used, the potentiometers can be omitted and the matching obtained by masking part of the surface of the more sensitive cell[35](see p. 54).

REFERENCES

1. VESZI, G. A., *J. Brit. I.R.E.* **13**, 183 (1953).
2. PRESTON, J. S., *Trans. I.E.S.* (*London*) **7**, 121 (1943).
3. PLEIJEL, G. and LONGMORE, J., *J. Sci. Inst.* **29**, 137 (1952).
4. BENSON, F. A., *Trans. I.E.S.* (*London*) **23**, 126 (1958).
5. WYATT, D. G., *J. Sci. Inst.* **34**, 106 (1957).
6. STEPHENSON, H. F., *Trans. I.E.S.* (*London*) **17**, 1 (1952).
7. CAMPBELL, N. R. and FREETH, M. K., *J. Sci. Inst.* **11**, 125 (1934).
8. WOOD, L. A., *Rev. Sci. Inst.* **7**, 157 (1936).
9. BERRY, R. G., *J. Sci. Inst.* **42**, 434 (1965).

10. CRAWFORD, B. H., *Physical Photometry*, HMSO, 1962.
11. CAMPBELL, N. R., *Opt. Soc. Trans.* **32**, 61 (1930).
    PRESTON, J. S. and McDERMOTT, *Phy. Soc. Proc.* **46**, 256 (1934).
12. DUNLOP, D. and FINCH, D. M., *Illum. Engng.* (*N.Y.*) **57**, 159 (1962).¹
13. RIGGS, W. G. and LAMPERT, A. R., *Illum. Engng.* (*N.Y.*) **58**, 736 (1963).
14. WILMAN, D., *Trans. I.E.S.* (*London*) **27**, 101 (1962).
15. BAUMGARTNER, G. R., *Illum. Engng.* **36**, 1340 (1941).
16. WILSON, G. H. and WEIR, W., *J. Sci. Inst.* **11**, 114 (1934).
17. HORTON, G. A., SPECK, R. C., ZAPHYR, P. A. and WENDT, R. E., *Illum. Engng.* (*N.Y.*) **53**, 591 (1958).
    ZAPHYR, P. A. and HORTON, G. A., *Illum. Engng.* (*N.Y.*) **49**, 403 (1954).
    HORTON, G. A. and ZAPHYR, P. A., *Illum. Engng.* (*N.Y.*) **53**, 341 (1958).
    ZAPHYR, P. A. and HORTON, G. A., *Illum. Engng.* (*N.Y.*) **53**, 236 (1958).
18. WALSH, J. W. T., *Photometry*, Constable, 1958.
19. BEAN, A. R., *Light and Lighting* **57**, 191 (1964).
20. KEITZ, H. A. E., *Light Calculations and Measurements*, Philips Technical Library, 1955.
21. SIMONS, R. H., *Monograph of I.ES.* (*London*) No. 5, 1962.
22. WALDRAM, J. M. *Trans. I.E.S.* (*London*) **14**, 187 (1951).
    HORTON, G. A., *Illum. Engng.* (*N.Y.*) **44**, 475 (1949).
23. COMMITTEE ON TESTING PROCEDURES OF THE I.E.S. (N.Y.), *Illum. Engng.* (*N.Y.*) **47**, 475 (1951).
    I.E.S. Lighting Handbook, IES, N.Y., 1959.
24. TAYLOR, A. H., *Sci. Pap. Bur. of Stand.* **17**, 1 (1922).
25. *Defence Specification*, DEF 1053, Method 12, HMSO, 1956.
    Paint Research Station Technical Paper No. 141.
26. *Defence Specification*, DEF 1053, Method 11, HMSO, 1957.
27. SCOTT, B. A., *J.O.S.I.* **37**, 435 (1960).
28. COLLINS, P. H. and HARPER, W. E., *Trans. I.E.S.* (*London*) **20**, 109 (1955).
29. FREUND, K., *Illum. Engng.* (*N.Y.*) **48**, 524 (1953).
    HORTON, G. A., *Illum. Engng.* (*N.Y.*) **60**, 217 (1965).
30. DUNN, J. F. and PLANT, G. S., *Phot. J.* **85**B, 114 (1945).
31. LUCKIESH, M. and TAYLOR, A. H., *J.O.S.A.* **27**, 132 (1937).
    LUCKIESH, M. and TAYLOR, A. H., *Illum. Engng.* (*N.Y.*) **32**, 235 (1937).
32. REDDING, C. S., *El. World* **65**, 85 (1915).
33. DOW, J. S. and MACKINNEY, V. H., *Opt. Soc. Trans.* **12**, 66 (1910).
    ENGLISH, S., *Public Lighting* **13**, 15 (1948).
34. JOHNSON, J., *Illum. Engng.* (*N.Y.*) **57**, 187 (1962).
35. LYNES, J. A., BURT, W., JACKSON, G. K. and CUTTLE, C., *Trans. I.E.S.* (*London*) **31**, 65 (1966).

CHAPTER 8

APPLIED LIGHTING CALCULATIONS

THE LUMEN OR FLUX METHOD OF DESIGN

The most frequently used method of calculation for interior lighting schemes is the lumen or flux method.[1] The calculation is based on the average illumination value required on the working plane (a horizontal plane at desk or work-bench height). The method is useful where the symmetry in the layout of lighting fittings ensures that the illumination at any point does not differ greatly from the average value. It has the important advantage of including both the direct and the interreflected components of illumination.

The illumination equation is formed in the following way:

$$\text{Average illumination (at the working plane)} = \frac{\text{Flux received on the working plane}}{\text{Area of the working plane}}$$

or

$$E = \frac{F \times N \times U \times M}{A},$$

where F = lamp flux, N = number of lighting points (i.e. $F \times N$ = total lamp flux), U = utilization factor (flux received by the working plane divided by total lamp flux), M = maintenance factor, A = area of working plane.

The procedure therefore consists of the following steps:

1. Select the type of lamp and lighting fitting.
2. Decide on the mounting height above the working plane (h_m) (Fig. 3.9, p. 80).
3. Using the spacing height ratio for the fitting, decide on the layout of the lighting points.
4. Select the appropriate value of illumination by reference to minimum value recommended in the Illuminating Engineering Society's Code.[2]

5. Select the maintenance factor (0·8 for a clean situation, 0·6 for a dirty situation, unless available data suggests a more specific value, e.g. I.E.S Technical Report No. 9).
6. Calculate the room index (K_r),

$$K_r = \frac{l \times w}{h_m(l + w)} \text{ (see Classification of Rooms, Chapter 3),}$$

and determine the utilization factor (from tables).
7. Calculate the required lamp flux and choose a suitable lamp size and number of lamps for each fitting.

THE BRITISH ZONAL METHOD

The lumen or flux method of design is both simple and rapid provided that the utilization factors may be obtained from tables.

If the utilization factors have to be calculated each time from first principles (Chapter 3), then the simplicity of the method is lost.

Many manufacturers therefore provide tables of utilization factors for their fittings.

The Harrison and Anderson method of calculating these factors, based on measurements in model rooms, was used for many years. The British Zonal method, based on mathematically derived data, was introduced in the Illuminating Engineering Society's Technical Report No. 2 published in 1961.

The method is intended to enable manufacturers and users to calculate utilization factors with a greater accuracy than was possible using the Harrison and Anderson data.

The BZ method can be stated as follows:

$$CU = LFU \times DLOR + UFU \times ULOR,$$

where CU = Coefficient of utilization (note the IES use the term coefficient of utilization instead of utilization factor),

    LFU = Lower flux utilance
       = The proportion of the total downward flux from the fittings which reaches the working plane, some directly and some after interreflections,

  DLOR = Downward light output ratio
       = The ratio of the downward flux emitted from the fittings to the total lamp flux,

UFU = Upper flux utilance
= The proportion of the total upward flux from the fittings which reaches the working plane after interreflection,

ULOR = The ratio of upward flux emitted from the fittings to the total lamp flux.

DLOR and ULOR

The downward and upward light output ratios may be obtained from the mean polar curve for the fitting, one of the methods described in Chapter 1 being used (e.g. zonal constants), and the total flux emitted by the lamp.

LFU and UFU

Tables of lower flux utilance are given in the report in terms of:

1. Room Index

$$K_r = \frac{l \times w}{h_m(l + w)}$$

(see Classification of Rooms, Chapter 3).
2. Direct Ratio (DR) (proportion of the total downward flux directly incident on the working plane). Obtained by the zonal multiplier method (see Chapter 3).
3. Wall and floor reflection factors.
4. Effective ceiling reflection factor (the BZ system employs the "cavity" method; see Chapter 3).

Since in the "cavity" method all the upward flux is directed into the cavity the upward "direct ratio" or "ceiling ratio" is unity and so the upper flux utilance is given in terms of:

1. Room index.
2. Wall and floor reflection factors.
3. Effective ceiling reflection factor.

BZ Classification

This is a method of classification of lighting fittings based on the downward light distribution. To have a particular classification at a given room index value the practical fitting must have a direct ratio for that room index close to that calculated for a standard distribution. The ten standard distributions, which are defined by mathematical functions, are given in Table 8.1.

TABLE 8.1. BZ CLASSIFICATION

Classification	Distribution
BZ1	$I_\theta - \propto \cos^4 \theta$
BZ2	$I_\theta - \propto \cos^3 \theta$
BZ3	$I_\theta - \propto \cos^2 \theta$
BZ4	$I_\theta - \propto \cos^{1\cdot5} \theta$
BZ5	$I_\theta - \propto \cos \theta$
BZ6	$I_\theta - \propto (1 + 2\cos\theta)$
BZ7	$I_\theta - \propto (2 + \cos\theta)$
BZ8	I_θ constant
BZ9	$I_\theta - \propto (1 + \sin\theta)$
BZ10	$I_\theta - \propto \sin\theta$

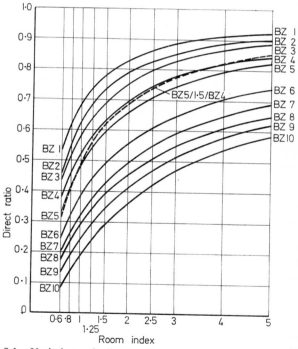

FIG. 8.1. Variation of direct ratio with room index for the BZ classification.

Figure 8.1 shows a set of curves taken from Technical Report No. 2 giving the direct ratios for these distributions. The figure also illustrates the classification of a practical fitting for which the direct ratio at each value of room index is known (broken curve). For this fitting the most appropriate classification up to a room index of 1·5 is BZ 5, but after that it is BZ 4, as indicated in the figure by the classification BZ 5/1·5/BZ 4.

When the BZ classification of a fitting is known the preparation of tables of coefficients of utilization (utilization factors) is easier since interpolation and the number of tables to be referred to is reduced. This short BZ method is not as accurate as the full method. The most important use of the classification is in connection with the calculation of the Glare Index of a lighting installation. The Glare Index method for the limitation of glare is given in the Illuminating Engineering Society's Code *Recommendations for Good Interior Lighting (1961)*. The BZ classification was used to define the fitting light distribution in the computation of the IES Glare Index tables.[2]

AVERAGE WALL AND CEILING ILLUMINATION

If the average values of direct illumination on the walls and ceiling are known as well as the total illumination on the working plane, then the total illumination on the walls and the ceiling can be obtained from the following equations:

Average ceiling illumination

$$E_1 = [XE_2 + E_{01} - E_{02}] \, Y,$$

Average wall illumination

$$E_3 = [E_{03} + Z(\varrho_1 E_1 + \varrho_2 E_2)] \, N,$$

where E_2 = average illumination on the working plane; E_{01} = average value of direct illumination on the ceiling; E_{02} = average value of direct illumination on the working plane; E_{03} = average value of direct illumination on the walls; ϱ_1 = ceiling reflection factor; ϱ_2 = working plane reflection factor; ϱ_3 = wall reflection factor; X, Y, Z and N are constants related to the room proportions and the surface reflection factors and are obtained from Table 8.2

TABLE 8.2. INTERREFLECTION TABLES

Factor	Reflection factor		Room ratio (R_r)									
			0·6	0·8	1·0	1·25	1·5	2·0	2·5	3·0	4·0	5·0
X	ϱ_2	0·1	1·025	1·034	1·042	1·049	1·055	1·063	1·069	1·073	1·079	1·083
		0·3	1·075	1·102	1·126	1·147	1·165	1·189	1·207	1·219	1·237	1·249
Y	ϱ_1	0·3	0·930	0·907	0·888	0·872	0·858	0·841	0·829	0·820	0·808	0·801
		0·5	0·889	0·855	0·826	0·803	0·784	0·760	0·743	0·733	0·717	0·707
		0·7	0·842	0·797	0·760	0·731	0·708	0·679	0·659	0·646	0·628	0·616
Z			0·225	0·264	0·29	0·319	0·338	0·37	0·388	0·405	0·420	0·425
N	ϱ_3	0·1	1·058	1·050	1·044	1·038	1·034	1·027	1·023	1·019	1·016	1·015
		0·2	1·124	1·104	1·092	1·078	1·070	1·055	1·047	1·040	1·033	1·031
		0·3	1·198	1·165	1·44	1·122	1·108	1·085	1·072	1·060	1·050	1·047
		0·4	1·282	1·233	1·202	1·170	1·149	1·116	1·099	1·082	1·068	1·064
		0·5	1·379	1·309	1·266	1·221	1·194	1·149	1·127	1·105	1·087	1·081
		0·6	1·493	1·395	1·337	1·278	1·242	1·185	1·156	1·129	1·106	1·099
		0·7	1·626	1·493	1·416	1·340	1·294	1·222	1·187	1·153	1·126	1·117
		0·8	1·786	1·607	1·506	1·408	1·351	1·263	1·220	1·179	1·147	1·136

Instead of room index the room classification is given in terms of room ratio (R_r),

$$R_r = \frac{l \times w}{h(l + w)},$$

where h is the distance between the working plane and the ceiling and not between the working plane and the fittings as in the room index equation [unless cavity method (p. 80) is used].

$$E_{02} = \frac{F \times DLOR \times DR}{A} \quad \text{and} \quad E_{01} = \frac{F \times ULOR \times CR}{A}.$$

While

$$E_{03} = \frac{F \times LOR - E_{01} \times A - E_{02} \times A}{A_w},$$

where CR = ceiling ratio = fraction of upward flux directly incident on ceiling, and is obtained from Table 8.3 (assumes a 3 : 1 spacing suspension ratio);

LOR = light output ratio = ULOR + DLOR; A_w = area of walls above working plane; A = area of working plane or ceiling (note: for cavity method CR = ULOR).

LUMINANCE DESIGN (DESIGN OF THE VISUAL FIELD)

The design of the majority of lighting installations is based on the average value of illumination required on the working plane. However, in many situations there are other lighted surfaces of equal importance. Examples of such interiors are: churches, showrooms, lounges, classrooms, and public halls. Road tunnels are a further example of a situation where it is the perspective view that is important rather than illumination on a working plane.

To deal with this type of problem a new method of design was evolved by Waldram and others,[3] which began by specifying the apparent brightnesses or brightness ratios that the observer was intended to see.

The link between the apparent brightness values and the corresponding physical brightness or luminance of the room surfaces is provided by graphs prepared from data obtained by various workers.[3,11]

Once the required luminance values for the various room surfaces have been fixed the solution depends upon the circumstances of the design.

TABLE 8.3. CEILING RATIOS

Upward intensity distribution	Room Index											
	0·6	0·8	1·0	1·25	1·5	2·0	2·5	3·0	4·0	5·0
Constant (broad)	0·370	0·440	0·490	0·550	0·600	0·660	0·710	0·746	0·802	0·835
Cosine (medium)	0·580	0·642	0·700	0·740	0·780	0·830	0·860	0·878	0·912	0·933

Method 1

If the room surface reflection factors are fixed then the procedure is aimed at determining the number and type of lighting fittings which will most nearly fulfil the luminance specification.

Method 2

If the room surface reflection factors are not fixed, then the type of fitting may be chosen, and the object of the calculation is then to determine the number of fittings required and the reflection factors of the room surfaces to fulfil the luminance specification.

The second method is more likely to come closest to the specification since the designer has more freedom. The first method sometimes results in the necessity for direct illumination patterns which are unobtainable using the lighting fittings available.

The calculations for either of these methods are simpler than those outlined in the section on interreflections in Chapter 3. In that section the purpose was to determine the performance of a given installation and so only the initial illumination values were known. In this case the same interreflection equations must be set up but since the final luminances are specified, there is only one unknown in each equation, and the solutions are easier.

Method 1

Consider one of the equations for the three-surface room dealt with in Chapter 4:

$$E_1 S_1 = H_2 S_2 f_{21} + H_3 S_3 f_{31} + E_{01} S_1,$$

which is the equation for surface 1, i.e. the ceiling.

The equation may be rewritten:

$$\frac{H_1 S_1}{\varrho_1} = H_2 S_2 f_{21} + H_3 S_3 f_{31} + E_{01} S_1.$$

For uniformly diffusing surfaces, the usual assumption, the luminous emittance H is equal to the luminance in foot-lamberts, or proportional to the luminance in candelas per square foot. In this equation the only unknown would be the initial illumination E_{01},

10*

and so the equation is solved for this quantity. The procedure is repeated for the other surfaces and E_{02} and E_{03} obtained.

The type and number of fittings must be selected to provide these values for E_{01} and E_{03}.

Method 2

In this case there are two unknowns in each of the equations, namely ϱ and E_0.

The solution is to set the reflection factor of one of the surfaces so that in one of the equations there is again only one unknown, i.e. the E_0 value. The E_0 value is calculated and the number of fittings required to produce this direct illumination determined.

Once the number of fittings is known, the E_0 values for the other surfaces are fixed and may be calculated. The E_0 values are then substituted in the remaining interreflection equations and the appropriate values for ϱ obtained.

Example. Steps required in the case of the simple three surface room (Chapter 3, Rooms):

1. Equation for working plane or floor

$$\frac{H_2 S_2}{\varrho_2} = H_1 S_1 f_{12} + H_3 S_3 f_{32} + E_{02} S_2.$$

It is usually convenient to fix the reflection factor of the working plane or floor; so fix ϱ_2.
Now only E_{02} is unknown.

2. Calculate E_{02} and from knowledge of the type of fitting chosen determine the number required.

3. Calculate E_{01} and E_{03} from the number and type of fitting used.

4. Substitute for E_{01} and E_{03} in the appropriate equations to obtain ϱ_1 and ϱ_3,

i.e., Ceiling reflection factor:

$$\varrho_1 = \frac{H_1 S_1}{H_2 S_2 f_{21} + H_3 S_3 f_{31} + E_{01} S_1}.$$

Wall reflection factor:

$$\varrho_3 = \frac{H_3 S_3}{H_1 S_1 f_{13} + H_2 S_2 f_{23} + H_3 S_3 f_{33} + E_{03} S_3}.$$

The above is an outline of what promises to be the lighting design method of the future. Further elaboration is beyond scope of this book, but the references relate to the original papers and these contain detailed examples.

ILLUMINATION FROM LINE SOURCES—ASPECT FACTOR METHOD

Sometimes the direct illumination at a point from a fitting or a row of fittings housing tubular fluorescent lamps is required. The aspect factor method [4] provides the simplest approach to this problem (the derivation of aspect factors is given in Chapter 2).

The basic equations give the illumination at a point directly opposite one end of a row of fittings, but all other positions may be calculated by the method of component sources described later.

The Basic Equation

Illumination in a horizontal plane (Fig. 8.2)

$$(E_h) = \frac{n \times I_\theta}{l \times h_m} \times \cos^2 \theta \times (AF_\alpha);$$

Illumination on a vertical or perpendicular plane parallel to the axis of the row

$$(E_{v_1}) = \frac{n \times I_\theta}{l \times h_m} \times \cos \theta \times \sin \theta \times (AF_\alpha)$$

$$= E_h \tan \theta = E_h \frac{X}{h_m} ;$$

Illumination on a vertical or perpendicular plane normal to the axis of the row

$$(E_{v_2}) = \frac{n \times I_\theta}{l \times h_m} \times \cos \theta \times (a.f._\alpha);$$

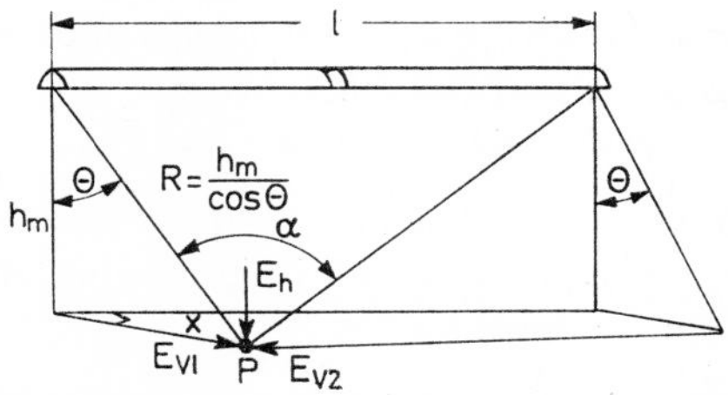

FIG. 8.2. Illumination at a point from a line source; point under end of source.

where n = number of fittings in the row or part of row contributing to illumination at that point; I_θ = intensity of one fitting in direction θ (from transverse polar curves, Fig. 8.3); l = length of row or part of row contributing to the illumination at that point;

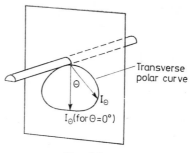

Fig. 8.3.

(AF_α) = aspect factor for the parallel plane; $(a.f._\alpha)$ = aspect factor for the perpendicular or vertical plane normal to the axis of the row; θ = angle between the downward vertical and the source normal passing through the illuminated point.

The calculation of illumination on an oblique or random plane is dealt with in the section on illumination vectors (Chapter 2). The above equations may be used for discontinuous rows, but when the distance between the ends of adjacent fittings reaches $h_m/4 \cos \theta$ the error will be of the order of 10%.

The Aspect Factor

Figures 8.5 and 8.6 give graphs of aspect factors for both the parallel plane and the perpendicular plane.

The aspect factor depends upon two things:

1. The aspect angle α, where $\alpha = \tan^{-1} l \cos \theta / h_m$ (Fig. 8.2).
2. The shape of the polar curve of the lighting unit in the AXIAL plane defined by angle θ (Fig. 8.4).

Many lighting units have axial polar curves which can be expressed approximately as cosine functions.

Classifications suitable for general use are given below:

Type of lighting unit	Type of axial distributions
Bare fluorescent lamp ⎫ Diffusing reflector fitting ⎬ Enclosed diffusing fitting ⎭	$I_x = I_\theta \cos \alpha$
Louvered fittings	$I_x = I_\theta \cos^2 \alpha$
Deep louvers or prismatic control	$I_x = I_\theta \cos^3 \alpha$
Specular louvers	$I_x = I_\theta \cos^4 \alpha$

If there is doubt concerning which of these will give the best approximation, the practical distribution can be compared with the mathematical functions by plotting both on rectangular coordinates.

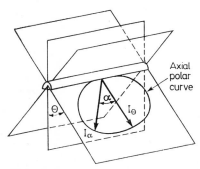

FIG. 8.4. Each axial plane will have its own particular polar curve, the shape of which may or may not vary with angle θ.

Method of Component Sources

When the point of interest is not directly opposite the end of the linear source the method of component sources may be used. Figure 8.7 illustrates the method. Similar reasoning may be applied to the case of rectangular area source calculations. The illumination on the horizontal plane directly opposite point D on the row of lighting fittings is obtained by considering the row to consist of two component sources, one of length AD and the other of length DE:

$$E_h = E_h \text{ (from } AD) + E_h \text{ (from } DE)$$

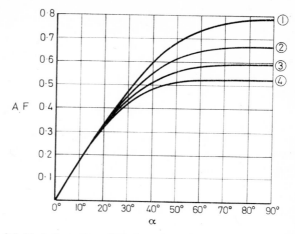

FIG. 8.5. Variation of parallel plane aspect factor with aspect angle α. Curve 1, axial distribution, cos. Curve 2, axial distribution, $\cos^2$. Curve 3, axial distribution, $\cos^3$. Curve 4, axial distribution, $\cos^4$.

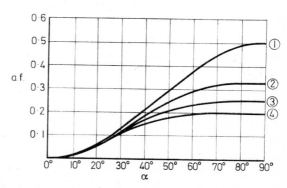

FIG. 8.6. Variation of perpendicular plane aspect factor with aspect angle α. Curve 1, axial distribution, cos. Curve 2, axial distribution, $\cos^2$. Curve 3, axial distribution, $\cos^3$. Curve 4, axial distribution, $\cos^4$.

giving

$$E_h \frac{nI_\theta}{lh_m} \cos^2 \theta \; (\text{A.F.}_{\cdot \alpha AD}) + \frac{nI_\theta}{lh_m} \cos^2 \theta \; (\text{A.F.}_{\cdot \alpha DE}),$$

where

$$\alpha_{AD} = \tan^{-1} \frac{AD \cos \theta}{h_m} \quad \text{and} \quad \alpha_{DE} = \tan^{-1} \frac{DE \cos \theta}{h_m}.$$

Since nI_θ/l is the intensity per unit length of the row it will have the same value for the component sources that it has for the whole source (i.e. the whole row) and AE may be taken as l if n is the total number of fittings in the row.

Therefore

$$E_h = \frac{nI_\theta}{lh_m} \cos^2 \theta \; [(\text{A.F.}_{\cdot \alpha AD}) + (\text{A.F.}_{\cdot \alpha DE})] \; \text{lumens/ft}^2.$$

Similarly for the vertical plane:

$$E_{v_1} = E_{v_1} \text{ (from } AB) + \text{E}_{v_1} \text{ (from } BE),$$

but $E_{v_2} = E_{v_2} \; (AC \text{ only})$, since section CE cannot contribute to the direct illumination on that side of the plane of incidence. When the point lies beyond the end of the source, e.g. opposite F, it is necessary to introduce an imaginary source extending the row until it is opposite the point under consideration.

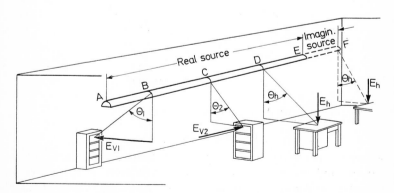

Fig. 8.7. Illumination at a point from a line source: point not under end of source.

In this case the horizontal illumination

$$E_h = E_h \text{ (from } AF) - E_h \text{ (from } EF)$$

$$= \text{illumination from imaginary plus real source}$$
$$- \text{illumination from imaginary source}$$

$$= \frac{nI_\theta}{lh_m} \cos^2 \theta \ [(\text{A.F.}_{\alpha AF}) - (\text{A.F.}_{\alpha EF})]$$

FLUX DISTIBUTION FROM LINE SOURCES—K FACTOR METHOD

An extension of the "aspect factor" method of calculation for line sources is the K factor method.[5] This method is useful when it is the average value of illumination from an installation of line sources that is required rather than the illumination at a point. K factors enable the flux received by a surface parallel to a line source to be calculated to a close approximation (better than 1 %). Consider the 10° sector solid shown in Fig. 8.8, which has a curved window marked $ABDC$.

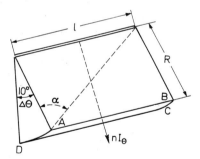

FIG. 8.8. The 10° sector solid.

The flux passing through window $ABCD$

$$F = nI_\theta K,$$

where K is determined by the axial distribution (polar curve) of the source, and the aspect angle α. The derivation of K is given in Chapter 3 and graphs of 10° K factors for a number of different axial distributions are plotted in Fig. 8.9 against $\cot \alpha$ $(= R/l)$. K factors are directly proportional to the sector angle and so if sectors of angle $x°$ are used instead of $10°$ sectors then the new K factor K' is given by $K' = (x°/10°) K$, e.g. for a $6°$ sector angle $K' = 0.6 K$.

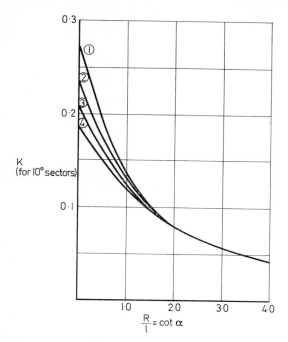

Fig. 8.9. K factors for $10°$ sectors. Curve 1, axial distribution, cos. Curve 2, axial distribution, $\cos^2$. Curve 3, axial distribution, $\cos^3$. Curve 4, axial distribution, $\cos^4$.

Using a series of sectors, we can calculate the value of flux received by a surface parallel to the axis of the row of fittings. Figure 8.10 illustrates the use of K factors to determine the direct flux to the floor from three rows of fluorescent fittings. Each row contains n fittings.

The procedure is as follows:

1. Measure or calculate R for each sector, and hence obtain R/l.
2. Read off the value of K for each sector from Fig. 8.9.
3. Read off the mid-sector value of I_θ for each sector from the transverse polar curve.

10a*

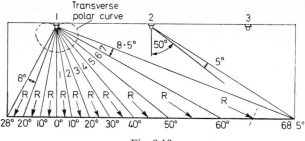

Fig. 8.10.

Row 1

$$F_{0-68\cdot5} = n[I_1K_1 + I_2K_2 + I_3K_3 + I_4K_4 + I_5K_5 + I_6K_6 + I_7K_7'],$$

where $K_7' = 0\cdot85 K_7$.

F_{0-28} only requires the calculation for the $8°$ sector since F_{0-20} may be taken from the previous calculation.

Row 2

F_{0-50} can be taken from the calculation for row 1 and only the $5°$ sector requires calculation. The result for row 2 is then obtained by doubling the value for F_{0-55}.

Row 3

Because of symmetry the result for row 3 is identical with that for row 1.

The flux to the parallel walls and the ceiling can be obtained in a similar manner, and the flux to the end walls is then obtained by subtraction, i.e.

Flux to one end wall $= \frac{1}{2}$[total emitted flux − flux to floor
− flux to ceiling − flux to parallel walls].

The method of dealing with rows which do not meet the end walls is given in Chapter 3.

ILLUMINATION AND FLUX DISTRIBUTION FROM AREA SOURCES

Illumination at a Point

In Chapter 2 we derived equations for the illumination at a point under one corner of a uniformly diffusing rectangular source, for both the horizontal (parallel) and vertical (perpendicular) planes

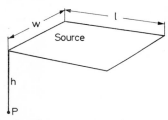

FIG. 8.11. Illumination from an rectangular source: point under one corner of source.

(Fig. 8.11). The graphs given in Figs. 8.12 and 8.13 have been developed from these equations. To obtain the required illumination value the factor read from the appropriate graph is multiplied by the luminance of the source in foot-lamberts ($= \pi \times$ luminance

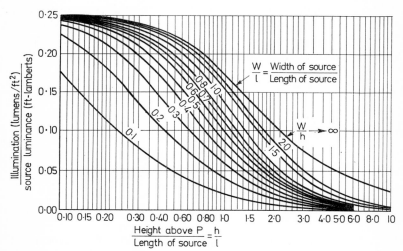

FIG. 8.12. Illumination from a uniform rectangular source in a plane parallel to the source.

in candelas/ft^2). When the point is not opposite one corner of the source the method of component sources should be used, i.e. the source should be divided up into a number of sources each

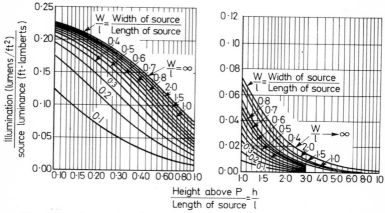

Fig. 8.13. Illumination from a uniform rectangular source in a plane perpendicular to the source.

having a common point above P. From Fig. 8.14 it can be seen that the illumination on the horizontal plane at P is given by $E_p = E_1 + E_2 + E_3 + E_4$. Graphs have been produced[12] which can be used in the same way for the more concentrating distributions obtained from louvered ceilings.

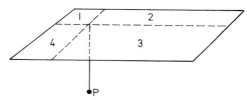

Fig. 8.14. Illumination from a rectangular source: point not under one corner of source.

Flux Distribution

Flux transfer from a rectangular ceiling to the floor beneath can be calculated by using the surface distribution factors given in Table 3.2 (Chapter 3), or for non-mathematically defined, but symmetrical distributions, by means of the zonal multipliers given in Table 3.1. Alternatively, the ceiling could be divided up into a series of strips and the flux from each strip to the floor or walls could be calculated by using the K factor method described in the section on line sources.

This method is applicable to both mathematically defined and practical distributions, and in addition as long as each curve is symmetrical about the vertical it is unnecessary for the axial and transverse polar curves to be the same.

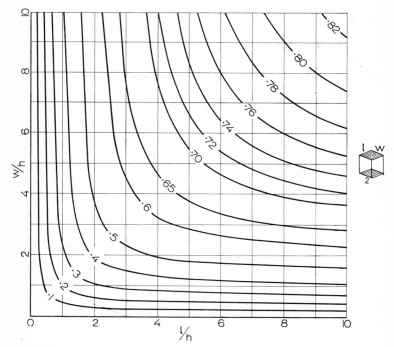

FIG. 8.15. Parallel planes; fraction of flux transferred from 1 to 2 (f_{12}).

Where the source is uniformly diffusing we may calculate the flux transfer by using the equations for illumination at a point already mentioned, and integrating over the illuminated area. The graphs given in Figs. 8.15 and 8.16 were obtained in this way.

The flux received by one surface is equal to the flux emitted by the other surface multiplied by the factor read from the appropriate graph.

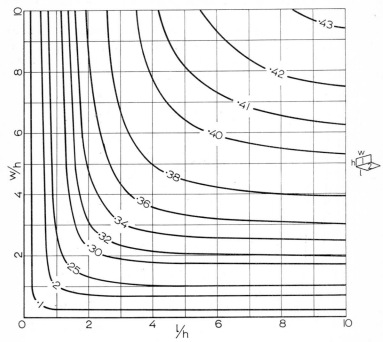

FIG. 8.16. Perpendicular planes; fraction of flux transferred from 1 to 2 (f_{12}).

POINT SOURCE CALCULATION

Although the inverse-square law and Lambert's cosine law are implicit in all illumination calculations, in its basic form for the horizontal plane, i.e. $E_h = (I_\theta \cos \theta)/d^2$, it is seldom directly used. The reason is that most practical problems involve average illumination from arrays of lighting units, and the utilization factor method is much more suitable for this type of calculation. In addition, considerable labour is involved in inverse-square-law calculations unless tables or graphs are used to reduce the amount of the work.

In Table 8.4 the illumination received at a point in a horizontal plane from a uniform point source of intensity 1000 candelas is given in terms of the mounting height (h_m) of the source and the horizontal distance (Z) to the point. In addition the angle (θ) from the vertical, of the direction of the point from the source, is given.

The illumination from a practical point source of known intensity distribution is obtained by multiplying this value of illumination (E_{1000}) by the intensity of the practical source, at angle θ (read from the polar curve), and dividing by 1000.

Thus

$$E_h = (E_{1000}) \times \frac{I_\theta}{1000} .$$

The effect of tilting the surface at an angle Φ (Fig. 8.17) to the horizontal can be quickly determined by multiplying E_h by a correction factor C_t. C_t is obtained from Fig. 8.18 (see Chapter 2 for derivation).

The illumination on a tilted surface (E_t) is given by

$$E_t = E_h C_t .$$

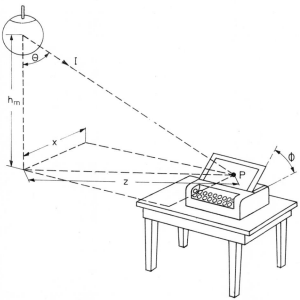

FIG. 8.17. The relation of a point source to a tilted plane.

TABLE 8.4. ILLUMINATION ON HORIZONTAL PLANE FROM SOURCE OF 1000 CANDELA INTENSITY

Z	$h_m = 5$ θ	E_{1000}	$h_m = 6$ θ	E_{1000}	$h_m = 7$ θ	E_{1000}	$h_m = 8$ θ	E_{1000}	$h_m = 9$ θ	E_{1000}	$h_m = 10$ θ	E_{1000}	$h_m = 11$ θ	E_{1000}	$h_m = 12$ θ	E_{1000}	Z
0	0·0	40·00	0·0	27·78	0·0	20·41	0·0	15·63	0·0	12·35	0·0	10·00	0·0	8·26	0·0	6·94	0
1	11·3	37·71	9·5	26·66	8·1	19·80	7·1	15·27	6·3	12·12	5·7	9·85	5·2	8·16	4·8	6·87	1
2	21·8	32·02	18·4	23·72	15·9	18·14	14·0	14·27	12·5	11·48	11·3	9·43	10·3	7·87	9·5	6·66	2
3	31·0	25·22	26·6	19·88	23·2	15·85	20·6	12·83	18·4	10·54	16·7	8·79	15·3	7·42	14·0	6·34	3
4	38·7	19·05	33·7	16·00	29·7	13·36	26·6	11·18	24·0	9·42	21·8	8·00	20·0	6·86	18·4	5·93	4
5	45·0	14·14	39·8	12·59	35·5	11·00	32·0	9·53	29·1	8·25	26·6	7·16	24·4	6·24	22·6	5·46	5
6	50·2	10·49	45·0	9·82	40·6	8·93	36·9	8·00	33·7	7·11	31·0	6·31	28·6	5·59	26·6	4·97	6
7	54·5	7·85	49·4	7·66	45·0	7·22	41·2	6·66	37·9	6·07	35·0	5·50	32·5	4·96	30·3	4·48	7
8	58·0	5·96	53·1	6·00	48·8	5·83	45·0	5·52	41·6	5·15	38·7	4·76	36·0	4·37	33·7	4·00	8
9	60·9	4·58	56·3	4·74	52·1	4·72	48·4	4·58	45·0	4·36	42·0	4·11	39·3	3·83	36·9	3·56	9
10	63·4	3·58	59·0	3·78	55·0	3·85	51·3	3·81	48·0	3·70	45·0	3·54	42·3	3·35	39·8	3·15	10
11	65·6	2·83	61·4	3·05	57·5	3·16	54·0	3·18	50·7	3·13	47·7	3·04	45·0	2·92	42·5	2·78	11
12	67·4	2·28	63·4	2·48	59·7	2·61	56·3	2·67	53·1	2·67	50·2	2·62	47·5	2·55	45·0	2·46	12
13	69·0	1·85	65·2	2·04	61·7	2·17	58·4	2·25	55·3	2·28	52·4	2·27	49·8	2·23	47·3	2·17	13
14	70·3	1·52	66·8	1·70	63·4	1·83	60·3	1·91	57·3	1·95	54·5	1·96	51·8	1·95	49·4	1·91	14
15	71·6	1·26	68·2	1·42	65·0	1·54	61·9	1·63	59·0	1·58	56·3	1·71	53·7	1·71	51·3	1·69	15
16	72·6	1·06	69·4	1·20	66·4	1·31	63·4	1·40	60·6	1·45	58·0	1·49	55·5	1·50	53·1	1·50	16
17									62·1	1·26	59·5	1·30	57·1	1·33	54·8	1·33	17
18									63·4	1·10	60·9	1·15	58·6	1·17	56·3	1·19	18
19									64·7	0·97	62·2	1·01	59·9	1·04	57·7	1·06	19
20									65·8	0·85	63·4	0·89	61·2	0·92	59·0	0·95	20

h_m = mounting height of source above plane (ft). Z = horizontal distance from source (ft). θ = inclination to vertical of direction from source (degrees). E_{1000} = illumination (lumens/ft²).

C_t consists of two factors. The first, A, depends only upon the value of Φ and is therefore constant for a given angle of tilt. The second, B, is a function both of Φ and x/h_m. A is given in a column adjacent to the appropriate value of Φ in the figure, and B is plotted against x/h_m.

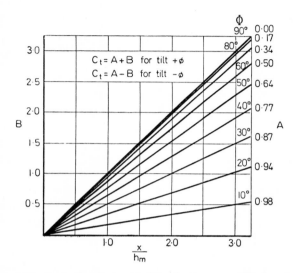

FIG. 8.18. Correction factor C_t (illumination on a tilted surface).

Forward tilt of the source is considered to give a positive value to Φ and tilt away from the source a negative value.

Thus $C_t = (A + B)$ for Φ positive and
$C_t = (A - B)$ for Φ negative.

STREET LIGHTING CALCULATIONS

The amount of actual calculation involved in the planning of a street lighting installation is very small. British Standard Codes of Practice give the geometry of standard layouts. However, utilization factors are often asked for from overseas, and their calculation is described at the end of this section.

Group A Roads

These are main traffic routes; they carry traffic other than purely local. British Standard Code of Practice, *Street Lighting*, CP 1004: Parts 1 and 2: 1963, gives full details for layout and installation. The actual geometry of the installation, that is the spacing of the lanterns, is given in tables. It depends on the following factors:

1. Lantern distribution: cut-off or semi-cut-off.
2. Arrangement: staggered, opposite, or single side.
3. Type of carriageway: single or dual.
4. Classification of carriageway: principal traffic route or A 1, normal traffic route or A 2, minor traffic route or A 3.
5. Mounting height: 25, 30, 35 or 40 ft.
6. Effective width of road.
7. Flux in lower hemisphere.

The maximum permissible overhang as well as the spacing can be read from the tables.

Which table is used and where the table is entered depends upon the street lighting engineer. For instance he has to decide whether to use cut-off or semi-cut-off lanterns. The former give less glare and are better suited to matt surfaces, but the spacing is less so that the initial outlay is more. Advantages cited for the semi-cut-off besides longer spacing are better performance with smoother surfaces, better appearance of buildings, and greater suitability for staggered arrangements. He then has to choose the lantern and the light source he wants, making sure that the lantern gives more than the allowable minimum of flux in the lower hemisphere. After deciding on the arrangement, the engineer can find the maximum spacing from the tables.

Group B Roads

The Code of Practice for Group B Roads has not yet been revised—it is dated 1956.

Other Groups

These comprise roundabouts and complex junctioos, bridges and flyovers, tunnels and underpasses, town and city centres, and special requirements such as motorways and airfields. The Codes of Practice are in course of preparation.

Coefficients of Utilization

This coefficient for a street lantern is equal to the fraction of bare lamp flux that falls on the road surface. To calculate this it is necessary to plot kerb lines on the isocandela grid and find the flux enclosed between these lines.

Kerb Lines

In Fig. 8.19 kerb lines are shown on Sanson's net and the normal zenithal projection. To understand how these are obtained imagine the eye to be positioned in place of the lantern and to be sur-

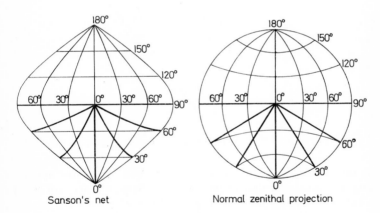

FIG. 8.19. Kerb lines.

rounded by a transparent sphere with lines joining points of equal elevation and equal azimuth scribed on its surface (i.e. lines of latitude and longitude). As the eye follows the kerb along, the locus of the intersection of the line of sight with the sphere will trace a kerb line. Kerbs at different distances will trace different loci.

Figure 8.20 shows how the kerb line may be calculated. *ABCD* is the roadway. The lantern is at *O* at a mounting height *h*. *b* is the width of the road. The angle of elevation, θ_1, of the point *E* directly across the road is given by tan $\theta_1 = b/h$. The angle of azimuth is obviously 90°. *F* is any point at a distance *d* from *E*. Its angle of elevation θ_2 and azimuth φ are given by

$$\tan \theta_2 = \sqrt{\left[\left(\frac{d}{h}\right)^2 + \left(\frac{b}{h}\right)^2\right]},$$

$$\tan \varphi = \frac{b}{d}.$$

Different values of *d* can be substituted in these equations and the kerb lines plotted, or the equations can be combined and the

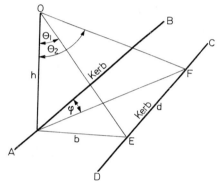

FIG. 8.20. Calculation of coordinates of kerb lines.

relation tan $\theta_1 = \tan \theta_2 \cos \varphi$ used instead. The advantage of using a normal zenithal projection over Sanson's net will be apparent by referring back to Fig. 8.19; the kerb lines are straight.

Flux between the Kerb Lines

The flux between the lines can be found in either of two ways:
1. By using the planimeter to find the area between the contours and making use of the relation found in Chapter 1:
   Flux in a zone = Mean intensity in zone × (fraction of total area of the diagram) × 2π.

If the diagram is taken as being representative of both sides of the lantern 2π must be replaced by 4π.

2. By dividing up the areas between kerb lines into equal areas and estimating the average intensity in each of these smaller areas. The flux between two adjacent kerb lines can then be found by averaging the appropriate intensity figures and multiplying the average so obtained by the solid angle subtended by the area between the two kerb lines. On the normal zenithal projection equal areas can be obtained by describing circles (about the centre of the diagram) which have radii of $\sqrt{\dfrac{1}{n}}$, $\sqrt{\dfrac{2}{n}}$, $\sqrt{\dfrac{3}{n}}$, etc., of the radius of the diagram, where n is the number of equal areas required between each pair of kerb lines. The division of Sanson's net into similar areas is more complex.[9]

Utilization Curves

Figure 8.21 shows the form in which the final results are plotted. The use of the curves is best shown by an example.

Suppose a lantern overhangs by 5 ft a road that is 30 ft wide, and suppose the mounting height is 25 ft. Find the flux falling on the road.

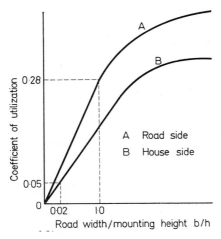

FIG. 8.21. Coefficient of utilization curves.

1. *House side*

$$\frac{\text{Road width}}{\text{Mounting height}} = \frac{b}{h}$$

$$= \frac{5}{25}$$

$$= 0.2.$$

From Fig. 8.21, coefficient of utilization = 0.05.

2. *Road side*

$$\frac{\text{Road width}}{\text{Mounting height}} = \frac{b}{h}$$

$$= \frac{25}{25}$$

$$= 1.$$

From Fig. 8.21 coefficient of utilization = 0.28.
The total coefficient of utilization will, therefore, be 0.33.
Hence flux on roadway from one lantern = 0.33 × bare lamp flux.
From this result the total flux from an installation can be found.

FLOODLIGHTING CALCULATIONS

Floodlighting calculations[6] are used for finding the illumination at specific points, for finding the number of floodlights needed to obtain a specified average illumination, and for making sure that the area to be floodlit is properly covered. The type of calculation needed depends on whether the floodlights have a linear source type of distribution or a symmetrical distribution.

Floodlights with Linear Sources

Tungsten iodine are the most common linear sources but sodium and fluorescent are also used. The data are usually published in the form of the vertical and transverse light distribution curves passing through the peak. Curves for a 1500 W tungsten iodine floodlight are shown in Fig. 5.35 (p. 165).

Suppose we want to find the illumination at the point P in Fig. 8.22. F is the fitting and this is aimed at A. To find the inten-

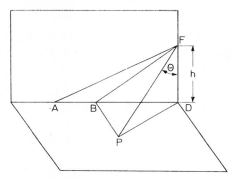

FIG. 8.22. Angular relationships for floodlighting calculations.

sity in the direction P, we must determine the angle AFB, the angle of declination from the peak, and angle BFP, the angle of azimuth.

$$\tan \angle AFD = \frac{AD}{h},$$

$$\tan \angle BFD = \frac{BD}{h},$$

hence $\angle AFB$ can be found by subtraction:

$$\tan \angle BFP = \frac{BP}{BF}$$

$$= \frac{BP}{\sqrt{(BD^2 + h^2)}}.$$

To see how these angles are used, refer to Fig. 5.35. Suppose the angle AFB is $10°$ and the angle BFP is $20°$. If we assume that the axial curves only change in magnitude and not in shape as their elevation is varied, we can find the intensity in the required direction by proportion.

At $10°$ of declination the intensity in the vertical plane of symmetry is 10,000 candelas (transverse curve).

At 20° of azimuth the intensity of the horizontal curve is 68,000 candelas for a peak intensity of 72,000 candelas. Hence if the peak intensity were 10,000 candelas, the intensity at 20° of azimuth would be

$$\frac{10,000}{72,000} \times 68,000 = 9400 \text{ candelas.}$$

Hence a value of 9400 candelas is used to find the illumination at P. The illumination can be found by using the inverse-square and cosine laws of illumination:

$$E_p = \frac{I \cos \theta}{(FP)^2} = \frac{I \cos^3 \theta}{h^2},$$

where $\cos \theta = \dfrac{h}{\sqrt{(PD^2 + h^2)}}$ and $I = $ intensity in direction of FP.

Floolights with Symmetrical Distribution

These usually employ tungsten or mercury vapour lamps.

Since the distribution is symmetrical, we need only find the angle AFP to read the intensity from the graph provided (Fig. 5.37, p. 166):

$$AF = \sqrt{(AD^2 + h^2)}$$
$$PF = \sqrt{(PD^2 + h^2)}$$
$$AP = \sqrt{(AB^2 + BP^2)}$$
$$\cos \angle AFP = \frac{AF^2 + PF^2 - AP^2}{2AF\,PF}.$$

Number of Floodlights Needed

The number of floodlights needed to obtain a required average level of illumination can be calculated by the lumen method. This is similar to the lumen method for indoor fittings; the number of lighting units required is found by dividing the flux required by the flux from one lighting unit.

The following are definitions of the terms used in association with the calculations.

Beam angle. The angle within which the diversity of illumination produced on a surface at right angles to the beam does not exceed 10 to 1. For symmetric floodlights there will be two beam angles, one in elevation, one in azimuth.

Beam lumens. The luminous flux contained within the beam as defined in beam angle. It is usually taken as being from 25–30% of the lamp lumens.

Number of floodlight required

$$= \frac{\text{Average illumination (lumens/ft}^2) \times \text{area (ft}^2)}{\text{Beam lumens}}.$$

Size of Light Patch

The circular or elliptical patches of light covered by the floodlights can be drawn on a plan of the area to be floodlit to find if the area can be covered evenly. The method[7] of finding the size of an individual patch may be understood by referring to Fig. 8.23.

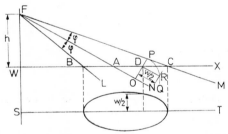

FIG. 8.23. Production of an elliptical patch by a floodlight at *F*.

The top part of the diagram is an elevation taken through the fitting *F*, and aiming point *A*. The beam is with in the cone *LFM*. The bottom part of the diagram is a plan of the resultant ellipse.

The major axis of the ellipse is found by dropping perpendiculars from *B* and *C* on to *ST*, which is drawn parallel to *WX*. The half-width at any point *D*, say, is found as follows. A perpendicular *DO* is dropped to *FN*. Let this cut *FM* in *P*. With centre *O* and radius *OP*, an arc *PQ* is described. *DR* is drawn parallel to *FN*, cutting the arc *PQ* in *R*. *DR* is the required half-width and this is transferred to the lower part of the diagram as shown.

It will be noted that the widest part of the ellipse does not occur below A, but below a point midway between B and C.

Training Plan

In lighting an area such as a football field it is convenient to train the floodlights so their beams lie in arcs round the tower.[8] In Fig. 8.24 the furthest arc from tower S is A, and its position

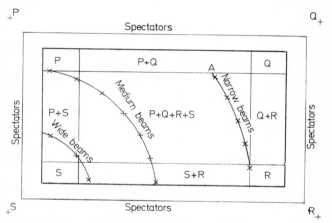

FIG. 8.24. Training plan for tower S, and the areas covered by towers P, Q, R, and S.

is fixed by the necessity to limit glare in the eyes of the spectators (an upper limit of 100,000 candelas per tower has been suggested). The spacing of the beams along the arc is determined by super-imposing plots of the light distribution of the floodlights on each other, and displacing them sideways as in Fig. 8.25 until the desired intensity is obtained by trial and error. A similar procedure is used for finding the spacing between the arcs, but the graphs have to be plotted in terms of illumination rather than intensity since the throw distance and the angle of incidence are being varied. Floodlights with a wider beam and a lower peak intensity will usually have to be used for the arcs closer in to the tower. Allowance has to be made for overlapping of the beams from the four towers. For instance in Fig. 8.24 each tower has to supply a quarter of the illumination to the central area (lighted by *P*, *Q*, *R* and *S*) than to a corner rectangle (lighted by either *P*, *Q*, *R* or *S*).

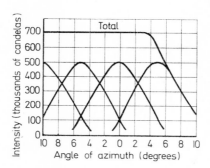

Fig. 8.25. Superposition of a number of beams to achieve desired intensity.

Flux Falling on an Area

The flux falling on an area is most easily found by using the type of diagram shown in Fig. 8.26, the use of which is recommended by the American IES.[10] The angles marked on the diagram are in the coordinate system shown in Fig. 7.27(b). The horizontal lines project onto flat surfaces as straight lines but the vertical lines project as curves.

As an example of the use of this diagram consider Fig. 8.27. Suppose we want to find the flux falling on the area *ABCD* from the floodlight mounted at *O*. It is mounted vertically over *G* and is aimed at *M*. The distances are as marked. From these it can be worked out that the angles are as follows:

$$\angle GOM = 11° \qquad \angle MOE = 28°$$
$$\angle GOC = 22° \qquad \angle MOH = 11°$$
$$\angle GOD = 11° \qquad \angle EOB = 17°$$
$$\angle MOF = 22° \qquad \angle EOA = 9°$$

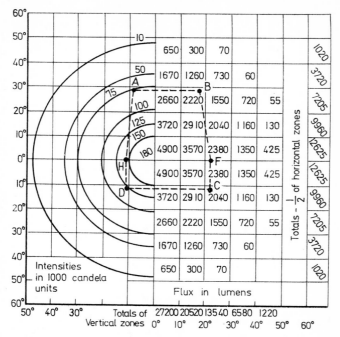

FIG. 8.26. Floodlighting diagram.

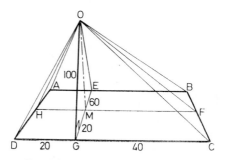

FIG. 8.27. Angles used in Fig. 8.26.

The positions of *A*, *B*, *C*, *D*, *E*, *F*, *G* and *H* can be marked on the diagram and the flux enclosed by the boundary line found. It will be noted that the lines *AB*, *HF* and *DC* appear on the diagram as straight lines, but all the other lines are curves. If desired these may be plotted more accurately by taking a greater number of points around the boundary of the floodlit area.

REFERENCES

1. HARRISON, W. and ANDERSON, E. A., *Illum. Engng.* (*N.Y.*) **11**, 67 (1916).
   HARRISON, W. and ANDERSON, E. A., *Illum. Engng.* (*N.Y.*) **15**, 97 (1920).
   JONES, J. R. and NEIDHARD, J. J., *Illum. Engng.* (*N.Y.*) **46**, 601 (1951).
   JONES, J. R. and NEIDHARD, J. J., *Illum. Engng.* (*N.Y.*) **48**, 141 (1953).
2. *The I.E.S. Code*, IES, London, 1968.
3. WALDRAM, J. M., *Trans. I.E.S.* (*London*) **19**, 95 (1954).
   HEWITT, H., BRIDGERS D. J. and SIMONS, R. H., *Trans. I.E.S.* (*London*) **30**, 91 (1965).
4. HOLMES, R. R., *Electrical Journal*, No. 7, 1963.
5. BEAN, A. R., Monograph of I.E.S. (London), No. 7, 1963.
6. *The Floodlighting of Buildings*, IES Tech. Report No. 6, IES, London.
7. LAMBERT, G. K., *Light and Lighting* **50**, 214 (1957).
8. DOVEY, G. M., PEIRCE, M. W. and PRICE, W. A., *Trans. I.E.S.* (*London*) **29**, 29 (1964).
9. SMITH, D. *Trans. I.E.S.* (*London*) **22**, 105 (1957).
10. *I.E.S. Lighting Handbook*, IES, N.Y, 1966.
    MCMILLAN, W. R., *Illum. Engng.* (*N.Y.*) **60**, 691 (1965).
11. PADGHAM, C. A. and SAUNDERS, J. E., *Trans. I.E.S.* (*London*) **31**, 122 (1966).
12. BEAN, A. R., Monograph of I.E.S. (London), No. 8, 1964.

NOMOGRAM FOR FINDING CORRE-SPONDING VALUES OF THE ANGLES OF INCIDENCE (*i*) AND REFRACTION (*r*)

Instructions: A straight edge is pivoted about the value of the refractive index for the material being used to find corresponding values of *i* and *r*.

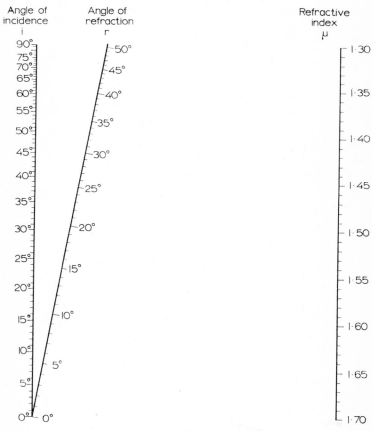

NOMOGRAM FOR FINDING THE DEVIATION $(i{-}r)$ WHEN THE ANGLE OF INCIDENCE IS KNOWN

Instructions: A straight edge is pivoted about the value of the refractive index for the material being used to find corresponding values of $i-r$ and i.

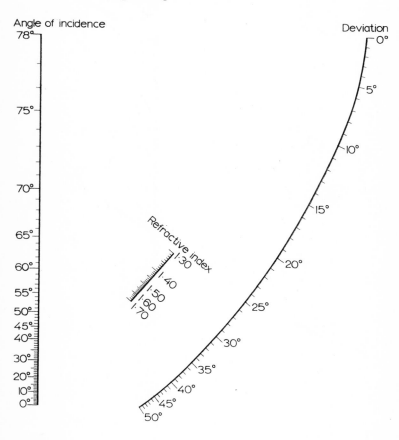

PRISM ANGLE CALCULATION CHART
FOR REFRACTIVE INDEX ($\mu = 1\cdot490$)

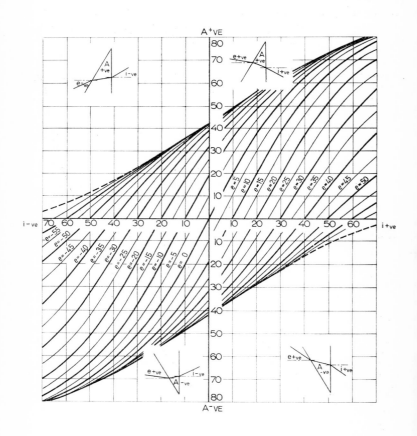

INDEX

Aberration, spherical 126, 177, 243
Accuracy 218
Aerodromes 166, 169, 177
Air handling fittings 213
Aluminium
 anodized 185, 191
 die cast 191
 louvers 191
 magnesium alloy 192
 silicon alloy 192
 welding 186
Amplifier for photocells 228
Apparent brightness 281
Apron floodlight 166
Area source, 2, 50
 flux distribution 294, 295
 illumination from 24, 293
 vector illumination 54
Aspect factor
 application 286
 definition 41
 use 41
Auxiliary lamp 251
Axial polar curve 9, 41, 44, 159, 286, 290

Baffles
 in distribution photometers 234
 in integrators 249
 in luminance measurements 267
Ballast 193, 194
Barrier layer cell 219
 (see Photovoltaic cell)
BAUMGARTNER, on fluorescent tubes 253
Beam
 angle 307
 centre 137
 floodlight 307
 lantern 137
 lumens 307

BLACKWELL, on illumination and contrast 163
Blended light fittings, photometry 257
Brewster's angle 110, 163
Brightness, apparent 281
British zonal classification 153, 277
British zonal method 276
BS 1788 137, 215, 253, 259
BS 3541 215
BS 3820 184, 215, 246, 253, 259
Buck-boost circuit 256
Buffon lens 128
BZ 153, 277

Calibration
 of floodlights 261
 of polar curves 253
 scalar illumination 273
Campbell–Freeth circuit 226
Candela 2
Capacitors 199, 206, 207
 high-frequency ballast 210
 interference suppressor for, 203, 204, 208
Cavity method 80
 application 281
Chokes 194, 195, 197, 198
Circuits
 buck-boost 256
 control gear 204, 205, 206, 207, 208, 209
 dimming 211
 photocell 224, 225, 226, 227, 228, 229, 231, 232
 vector illumination 273
Classification, British zonal 153, 277
Coefficient of utilization
 in street lighting 303
 (utilization factors) 79, 275
Collimating lens 243

11 a*